Advance Praise for *The Cell and the Soul*

'Anand Teltumbde is one of the most important intellectuals at work in India today. He is one of the few who takes on the bigotry of caste and the depredations of big capital that reinforces both caste and class. His arrest and incarceration only underlines how important he is and how much we need him.'

Arundhati Roy

'This is a truly remarkable book, at once a richly textured personal memoir and an absorbing (if also chilling) ethnography of life in jail, with finely sketched portraits of prison staff and prisoners, many from subaltern backgrounds. Beyond what it tells us about life in prison, the book is deeply insightful about the amorality of the Indian state, the complex nature of Ambedkarite politics, the precarious position of Dalits and Muslims, and much else. Written with a rare courage and intellectual clarity, the author gives us a searingly honest indictment of an India "where destroyers of the nation become *deshbhakts* and selfless servers of people become *deshdrohis*".'

Ramachandra Guha

'What do you do if you are summarily put behind bars on false charges while you are busy reading, writing, teaching and trying to better a flawed world? If you are Anand Teltumbde, you make notes, you talk to people and discover their stories, and you analyse the judicial system in which law-keepers break laws with impunity and casual injustice goes by the name of justice. *The Cell and the Soul* gives us an intimate view of prison life, its lingo, its relationships, its human bonds and its hierarchies, which, as in the outside world, are good for the rich and powerful and often tragic for the disempowered.

'When Anand Teltumbde, the renowned academic, writer and social activist finds himself suddenly thrown into Taloja prison as a "dreaded anti-national terrorist", he overcomes the initial shock to comprehend his new world of hardened and newbie criminals, with its class hierarchies and economics, the built-in sadism of the system and the humanity of its inmates, to give us this memoir of crystal clear analysis, deep human feeling and sheer narrative power that holds us from prologue to epilogue and leaves us with fundamental questions about justice and democracy.'

Shanta Gokhale

'Anand Teltumbde's memoir of his years in prison is an incisive, and deeply moving, archive of the contradictions of life behind those high walls. Equally, it is a conversation that bridges the world he was forced to inhabit and the one he left behind, and his profound realisation that the world inside is only a cruel microcosm of the outside. Within both exist the unresolved ethical quandaries of power, justice and freedom. By collapsing this boundary, Anand also brings to life ideals of kindness and sharing that human beings everywhere are capable of. An intent listener, he receives all that courts, policemen, inmates, activists, lawyers, colleagues, friends and family have to say and turns these dialogues into a dispassionate interrogation of society. And yet, this is no dry account of distressing truths. It is also figuratively a book of songs. And of stories. Stories of loss, compassion, protest, anger, dejection, hope and relief.'

T.M. Krishna

The Cell and the Soul

THE CELL AND THE SOUL

A Prison Memoir

ANAND TELTUMBDE

BLOOMSBURY
NEW DELHI • LONDON • OXFORD • NEW YORK • SYDNEY

BLOOMSBURY INDIA
Bloomsbury Publishing India Pvt. Ltd
Second Floor, LSC Building No. 4, DDA Complex, Pocket C – 6 & 7,
Vasant Kunj, New Delhi, 110070

BLOOMSBURY, BLOOMSBURY INDIA and the Diana logo are trademarks of Bloomsbury Publishing Plc

First published in India 2025

Copyright © Anand Teltumbde, 2025

Anand Teltumbde has asserted his moral rights to be identified as the author of this work in accordance with the Indian Copyright Act, 1957

All rights reserved. No part of this publication may be: i) reproduced or transmitted in any form, electronic or mechanical, including photocopying, recording or by means of any information storage or retrieval system without prior permission in writing from the publishers; or ii) used or reproduced in any way for the training, development or operation of artificial intelligence (AI) technologies, including generative AI technologies. The rights holders expressly reserve this publication from the text and data mining exception as per Article 4(3) of the Digital Single Market Directive (EU) 2019/790

Bloomsbury Publishing Plc does not have any control over, or responsibility for, any third-party websites referred to in this book. All internet addresses given in this book were correct at the time of going to press. The author and publisher regret any inconvenience caused if addresses have changed or sites have ceased to exist, but can accept no responsibility for any such changes

ISBN: HB: 978-93-69521-88-3; eBook: 978-93-69529-86-5

2 4 6 8 10 9 7 5 3 1

Typeset in Minion by Manipal Technologies Limited
Printed and bound in India by Thomson Press India Ltd.

To find out more about our authors and books visit www.bloomsbury.com and sign up for our newsletters

To the memory of my brother Milind

Contents

Prologue   1

1. Portent of the Peril   5
2. Hope and Dejection   13
3. Brush with Arrest   19
4. Protests and Support   35
5. Theatre of the Absurd   41
6. Surrender during the Pandemic   46
7. Entering the Hellhole   57
8. Black Flag over Rajgruha   64
9. My New Address   70
10. And I Survived COVID-19   79
11. We Lost Stan   88
12. The Killing of My Brother   99
13. In Lieu of an Ode to Stan   110
14. A Broken System   116
15. And Bhola Hanged Himself   128
16. The Proximity of Captivity   135
17. Jai Bhim Syndrome   151
18. Thou Shalt Not Speak   161
19. POCSO's Dalit Victims   171
20. Abolish Prisons?   180
21. A Nation of Anti-Nationals   190
22. Of Labels and Labelling   199

Epilogue   207

Appendix 1 Orders of Violence Program   219
Appendix 2 Some Salient Draconian Laws   222
Acknowledgements   224

Notes	227
About the Author	245

Prologue

As a society, our decision to heap shame and contempt upon those who struggle and fail in a system designed to keep them locked up and locked out says far more about ourselves than it does about them.

Michelle Alexander

Nekhlúdoff clearly saw that all these people were arrested, locked up, exiled, not really because they transgressed against justice or behaved unlawfully, but only because they were an obstacle hindering the officials and the rich from enjoying the property they had taken away from the people.

Leo Tolstoy

INCARCERATION IS OFTEN SEEN as a fate worse than death – prison is a place where time stands still, life is stripped down to its bare essentials and the human spirit is tested to its limits. For many, prison is a distant reality, a shadowy realm that lies beyond the periphery of everyday existence. But for those who have lived within its confines, it becomes a world unto itself, with its own rhythms, rules and harsh realities.

The Cell and the Soul is a memoir that seeks to bridge the chasm between the incarcerated and the free. It comprises the notes I penned down while in jail, reflecting upon the events and processes that culminated in my imprisonment. I wrote through my thirty-one months in Taloja Central Prison as an undertrial prisoner until my release on bail. Writing was my survival strategy; without my penmanship, I could not imagine surviving prison life.

Each person navigates life in their own way. Mine was to work tirelessly – partly for my family's survival but mostly to better the world I found deeply flawed. I invested my intellectual energy, beyond the confines of my profession, to contribute to the process of making the world a little better place to live for all. It was this latter pursuit that landed me in prison.

Our case (Elgar Parishad or Bhima-Koregaon or simply BK) has already been exposed extensively by journalists in India and abroad, written on by scholars and intellectuals, and commented upon by legal and political commentators, with much more surely to follow. As I write this prologue, there are at least two books on the case making waves in the society – Alpa Shah's *The Incarcerations: Bhima-Koregaon and the Search for Democracy in India* and Ajaz Ashraf's *Bhima-Koregaon: Challenging Caste: Brahminism's Wrath against Dreamers of Equality*. It is bound to be a landmark case, not from the point of view of legal experts but for all those who take their liberties for granted in the so-called democracies of the world. For Indians, it is a matter that can be ignored only at their peril.

I am not discussing the case here, as it is sub judice. However, much has transpired around it since my world was upended when Pune police raided my home in the idyllic campus of the Goa Institute of Management. Inevitably, the impact of that moment has seeped into these memoirs, like fluid from a festering wound. The story of my world suddenly being turned upside down, thrusting me into the unfamiliar realm of courts and legalese, fraught with uncertainty and certain to bring humiliation and ignominy, no longer feels solely mine; it has taken on a representative character, reflecting the potential fate of any conscientious citizen of this republic.

When I entered Taloja prison as accused no. 10 in the BK case, naturally memories of the past came back to haunt me. I came from a very poor family, perhaps the poorest of poor, but strangely I was spared certain predictable hardships that so often accompany such poverty. As a scholar, I was esteemed in my surroundings, lived in the hostels of elite institutions, and thereafter led a reasonably cushy corporate life that ended up in an exalted position of CEO for me. Resisting the temptation of lucrative offers that go with such a career, it was the activist in me that prompted me to accept a professorial position offered by the prestigious IIT Kharagpur, which promised to sustain my standard of living. So the prospect of living in an unhygienic environment, sleeping on the floor, eating tasteless and unhealthy jail food, being locked up with strangers, being ordered around and suffering the infinite humiliations that go with jail life, worried me. I wondered if I would be able to endure those conditions.

In addition, my health had been in a precarious state; there was hardly a fortnight when I did not visit my family doctor for some health issue or the other. So it was that I entered the jail not with fear but with mental preparedness to die. However, like any organism that learns to survive, I too came out alive, with these writings as my testament to it.

I entered prison during the COVID-19 pandemic and witnessed the joke called social distancing. The already socially distanced lower classes barely had space to lie down where they lived. Train and bus stations were packed with them, desperate to return to their villages. Thousands embarked on foot journeys, tragically losing their lives en route. Reports emerged of migrants being fatally struck by trains or subjected to police beatings. But they are absent in the records as well as in public memory. Their deaths were inconvenient statistics. They quietly exited, leaving behind a world of grief and unanswered questions for the families they left behind.

In custody, the irony of 'social distancing' struck me keenly when two hefty cops squeezed me into a vehicle every time I had to be moved. In prison, the overcrowding was relentless. The prison authorities repurposed a school for quarantine, cramming thirty-five to forty inmates into each classroom, sleeping shoulder to shoulder. Article 21 of the Constitution helplessly stared at the fact of three toilets, seven urinals and no bathrooms for nearly 400 prisoners. Rather than containing the virus, this kind of quarantining actually accelerated its spread.

In the hospital barrack of the Taloja prison, where I was held in a cell, over fifty-five people jostled for space meant for thirty or thirty-five. Single-prisoner cells housed five, leaving barely enough room for the inmates to huddle. Many contracted COVID-19, yet officials insisted there wasn't a single case as a result of 'excellent management'. Deaths occurred but were never recorded as COVID-19 fatalities. After all, nobody dies of COVID-19!

The same thing was happening nationally. COVID-19 deaths were vastly underreported. Studies suggested the actual toll could be eight to ten times higher than the official figures, with millions of excess deaths. The World Health Organisation estimated 4.7 million deaths in 2020–2021, nearly ten times the official count and a third of global COVID-19 deaths.[1]

I myself barely escaped becoming another 'excess death' statistic. Stan wasn't as lucky. For four days, I suffered relentless vomiting and convulsions, yet no doctor attended to me. The *kamwallas* struggled to insert a needle into my veins, administering saline with some unknown medication. Only later did the prison begin testing select inmates for COVID-19. And found that many, including me, had COVID-19 antibodies. It only confirmed what we had long suspected: we had all been infected. Some of us survived. Others like Stan did not.

There was a constant scare in our minds about our families outside. There was almost no communication with them for days and weeks, mainly because of the maladministration and the sadistic attitude of the prison authorities. The guards served as messengers for hefty fees. I lost many of my friends, one uncle and two aunts to COVID-19. Most of it I learned only after coming out.

These notes, selected from over a hundred, not only offer a glimpse of jail life but are also a commentary on the system that perpetuates problems while pretending to solve them. With four decades of civil rights activism, I was not entirely unfamiliar with the systemic injustice in our country, yet experiencing it first-hand surprised me for its sheer enormity. Writing these notes in longhand after forty years was both a cathartic and challenging process. Though I am not accustomed to emoting, there were moments when I was deeply moved, allowing the words to flow naturally. I decided to include some of the emotional outpouring, along with notes on related events. I am not concerned with fitting them into any particular literary genre.

This book surely presents stark truths of prison life in India, the inherent sadism of the jail system and the unyielding spirit of prisoners. It chronicles not only my personal struggles but also those of my co-accused as we confronted the injustices we encountered. It stands as a testament to the resilience of countless others who were imprisoned alongside us. However, this memoir goes beyond these narratives; like much of my writing, it seeks to provoke you to rethink about a system that thrives on the pain and suffering of the people and from perpetuating injustice in the name of justice.

1

Portent of the Peril

> False accusations are like the venom of a snake – deadly and destructive.
>
> Stefan Molyneux

It all started on the evening of 31 August 2018, when Pune police held their first press conference on the Elgar Parishad case. I had just returned from the institute and found Rama watching it seriously on TV. Earlier, on 6 August 2018, Pune police had raided the houses of five activists – Sudhir Dhavale, a social activist and editor of *Vidrohi*, a periodical in Marathi from Mumbai; Surendra Gadling, a human rights lawyer and a member of the Indian Association of Peoples' Lawyers; Rona Wilson, a researcher and an activist of the Committee for Release of Political Prisoners (CRPP); Shoma Sen, professor and head of the English department at Nagpur University; and Mahesh Raut, an activist working among the Adivasis of Gadchiroli, his home district, and a co-convener of the Visthapan Virodhi Jan Vikas Andolan (VVJVA). The police had seized all their electronic devices during the raid and arrested them, alleging they had engineered the violence at Bhima-Koregaon on 1 January 2018. It had shocked many people across the country, including me.

I saw Param Bir Singh, additional director general of police (law and order), telling the press that they had extracted multiple letters from the seized electronic devices of the five arrested people, which revealed that the violence at Bhima-Koregaon was a conspiracy of the banned CPI (Maoist). He said there were many more names that surfaced in those letters, and among some he stressed mine. Someone from among the journalists asked him about my involvement, and Singh, as though anticipating the question, enthusiastically arranged for a letter and read out from it. This letter was allegedly written by some Maoist member and addressed to me.

It was so clumsily worded that I simply laughed at its comic content. I soon realised that it was fabricated, and that it was based on the published programme of a seminar put up on the website of the American University of Paris. The programme included the names of the participants and the topic of each one's presentation. Professor Etienne Balibar, whose name figured as the keynote speaker, was said to have been organised by the CPI (M) to interview me as though he were a petty journalist. Professor Balibar, the most celebrated student of the very influential French Marxist philosopher Louis Althusser, is considered one of the greatest living Marxist philosophers and is associated with many American and European universities. Anupama Rao and Shailaja Paik, the only two Indian names besides mine, appeared in the seminar programme as participant scholars. It was one of the tiniest international seminars I had ever attended and had just ten participants, including the organising professor. It was held in a typical seminar room. However, it was projected as a 'convention' in the letter. (The programme, as it existed on the university's website, is provided in Appendix 1.) Clearly, the letter read out by Param Bir Singh, purportedly recovered from the seized computers, was a fabrication based on information in the public domain to weave a hilarious story to frame me and others.

Interestingly, my Budapest visit, which was embedded in my itinerary to Paris, did not find any mention in the fabricated letter as it was not in the public domain. When I accepted an invitation from the American University of Paris, I thought I could economise on my time if another pending invitation from the Central University of Europe (CEU) in Budapest to deliver a lecture could be scheduled after the Paris seminar. The university professors accommodated my proposition and booked my programme accordingly. I took an opportunity to also schedule meetings with the concerned faculty and university officials for possible associations between the CEU and my Big Data Programme at the Goa Institute of Management (GIM). The entire programme had been approved by GIM.

The clumsiness of the letter was on multiple counts. Every word of it could be proved to be factually wrong and mal-intentioned. However, I will not elaborate on that here as my case is sub judice.

In my naiveté, I imagined that the letter, since it was now in the public domain, would be dismissed by the entire academic community, who would find it laughable, as I did. But it was not, even though all the letters that were claimed to have come out of the computers of the two arrested persons – not named in the initial first information report (FIR) but specially included by the police to be raided – were adversely commented upon by some domain experts and even a Supreme Court judge. However, I felt sure that whatever the purpose behind the fabrication of such a letter, they could not incriminate me on the basis of a letter filled with such obvious idiocy.

Most of the news channels and newspapers, especially in Maharashtra, had sensationalised the letter by organising panel discussions on it. These discussions were dominated by a so-called Maoist expert, hitherto unheard of, who I was later told belonged to the Forum for Internal National Security, Pune, an outfit associated with the Rashtriya Swayamsevak Sangh (RSS). It was distressing to see my hard-earned academic and professional credentials being projected as a guise for Maoist activities by people who hardly knew that I had basically trained in technology and business management and had even practised capitalism for the major part of my life. Most of the international conferences I had attended were connected with those domains, and I had been invited either to deliver keynotes or to preside over sessions. Only lately had the academic world taken note of my work on caste, class, Ambedkar, Marx and public policy, and begun inviting me to seminars and conferences related to these issues. Even at the Paris seminar, my topic was 'Political economy of caste', as may be seen in Appendix 1. Initially, I was aghast to see such brazen defamation in the media, but then realised that there was no easy succour for an individual like me in this country. I complained against a TV channel to the News Broadcasting Standards Authority once but did not even receive an acknowledgement. I slowly prepared myself to live with it and even much worse calumny that might follow. What pained me most was the silence on this dangerous canard on the part of the intellectual class that I assumed existed.

These letters, purportedly recovered from the computers of two accused, Rona Wilson and Surendra Gadling, were so clumsily concocted that they were trashed by real experts in the field. Ajai Sahni – founding member and executive director, Institute for Conflict Management and South Asia Terrorism Portal; editor, *South Asia Intelligence Review*; executive editor, *Faultlines*; researcher, analyst, writer, TV and radio commentator on terrorism and insurgency – had publicly raised doubts about the veracity of these letters, saying, 'Which fool would disclose sources like that, referring to Maoists?'[1] He said it was 'impossible' that operational requirements would be mentioned so openly. 'There are code words which keep changing from time to time and region to region: book/umbrella for guns, magazine/copies/buttons for ammunition, raincoats for explosives,' he said. He mocked the claim that Maoist leaders could be conferring with anyone on operational details. 'Established overground workers or sympathisers would rarely be jeopardised by direct involvement in operational matters, nor would such individuals be directing operations and conspiracies,' he observed.[2] However, Vishwa Ranjan, a former director general of police in Chhattisgarh, claimed the use of terms like 'M4' was not uncommon in Maoist communication with overground cadres.[3] Vishwa Ranjan also sought to explain the lack of secrecy on the part of the Maoists, saying, 'For a long time Maoists believed that emails are tough to intercept.'[4] Neither of his remarks was an answer to Ajai Sahni's specific observations. Ranjan's reference to Maoists' faith in emails to explain their lack of secrecy was well off the mark as the incriminating letters were not emails; their source still remains unexplained.

In an interview with Scroll.in on 30 August 2018, just two days after the second police raids, Ajai Sahni presciently stated:

If I had read these excerpts without knowing the context, I would have thought them the work of a satirist or comedian. Obviously, not a single charge will actually stick, but that is clearly not the intention. The case will drag on in what I have described as a process of 'punishment by trial'. The judicial system is slow, and is willing to pretend that it does not notice the utter silliness of the prosecution's submissions. The accused will either continue to languish in jail or, even if enlarged on bail, will be harassed for years by the judicial process. This alone is the objective. In any civilised country, this would be regarded as malicious prosecution, and the people responsible would be severely penalised. In India, however, officers putting up such cases face no consequences beyond a rare dressing down by a conscientious magistrate.[5]

I had almost forgotten about the letter, steeped as I was in my academic work. Besides teaching, I had to recruit faculty, monitor the progress of the students, arrange for live data sets, design and approve appropriate evaluation methods for the students, constitute the board of studies, and arrange for industry associates in certain select domains amenable for application of Big Data analytics for my programme at GIM, the first such programme in the country, acclaimed for its design and creative execution. During my long professional career, I have had the good fortune of leading a series of innovative projects, consistently delivering outstanding results. As this could be my last project, I was determined to uphold that record of excellence.

On 28 August 2018, my wife woke me at about 7 a.m. informing me about a call from my colleague Ajit Parulekar, director of GIM. I had reached Mumbai barely a few hours before by a late-night flight for a scheduled meeting with officials of Bharat Petroleum Corporation Ltd (BPCL) at 10 a.m. to discuss the possibility of BPCL becoming a corporate associate for my programme. My wife had already come to Mumbai to see off my daughter, who was leaving for the US, where she lived. I reluctantly got up and called back the director. What he said on the phone numbed me. He said that the Pune police had raided the campus early in the morning and were looking for me. He assured me not to worry as he was rushing to the campus (he lived a forty-minute drive away) and would manage the situation. I thanked him and asked him to call me after he reached and had interacted with the police. I did not get any phone call until I switched off my phone for the meeting with BPCL officials. When I switched on the phone after the meeting, I saw a spate of messages and missed calls, most of them from my wife. Soon the phone rang and there she was again, sounding panicky and breathless as she informed me that the police had broken into our house (she did not know then that the police had forcibly got duplicate keys to our house from the security) and it was being shown on TV. She also informed me that there had been simultaneous raids on the houses of Sudha Bharadwaj, Gautam Navlakha, Varavara Rao, Arun Ferreira and Vernon Gonsalves, and news of their arrest. This was terrifying and sent shivers down my spine.

I straightaway went to my lawyer friend Mihir Desai, who as a human rights activist already had an idea of what was happening from the time of the previous arrests in this case. He advised me that one of us should rush back to Goa, check if any object had been planted in our house by the police and file a complaint at the local police station to say our house had been opened in our absence and that we would not be responsible if they had planted any incriminating evidence in there. He informed a lawyer friend in Goa to assist us. Since I had some more meetings scheduled in Mumbai, my wife took the next available flight and completed the tasks as per Mihir's advice.

There was news of the arrest of all five people whose houses were raided along with mine. It meant that if I had been home, I would also have been arrested. What foxed me was that if the police wanted to arrest me, it was not difficult for them to locate me for the purpose. They did know about my whereabouts in Mumbai. Or could it be that they did not want to arrest me? There was no way to know what their plan for me was.

On 30 August 2018, a petition was filed before the Supreme Court under Article 32 by five illustrious persons: Romila Thapar, India's noted historian; Devaki Jain, feminist economist and Padma Bhushan awardee; Prabhat Patnaik, eminent Marxist economist; Satish Deshpande, noted sociologist; and Maja Daruwala, a barrister and civil rights activist, challenging the arrests of the five human rights activists – Gautam Navlakha, Sudha Bharadwaj, Vernon Gonsalves, Arun Ferreira and Varavara Rao – and praying for constitution of a special investigation team (SIT) to conduct an investigation into what had happened. The honourable Supreme Court admitted the petition and, pending the hearing, directed that the five persons be kept under house arrest. The FIR charged them with hatching a conspiracy for the CPI (Maoist) to organise the Elgar Parishad at which inflammatory speeches were delivered, as a result of which violence broke out the next day at Bhima-Koregaon, culminating in a death. There were many holes in the police story, but I will not discuss them here as the case is sub judice.

The arrested persons variously managed to get relief from the court until the final decision on the petition by the Supreme Court.

On 28 September 2018, the Supreme Court gave a majority decision by Chief Justice of India Dipak Misra and Justice A.M. Khanwilkar, Justice D.Y. Chandrachud dissenting, rejecting the petition. Justice Chandrachud, in his dissenting opinion, raised concerns about the investigations conducted by the Pune police. He also expressed doubts about the authenticity of the letters purportedly recovered from the computers of the accused. Picking up one, purportedly written by some Maoist Prakash to Sudha Bharadwaj, he observed that it 'does not contain any details including the e-mail header', and that 'Sudha Bharadwaj, who does not belong to Maharashtra and is not Marathi speaking, could not possibly have written a letter in Devanagari utilising essentially Marathi forms of grammar or address'. He also questioned the conduct of the Pune police in approaching the media while investigations were still underway. According to him, the selective disclosure of details by the police to the media created public bias against the accused and cast doubts on the impartiality of the investigations, therefore necessitating the need for an SIT.[6] With the majority Supreme Court decision, the house arrests of the five persons came to an end. Four persons – Sudha Bharadwaj, Varavara Rao, Vernon Gonsalves, Arun Fereira – were arrested and sent to Yerwada Central Jail in Pune. In the thick of the moment, Gautam managed to obtain relief from the court, shielding him from arrest. As for me, there were no signs of the police wanting to arrest me. I was under the delusion that because of my qualifications, the exalted positions I had held in the corporate world, my impeccable record of integrity and my general public image, I might not qualify for arrest.

2
Hope and Dejection

Corrupt and incompetent police officers have a long history of being protected by their colleagues, police internal affairs and the government.

Steven Magee

As a civil rights activist, I was very concerned about these unsavoury developments right from the beginning. But as an individual, I was more concerned about my reputation being sullied by the police in the unbecoming manner they were going about it. I knew the letter Param Bir Singh read out at the press conference was fake as I had material to disprove each word of it with concrete documentary evidence. So I decided to file a defamation case against him. Some of my journalist friends also disclosed to me that Param Bir Singh had not only read out the letters but also had their copies distributed among the attending journalists. After a few days, one of them even shared the entire set with me, as received from the police. Interestingly, this evidence was 'distributed and discussed in public' before its submission to court, which was a grave violation by the police.

The courts took note of this misdemeanour. On 3 September, while hearing a petition filed by Satish Gaikwad, one of the victims of the Bhima-Koregaon violence, a division bench of Justices S.S. Shinde and Mridula Bhatkar of the Bombay High Court questioned how the police could read out from documents which may be used as evidence in the case.[1] Two days later, the Supreme Court bench headed by Chief Justice Dipak Misra took umbrage at the statements made by the assistant commissioner of police of Pune in the matter, saying he was casting aspersions on the court.[2] Asserting that he had viewed the 'press conference carefully', Justice D.Y. Chandrachud reportedly said the police officers had attempted to make an insinuation against the court in the matter. In response, Additional Solicitor-General Tushar Mehta then apologised on behalf of the government of Maharashtra.[3] It also reprimanded Maharashtra police, especially over the press conference that they held revealing the details of the case.[4] The unfortunate thing is that our courts make all kinds of moralising observations during hearings but do nothing against delinquent officers for wilful violation of rules and laws.

Despite the police being reprimanded by the Bombay High Court and the Supreme Court for their misdemeanour of holding press conferences and sharing evidence in a case with the media before it was submitted to the court or provided to the defence, Assistant Commissioner of Police (ACP) Shivaji Pawar, who was the investigating officer for the case, later committed another violation by arresting me on 2 February 2019 while I was under the protection of the Supreme Court. The Special Court set up to hear this specific case not only declared my arrest illegal but also in contempt of the Supreme Court, and marked a copy of the verdict to the Supreme Court. Retired Supreme Court Justice P.B. Sawant had slammed this very gentleman and his senior colleagues for turning an informal conversation with him, that is, Judge Sawant, into a formal 'statement' without his knowledge and annexing it to a charge sheet filed in the Elgar Parishad case.[5] Notwithstanding all this misconduct and incompetence, this ACP was awarded the Union home minister's Medal for Excellence in Investigation for his work in the Bhima-Koregaon case for the year 2020.[6]

I had been quite engrossed in my new programme, which was the first of its kind in the country and perhaps in the world to embed Big Data analytics in management decisions. The two-year residential programme was for a postgraduate diploma in management (Big Data analytics). In the very first year, even before the first term was completed, the programme was adjudged as one among the top ten 'analytics' courses on the basis of its creative course content and the market opinion. This rank, of course, improved substantially the next year, and the programme was adjudged fourth in the broader category of Data Analytics courses, there being no peer in Big Data yet.[7] The first rank was bagged by the business analytics course offered jointly by IIT, Kharagpur, ISI Kolkata and IIM Calcutta, with the design of which too I was associated prior to joining GIM.

In order to prosecute Param Bir Singh, I needed permission from the Maharashtra government. Accordingly, I sent a letter through my lawyer on 5 September 2018 to the Principal Secretary, government of Maharashtra, asking for the required permission. There was no response from the government to this letter until I surrendered on 14 April 2020 in Mumbai. After my coming out of the jail in November 2022, when we began to open the packages containing my books, documents and letters during my incarceration sent by GIM in September 2024, I was surprised to find an unopened letter from the government of Maharashtra informing me of its decision not to grant this permission. The letter was in Marathi, numbered ENQ-1218/Pra. Kra. 328/Pol-2, Gruh Vibhag, 2nd Floor, Mantralaya, dated 17 June 2020, two months after my arrest. The government had ensured in various ways that I would not be able to file a defamation case against Param Bir Singh.

I couldn't help but feel dejected at the thought of this system, which is not accountable to the people. On what grounds can the government refuse anyone permission to prosecute an officer who had blatantly violated the law – and so egregiously that both the Bombay High Court and the apex court had reprimanded him? It was, in fact, the government's duty to take cognisance of his misconduct and initiate action against him. Yet, not only did it fail to act but it also sought to prevent me from doing so.

Was the Principal Secretary not committing an unlawful act by not granting me permission to prosecute Singh? Was it not his or her duty to respond to my letter within a reasonable time? Is he not paid to perform his duties with taxpayers' money – including mine? These seemingly small transgressions on the part of government servants go unaddressed, accumulating into a thick crust of systemic impunity.

The Param Bir Singh episode took an even murkier turn in the following months. He was accused in an extortion case, leading to a non-bailable warrant being issued against him.[8] He absconded, prompting the state criminal investigation department to issue a lookout notice on him,[9] and was later declared a proclaimed offender by the Mumbai additional chief metropolitan magistrate's court – the first such instance involving a Mumbai police commissioner.[10] The Supreme Court refused to grant him relief from arrest,[11] and he was ultimately suspended. Disciplinary action was initiated against him for lapses and irregularities, including unauthorised absence from work.[12]

However, despite these serious allegations against him, Param Bir Singh had the last laugh when the Uddhav Thackeray government collapsed and the Bharatiya Janata Party (BJP), in alliance with the Shinde-led Shiv Sena, came into power in Maharashtra. The new state government dropped all the charges against him and revoked his suspension, citing a Central Administrative Tribunal (CAT) order that deemed the suspension void due to the government's failure to review it in time.[13] Notably, no action has been taken against anyone responsible for this 'failure' to review his suspension. The message is clear: regardless of his alleged crimes, Param Bir Singh enjoys the protection of the BJP.

Although there were no immediate signs of my arrest, it remained a looming possibility. The charge sheet against the first batch of five arrestees had been filed, and I was named as an accused in it. This charge sheet laid bare all the allegations the police had levelled against me. After examining its contents, we moved a petition in the Bombay High Court to quash the FIR against me. Similar petitions were also filed for Father Stan Swamy and Gautam Navlakha. In Stan Swamy's case, the police submitted to the court that he was merely a suspected accused, whereas in my case the hearing proceeded.

I had travelled from Goa to Mumbai for a meeting and attended the first hearing dressed in full executive attire, in the innocent belief that the court would see the incongruity of the charges against me. The prosecution, besides presenting its arguments in court, submitted some documents in a sealed envelope. On 21 December 2018, the court rejected my petition. However, it granted me three weeks to appeal the judgement.

All this while I remained engaged in my academic work at the institute, placing full faith and confidence in my lawyer and the judiciary. However, the first rejection jolted me. Had I not witnessed the court proceedings first-hand, it might not have hit as hard. With no other option, we proceeded with an appeal to the Supreme Court.

At the Supreme Court, the same pattern repeated – after all the arguments, the prosecution submitted some documents in a sealed envelope, and the court rejected the appeal. This decision came on 14 January 2019. As a small relief, however, while dismissing my quashing petition, the Supreme Court granted me four weeks' protection to seek pre-arrest bail from the appropriate court.

It seemed the prosecution was determined to keep fabricating claims in sealed envelopes and submitting them to the courts to deny us relief. Though technically permissible under Rule 7 of Order XIII of the Supreme Court Rules and Section 123 of the Indian Evidence Act, 1872, the rampant misuse of this provision has reduced the legal process in the country to a farce, eroding transparency and due process. The menace of these sealed envelopes had not only obstructed the court's consideration of my application for quashing the case and thereafter for anticipatory bail but also played a sinister role in the Pegasus spyware case.[14] Fortunately, the Supreme Court recognised this blatant abuse of the legal system by the state and put an end to the practice.[15]

For the first time I grasped the gravity of the situation. What had so far seemed like a ludicrous farce now loomed as a potential catastrophe. My faith in the system was completely shattered. Determined to bring the matter before the public, I wrote a detailed account titled 'I Need Your Support' and emailed it to a group of readers of my *Economic & Political Weekly (EPW)* column on 17 January 2019.[16]

The write-up leaked to the media, and numerous digital platforms picked it up, giving it wide publicity. However, apart from a few articles and social media discussions, it did not lead to any substantial impact. It was then that I truly understood the haunting words of Pastor Martin Niemöller:

> First they came for the socialists,
> and I did not speak out – because I was not a socialist.
> Then they came for the trade unionists,
> and I did not speak out – because I was not a trade unionist.
> Then they came for the Jews,
> and I did not speak out – because I was not a Jew.
> Then they came for me
> – and there was no one left to speak for me.[17]

3

Brush with Arrest

> We must always take sides. Neutrality helps the oppressor, never the victim. Silence encourages the tormentor, never the tormented.
>
> Elie Wiesel

I HAD NEVER SEEN a jail – not even from the outside – before I went to high school. Perhaps no one from our village had. Yet I was not entirely unaware of it. Jail was an integral part of our socialisation, associated with socially undesirable behaviour. It was a scarecrow planted in our minds from childhood. Mothers warned their children to behave or else the police would take them away to jail. Jail was portrayed as a living hell, an inferno, a *jahannam* created on earth for those who deserved it. But who decided who deserved it?

My father used to sing us ballads about those who had fought against the oppression of the local zamindars – heroes immortalised in songs, stories and folklore. Yet those stories are not remembered any more, disappearing well before the rise of WhatsApp university and the post-truth world, where men of straw are turned into heroes, and real heroes are buried under layers of manufactured trash. The heroes in my father's stories were not only imprisoned by the police but were sometimes even gunned down. Every time he sang them, tears would well up in my eyes.

I still remember a ballad of 'Balya Dhiwar', though the exact words escape me now. Balya Dhiwar – a Robin Hood figure, do-gooder, and rebel against the British – was killed in a trap laid by the police in collusion with a local landlord. That struck me as deeply unsettling. If these people had sacrificed their lives fighting injustice – so much so that the people celebrated them in folk songs – how could they be considered criminals? Who decided what crime was? Even as a child I sensed that something was fundamentally wrong in the relationship between the people and the police. Why were they always at odds with each other? Why were children raised to fear the police?

Back then, I did not yet understand that the police were merely pawns, obeying the orders of someone far more sinister.

I remember being terrified of a policeman who was a tenant at my uncle's house in town, despite his occasional attempts to win me over with sweetmeats. I was too young to grasp the contradiction – how could someone who seemed so kind turn against those who fought against injustice? I could not reconcile the man who offered me sweets with the image of a uniformed enforcer who gunned down heroes like Balya.

Each time he handed me a sweet, I would accept it fearfully, only to throw it away later, making sure he didn't see me. In my mind he was the very one who had pulled the trigger on Balya. Many times I asked my father why the police had killed Balya, but he never gave me an answer that fully satisfied me. I realised that if I wanted to understand his killing, I would have to search for the answer myself.

The first time I read about jail was in a small biography of Joseph Stalin, a book my school had awarded me as a prize for topping my class. In it, I came across the story of Aleksandr Ulyanov, Lenin's elder brother, a student at the Imperial University of St Petersburg, who was imprisoned and hanged at the age of twenty-one along with four comrades. Their crime? Plotting to assassinate Tsar Alexander III, the head of Russia's oppressive autocracy.

Later, I discovered another book in my school collection – this one about Bhagat Singh. He too was imprisoned and hanged at the age of twenty-three, alongside his comrades Sukhdev and Rajguru. Their crime? Fighting to free India from British imperialism.

These stories unsettled me. Who exactly had they wronged – society? Humanity? I did not think so. Ulyanov's defiance was born out of the people's suffering under Tsarist rule, just as Bhagat Singh's struggle had been against British exploitation of India. I knew that Bhagat Singh, Sukhdev and Shivram Rajguru were charged for the murder of John Saunders, a British police officer. But it was part of their struggle against oppressive British rule. After all, they wanted to avenge the brutal lathi-charge on the anti-Simon Commission protesters by the police. Lala Lajpat Rai had been killed in that violence. Was it, then, that those who resisted oppression were the ones who got jailed and executed? This question gnawed at me, unsettling the simplistic notions of crime and justice I had absorbed as a child.

A vague sense of admiration began to take root within me for those who were imprisoned. I read and reread these books, slowly identifying with Aleksandr Ulyanov and Bhagat Singh, each time imagining myself in their place as they walked to the gallows. Instead of fear, I felt pride. Sometimes, I was overwhelmed with anger at the injustice of the world; at other times I cried silently, unable to understand why. I was barely eight years old, in the third standard – too young to grasp why the world had to be so unfair. Why did Tsar Alexander have the right to rule? Who made him king? Why were the British entitled to rule over distant lands?

I couldn't ask my teachers these questions as they weren't part of the school syllabus. Nor could I ask my illiterate parents, who had never heard of Aleksandr Ulyanov or Bhagat Singh. They first learned about them from me when I read their stories out to them. Yet, in their own way, they seemed to approve of their heroism. My father admired Balya, a local rebel, while my mother reacted with fierce defiance to anything she perceived as unjust. I instinctively shared their hatred for oppressors, though to me the oppressors remained abstract – just as abstract as the world beyond the villages surrounding mine.

Ulyanov was distant, somewhere in Russia. But Bhagat Singh was different, being an Indian. He was real, tangible. He became my childhood hero, and he remained so for the rest of my life.

I had dedicated my first book to him.

Years later, these childhood memories unconsciously drew me to the very places associated with them. On my first visit to St Petersburg in 1990, the first thing I did after checking into my hotel was to rush to the grim Trubetskoy Bastion of the Peter and Paul Fortress, known as the 'Russian Bastille'. Now a museum, it depicted the lives of political prisoners during the rule of Tsar Alexander III. There I stood, outside Ulyanov's cell, unmoved, trying to feel his plight, to touch his soul. I also felt a strong urge to visit the site of his execution in the fortress at Shlisselburg, some thirty-five kilometres from St Petersburg, but my local friend dissuaded me.

Similarly, during my first visit to Lahore, I had the unusual privilege of being hosted by Salman Taseer, then governor of Punjab. When I expressed my desire to see places associated with Bhagat Singh, he graciously sent his car and aide-de-camp to take me to Singh's birthplace in Chak Banga, a village in Jaranwala tehsil of Faisalabad district, about 150 kilometres from Lahore. On our return, we stopped at Shadman Chowk, the site in Lahore Central Jail where Bhagat Singh, Sukhdev and Rajguru were hanged. He also showed me the Government Islamia College on Civil Lines – formerly Dayanand Anglo-Vedic High School – and the National College of Arts, where Bhagat Singh had studied and evolved into a revolutionary.

Over lunch, I expressed my surprise that Shadman Chowk had not been renamed after Bhagat Singh. To my astonishment, Taseer sahab admitted that the thought had never occurred to them and assured me he would do whatever he could to push the idea forward. I do not know what steps he took, but soon after, a movement emerged to rename Shadman Chowk as Shaheed Bhagat Singh Chowk. However, it also provoked opposition, and the proposal was suspended.

Tragically, before I could follow up with him during my next visit in 2012, Taseer sahab was assassinated at Kohsar Market in Islamabad by his own bodyguard, who was enraged by his vocal opposition to Pakistan's blasphemy law, seeing it as an insult to Islam. I felt a deep sense of sorrow. His personal gifts – a framed picture of the Red Fort in Lahore, a coffee table book on the history of the Governor's Palace, and a signed copy of *Poems by Faiz* – still adorn my bookshelves and wall, reminders of a conversation left unfinished.

Within months, another person who became friends with me in Lahore – Shahbaz Bhatti – a young minister of minority affairs in the prime minister Yousuf Raza Gilani's cabinet, was also gunned down for his call for reform in the controversial blasphemy laws of Pakistan.

While I instinctively made Bhagat Singh my hero, we Dalit children had an inherited role model in Babasaheb Ambedkar. I do not remember how my parents conveyed it, but it was deeply ingrained in my mind that I had to become an Ambedkar. However, I had little understanding of what that truly meant, beyond the blaring of his praises in songs over loudspeakers and the local leaders extolling him in their evening meetings where we, children, always sat closest to the speakers. From these meetings I gathered that Ambedkar meant four things: excelling academically, asserting our Buddhist identity, opposing Mahatma Gandhi and wearing coat and a tie, the meaning of the latter I hardly understand even today.

I instinctively embraced the first, monopolising the top rank in every exam in school. This endeared me to the entire village, as I brought prestige to our village in the fourth- and seventh-standard exams, which were held for a cluster of villages. Casteism, if it existed, was not something we acutely felt. I recall only one old shopkeeper, a Teli by caste – a traditional oil-pressing community, classified as an Other Backward Class (OBC) in Maharashtra – owning a double-storeyed brick house, who would avoid touching us while handing over goods. I would deliberately brush against him, and he would curse as I ran away, later complaining to my mother while passing by our house on his way to relieve himself in the open fields. To us, it was just a mischievous game. Strangely, he was supposed to be our grandpa, since he called my mother daughter-in-law.

All the so-called upper-caste Kunabis and others who belonged to the classical Shudra castes – the lowest in varna hierarchy and today the OBCs – were simply uncles, aunties, grandfathers and grandmothers. They had their own well, and we had ours, but the rigid social hierarchies I would later read about seemed distant and unreal. It was only after moving to Nagpur after my tenth standard that I encountered first-hand accounts of caste discrimination from friends who had experienced it more starkly elsewhere.

As a pre-university student at the Institute of Science in Nagpur, I finally began to understand Ambedkar through books in the university library, not far from my hostel. Every day, as soon as my morning classes ended, I would gulp down a hurried lunch and rush to the library with a notebook and a dictionary in hand. I would immerse myself in books on and by Ambedkar, reading until the library staff asked me to leave. By the time I returned to the hostel, the mess would be closed, leaving me with the choice of staying hungry or grabbing something from a wayside stall. It was through this relentless routine – alongside my studies in physics, chemistry and mathematics – that I began to grasp Ambedkar's ideas.

I entered student politics, carrying Bhagat Singh as my hero, and read books with Ambedkar as my guiding inspiration. To me there was no contradiction between them – they coexisted effortlessly within me.

Returning to my first real encounter with a jail, it wasn't until I left my village school and joined a high school in Wani, a taluka town, that I caught my first glimpse of both a prison and a prisoner. One day, I accompanied a friend to the *kutchery* – a fortress-like, stone-built compound of British vintage – to get a school form attested by the tahsildar. As we entered, my eyes fell on a dimly lit room behind steel bars. Inside, two men stood there, locked away in the darkness.

That was the jail.

The room was bare except for a lone pitcher in a corner. There perhaps was an enclosure in lieu of a toilet, but we could not see it. The prisoners stared outside – pitifully, blankly. Their eyes lacked the fire I had imagined in those of revolutionaries like Aleksandr Ulyanov or Bhagat Singh. There was no defiance, no spark of rebellion. My heroes could not look so defeated.

No, these men belonged to a different world – a different class. Perhaps they had stolen something, assaulted someone, or even committed murder and gotten caught. They were not the kind of prisoners I had read about.

But why might they have done what they did? What drove them to commit the crime? Was it right to incriminate them without knowing why? They might have stolen money as they had nothing to feed their children. They might have beaten someone who harassed their families, done something unseemly or murdered someone who had been oppressing people around, like Balya. I was not convinced as I am today. They did not appear to be men driven by an ambition to become rich. And what if they were? It was confusing then, as it is now.

If they thieved because of their penury, is not the system responsible for normalising inequality between thieves and the thieved ones. Is it not responsible for their not getting a job to earn enough to feed their children in a decent way? Thus, there may be a cascading chain of reasons for every crime, which would tend to decriminalise the victim and externalise the responsibility for his crime. In most cases, this chain of reasons may incriminate his situation, which is created by the society or the state, they being more responsible for the crime than his own self. How do I decide then that they were not innocent?

Years later, when I found myself in IIM Ahmedabad, Pulin Garg, a maverick professor who taught us organisational behaviour, wrote an equation on the board that seemed to answer my long-standing doubts:

$$\text{Behaviour} = f\,(\text{self, situation})$$

I wasn't entirely sure about the *self*, but in India, *situation* seemed to be the stronger explanatory variable.

Oh no – by *self* or *situation*, or both, I could never have imagined myself in the place of those prisoners I had seen in Wani. I was the hero of my village, the boy who had brought it laurels by standing first in every exam. As a child, I had once felt an urge to die like Bhagat Singh, but the world had changed before I was even born. The British had left. India was now independent, a republic with a grand Constitution that declared all citizens equal, granting them each one vote, of one value. It abstracted the rulers as the people's choice.

My own journey had slowly drifted away from the path my hero had walked. Instead, I was channelled into the path laid out for a child like me – becoming an engineer, earning an MBA, securing a well-paying corporate job and everything that came with it. Though I never let myself be fully consumed by the capitalist lures and remained engaged in struggles against injustice, my formal positions in the corporate world inevitably overshadowed these commitments.

At the age when Bhagat Singh was hanged, I was immersed in projects, adding to my company's coffers – a cycle that continued for five decades. Though my pro-people activism ran parallel, the accolades I earned in the capitalist world always overshadowed it. People in similar positions could be entangled in corruption, sexual misconduct or domestic-violence scandals. Yet even my harshest critics could vouch for my integrity. Arrest or imprisonment seemed like an impossibility in my life – until it wasn't.

Yes, it happened – at a time when it seemed utterly unthinkable. By then I had long left my corporate career behind, having risen in it to the rank of executive director at Bharat Petroleum and CEO of a holding company incorporated to develop petroleum infrastructure in India and abroad. I had earned recognition as an author, public speaker and intellectual, with books, articles and academic honours to my name. I held a professorship at a prestigious B-school in an IIT, pioneered a Big Data programme at a leading management institute in Goa, and was decorated with numerous public awards. These formal accolades made even the thought of being arrested seem absurd – let alone the reality of it.

And yet, when they raided my house on the GIM campus, it came startlingly close. Every other person whose home was raided that day had been immediately arrested. I was spared, not because of any special immunity I had but simply because

Brush with Arrest

I was not present there at the time. Yet, as days passed and they made no move to arrest me despite knowing my whereabouts, it seemed, strangely, as if they had lost interest in me.

And then it happened.

I had a brief brush with arrest when the Pune police held me at Mumbai airport in the early hours of 2 February 2019. It was past 2 a.m. and I was half-asleep as I walked out of the airport, trying to book a cab. Suddenly I heard a voice behind me: *'Chala saheb'* (Let's go, sir). There were two cops by my side who appeared to have followed me from the arrival gate of Terminal 1.

I knew about the rejection of my anticipatory bail application in the Pune court while I was in Thrissur. I had travelled there at the invitation of a group of activists to speak at a gathering on the theme, 'Is India a democratic country?' As the chief guest, I shared the stage with several prominent speakers, including former senior bureaucrats.

I recall invoking Babasaheb Ambedkar, who had cautioned that democracy was not to be taken for granted – it depended on the people imbibing constitutional morality, which had to be cultivated. He had famously warned, 'Democracy in India is only a top dressing on an Indian soil which is essentially undemocratic.'

In my speech, I had pointed out how in the Constituent Assembly itself, over 80 per cent of the population was excluded from representation. Their exclusion did not end there; it persisted in the making of the Constitution and thereafter. That exclusion distinctly showed up in the plight of the majority of our people. After seven decades of independence and constitutional rule, those excluded from representation in the Constituent Assembly – mostly Dalits, Adivasis, religious minorities and property-less masses – still suffered exclusion and acute deprivations.

I was aware of the hearing on my anticipatory bail application, but experience had taught me equanimity. Just before heading to Kochi airport, I made a quick call and learned that my application had been rejected. Yet I hardly expected it to lead to my arrest. My lawyer had assured me that the Supreme Court had granted me a month to seek anticipatory bail, meaning I still had legal protection. But what does legal protection mean when a policeman descends on you and simply says, '*Chala*'? There was no point in arguing. They were just constables following orders.

I was taken to a police station at the end of the terminal. I must have driven past this place countless times while visiting Bharat Petroleum's aviation station, or for resting there when a flight was delayed. But I had never noticed that a police station existed there. That's the peculiarity of police stations – ordinary people never see them. But they are always there, waiting.

I didn't know what to say or do. The cops initially stopped me from using my phone, but after a brief argument they relented. I dialled my wife, who was waiting for me at our home in Dadar. I told her I had been arrested and asked her to contact our lawyer and come to the airport. But who would pick up a call at such an ungodly hour? After about thirty to forty minutes, she arrived with her younger brother and his wife. The police told us they were merely following orders from their higher-ups. The Pune police were on their way to complete the formalities.

A while later, the Pune police arrived. They completed the paperwork and asked my wife to take my belongings – my bag, phone, watch and wallet. They then bundled me into their rickety jeep, sandwiched between two cops. I worried about my spondylitis as the jerks of the vehicle jolted my neck. I knew we were on the Mumbai-Pune road – a route I had travelled hundreds of times – but this time I felt as if I were being taken to an unfamiliar, faraway place. There was no sense of time either, as my watch was given to be taken home. Despite the tension, I couldn't fight my exhaustion and drifted off to sleep.

When the vehicle finally stopped, I was led into an unlit room where people lay packed like sardines. I was lucky to find an empty bench and stretched out for a nap. But barely had I closed my eyes when I was woken up and shoved into another police jeep.

The most painful part of being arrested is the complete loss of control over yourself. A petty policeman tells you to get up, and you get up. By now it was morning, but I had no idea where we were heading. The cops remained silent and unfriendly. Eventually, we stopped at what I recognised as a hospital. A man sitting behind a wooden desk glanced at some papers handed to him by the police and, without looking up, asked, *'Koi taklif hai kya?'* (Did I have any problems?) But before I could respond he scribbled his signature and returned the papers. That was the doctor. He too seemed like an extension of the police – indifferent, mechanical, almost monstrous.

Back in the vehicle, I was taken to a larger police station. They walked me through a dimly lit corridor and into a narrow holding cell. Before I could grasp what was happening, the steel-barred door clanked shut with a finality that sent a chill through me. A frail old cop at a desk asked me to surrender everything in my pockets – even a small piece of paper and my medicines. Then came the inevitable question: 'Caste?'

'I don't have one,' I said.

He looked up, irritated.

'Write Muslim,' I added.

He muttered something under his breath and moved on, instructing me to pick a sleeping mat from a filthy pile in the corner. They were so grimy that one wouldn't touch them under normal circumstances. But I was in a different world now. I sifted through the tattered heap and gingerly picked up one, holding it at its edge like a dead lizard.

The cell they shoved me into was pitch-dark. For a few moments I couldn't see anything. There was no light bulb inside, only a faint, flickering light from a low-wattage bulb outside the bars. Slowly, my eyes adjusted. The room was packed with people, curled up on the floor. I stood motionless near the door, careful not to step on anyone. It was freezing, and I shivered. Eventually, I slid down against the wall and sat, stretching my legs into whatever small space was left in the corner.

I believe there were two more cells. Every few minutes, one of the doors would open and slam shut with a metallic clank. The main door at the entrance did the same whenever a cop entered. If an inmate needed to relieve himself, the guard would unlock and relock the doors for every single movement of anyone in and out. The clanking never stopped.

After some time, a pot-bellied cop arrived and muttered something to the guard at the desk. Within minutes my cellmates were shuffled into another cell, leaving me alone. Perhaps it was because I belonged to a *special* category – an intellectual, a supposed anti-national, a *dangerous terrorist*.

A little later, the guards opened the door and told me to freshen up. They pointed me to a makeshift washroom at the far end – a wet, stinking enclosure with a grimy Indian-style toilet, yellowed with filth. A leaky tap stood behind a half-broken wooden shutter. I had left my shoes at the entrance, walked in barefoot, relieved myself, splashed water on my face and returned.

Shortly after, the guard pushed in a parcel wrapped in a newspaper – it was breakfast. Inside were two idlis with chutney. A tiny paper cup of tea followed. I set the food aside and sipped the tea in one gulp. When I asked for another cup, I was met with silence.

After some time, the cell door opened again and a hefty man in his late twenties or early thirties was shoved inside. He carried his bedding of the better of those dirty dhurries outside with him, spread it out, and lay down. Then he handed me a spare dhurrie and told me to lie down too. I just sat on it.

After a while, he began talking.

'*Kya case?*' he asked.

'Bhima-Koregaon.'

He had not heard of it.

'*Woh kya hai?*' What was that, he wanted to know.

'*Woh last year Puna ke pas maramari huwa tha, woh.*' (The skirmish last year near Pune.)

'*Acchha ... woh Jai-Bhim-wala ... jhamela.*' (Oh, right ... that Jai Bhim mess.)

'*Han ... tum?*' I asked him. What about him?

'Extortion', he proudly said. '*Saala, thoda gochi hua aur andar aa gaye ... vaise humara andar bahar chalta rahta hai ... abhi court shuru hone par hamara vakil chhuda lega ...*'

Barely a mishap and had to be incarcerated, he was saying. Going in and out was routine for him, and as soon as court resumed, his lawyer would be able to get him out. He sounded pretty confident.

He suddenly got up, as if he recollected something, went up to the door and began shouting at the police for something. He was hurling full-throated abuse at them for some five minutes, but the cop did not utter a word. I did not understand what was going on. He would take a pause and again start shouting abuses at them. I was wondering how the police there, two of them now, were quietly tolerating it.

After he finished, I asked him what had happened. He murmured something, which I again could not understand. Was he not afraid of the police, I asked him. '*Yeh bhadkhau saale kya bolenge, inko paise jo milte hai . . . ham khilate rahate hai paise . . .*' (What will these bastards say, they keep getting money . . . we keep feeding them money . . .) True or not, but I was witnessing the muteness of the police in the face of shouts of 'motherfuckers' and 'sisterfuckers' from a prisoner. After some time, an officer came up and said something to him and, equally surprisingly, he cooled down.

I asked him what exactly he had done. '*Oh, ek yahanke bhadve se pachas peti ki baat hui . . . lene gaye, to police ke jaal me fas gaye . . .*' (Oh, there was deal of fifty lakh rupees with one guy . . . when went there to collect it, fell into a police trap.) I mustered up the courage to ask him about the details of the case and he blurted it all out without the slightest hesitation in a single breath, explaining to me how the extortion racket is run, how their gang operates, how they choose their target, who in the gang does what, how the police are hand in glove with the gangs and get regular hafta from them, and how sometimes the police assist them, and everything . . . One does not read as much about extortion cases in the newspapers as one used to earlier. But he said extortion would never stop. As long as there are police, crime will not stop, he said prophetically.

He was from a village near Pune, educated up to ninth standard, came to Mumbai, worked on odd-jobs, and one day became part of a gang (which one, he did not reveal). There were many gangs that operated scrupulously within their territories.

As we gossiped, the door clanked open and the guard announced lunch. Everyone picked up one of the melamine plates piled up on a heap of soiled and tattered dhurries, took a plateful of rice with watery dal served out of a plastic bucket by two boys, and started gulping it down, sitting on the floor. I couldn't muster up the courage to venture into eating it. I just watched the others eat, standing near the door. My friend consumed two courses of rice and dal and came back. He advised me to eat, saying it was good, better than what was served in prisons. I shuddered at the thought of having to eat that kind of food in that condition in a prison for weeks, months and years.

After a while, the door clanked open again, and this time my friend was called out. He hurriedly said he was being taken to court and wouldn't be coming back. I was left alone in the cell, as dark as night even if it was noon outside. I sat leaning against the wall and closed my eyes, trying to steal some sleep, but couldn't. After some time, the door clanked open again, and I was called out.

I was surprised to see Rama, my wife, with a police officer near the entrance of the lock-up. She looked sick and dishevelled, appearing years older than when I had last seen her at the airport police station some hours before. She was seated in a chair. She had brought a chocolate for me, but the cop didn't allow me to take it. She requested him to let me sit in a chair, but he again declined permission. I had to stand as she spoke. I told her to send a sweater as I felt very cold inside. She informed me that people had put up posters everywhere protesting my arrest and had gathered in huge numbers around the police station, though they weren't allowed to approach it.

She left, and I was locked in again. A while later, the sweater came, and I was taken out. The guard checked every inch of it, as though there might be nano bombs hidden in its stitches. As I stared at him with contempt, the poor chap felt ashamed and said, 'What to do, saheb, it is our duty.' He abruptly stopped his 'duty' and handed it to me. I was locked in again.

With the warmth of the sweater, I fell asleep for an hour or so, only to be woken by the loud clank of the door and a call to come out. Two cops escorted me to a vehicle parked at the rear. I was seated, sandwiched as usual between cops, and was driven out through the back gate. Journalists, already expecting this, ran after the vehicle as it sped away, but they couldn't catch us. Some people followed us on bikes, shouting, 'Anand sir, don't worry. People are with you.'

One journalist daringly drove his bike dangerously close to the jeep, with his friend constantly clicking me on his camera from the pillion seat until we reached the court. The cop sitting by the window turned his torso, virtually blocking the view with his back. As we arrived at the court, we saw a huge crowd. The cop on my right alighted and told me in Marathi, *'Chal, utar'* (Come, get down). I retorted in annoyance, 'Do you speak to your father like this?' He looked shamefaced. The police whisked me into a lift and we reached the courtroom on some upper floor. The courtroom too was packed with people, among them many friends and relatives.

I was left in the dock for the accused. My lawyer, Rohan Nahar, came over and assured me not to worry, comforting me that we had a strong case. Either way, I was beyond feelings, having had a glimpse of jail life. Now it was just a matter of standing by, whatever happened next.

After some time, the judge arrived and the arguments began. I remained nonchalant, uninterested in the proceedings. They were not audible to me, moreover. The prosecution lawyer started off aggressively, but as my lawyer began to speak she slowly fell silent. The judge adjourned the court for some time. There was a commotion among the people there. Some who heard the arguments already expected the verdict to be favourable to us. The judge returned and announced that my arrest was illegal. People shook hands and rushed to me showing solidarity. My lawyer came over and took me outside, where I was surrounded by journalists.

That perhaps was the first positive verdict in the Bhima-Koregaon case!

The investigating officer responsible for my arrest approached and said to me that he needed some time to finish the paperwork before I could leave. I curtly asked him to expedite it. Outside the courtroom, I was surrounded by journalists, with my lawyer at my side. After a while, we left for our vehicle, surrounded by a crowd of journalists and well-wishers. Before we started off, I suddenly remembered that I had left my things – medicines and papers – back at the police lock-up. With my experience of the courts so far, I couldn't dare to think positive and thought I might be brought back. Rama organised with some activists to collect them and have them sent to us.

The court not only declared my arrest illegal but also conceded to my lawyer's argument that it was contempt of the apex court. The judge sent a note to the Supreme Court, stating that the police had violated their order by arresting me despite their protection.

This was in the court. But who would account for the lies of the police issued for public consumption? As the Press Trust of India reported, Shivaji Bodkhe, joint commissioner of Pune police, had said that 'Teltumbde was interrogated and later arrested by the Pune Police. He would be produced in the court later in the day.'[1] It could easily be verified that no police officer met me, let alone interrogated me. Should Bodkhe, in a responsible position, not be punished for telling lies to the public?

4

Protests and Support

Injustice anywhere is a threat to justice everywhere.
Martin Luther King Jr.

THERE WERE SPONTANEOUS PROTESTS by students and civil rights organisations against my arrest all over the country and abroad. The IIM Ahmedabad community, to which I belonged, said:

> He is a role model for so many of us, faculty and students alike. It's rare to find someone from IIM A with such a distinguished corporate career, to stand up for democracy and social justice. He provides our campus with a guiding hope for a better future for this country.[1]

Both IIM Ahmedabad and IIT Kharagpur, two premier institutes I was associated with, came out in unflinching support of me. Some faculty members of the former issued a statement:

> As faculty members, we are proud not only of Professor Teltumbde's achievements in the corporate world but also of the extremely rich scholarship he has produced on a diverse range of topics, including the Constitution of India. We are alarmed that a public intellectual who has made selfless contributions to the nation through his scholarship, can be under the threat of imprisonment on the basis of extremely questionable and prima facie motivated evidence.[2]

Another statement issued jointly by students and faculty said: 'Professor Teltumbde has contributed significantly to the cause of social justice and his actions have been in the interest of strengthening Indian democracy. We are concerned about the repression faced by persons who speak for social justice, and those who serve as role models for the aspiring youth.'[3] IIT Kharagpur students and faculty demonstrated on campus and also issued a statement condemning the arrest.[4]

Most notable was the response of my current institute, Goa Institute of Management, which stood resolutely by me. The print edition of *Times of India* in Goa featured a boxed news item on its front page: 'GIM stands with its Big Data Boss'.[5] Upon hearing of my arrest, my students collectively had approached the director, anxious about the future of their programme. The programme, the first of its kind,[6] entirely conceived and designed by me, was identified with me in the market, and now I was in police custody! The programme, though well received in the market,[7] was only in its second year and required continuous nurturing and updating to keep pace with the rapid technological advancements that were happening. My sudden absence raised fears that everything would come to a standstill. When news of my release by the court arrived, a wave of relief swept through the campus.

A couple of days later, a senior member of the GIM Society and Governing Board, accompanied by the director of the institute, came over to Mumbai and met me at our house. I was pleasantly overwhelmed by this moral support from the institute that dared to stand by me.

Our court battle resumed. At one point the Bombay High Court ordered the investigating officer who had insisted on my custodial interrogation to interrogate me as much as he wanted. We drove all the way to Pune for two consecutive days along with a lawyer for the so-called interrogation, which comprised merely the drawing up of the family tree and nothing remotely related to the case. The officer concluded the interrogation in just over a day and a half. Obviously, he had no questions left to ask me, but still he would say to the court that I had not cooperated and so custodial interrogation was required. One did not understand this business of custodial interrogation, which the courts keep silent on or worse, conceded to the police demand for. Later, in jail, I was pleasantly surprised to read about a senior police officer of inspector general rank, incidentally in charge of the entire prison system in Maharashtra during my incarceration, expressing similar doubt in his fictionalised account of his experiences in his debut novel, *Cops in a Quagmire*.[8] I was so impressed that I wrote a review of it in prison. It was published by The Wire when I came out of prison.[9] I feel tempted to cite him (the protagonist in the book):

> We apply to the magistrates for police custody remand of the accused and they grant it. Reasons quoted – custodial interrogation of the accused and recovery of stolen goods or weapons used to commit the crime. Isn't it implicit that we intend to beat the hell out of the fellow? Internationally, any person arrested for a crime has a right to silence, meaning he has a right not to answer any of the questions asked by the police. Even the Constitution of our country has a similar provision. Doesn't that make police custody remand unconstitutional, especially if the accused has no wish to cooperate with the investigation?[10]

My wife and I stayed in Mumbai until the process was complete. When we returned to Goa, I immediately went with some of my faculty to the data lab where the students were working on their assignments. As soon as they saw me, they began to clap and continued until I interrupt their clapping with a 'thank you'.

These students, aspiring to enter the corporate world, might have been apprehensive about openly expressing their support for me, but their applause within those four walls spoke volumes. It was an expression of their faith and confidence in me. I was overwhelmed with emotion but managed to address their key concern. I said they should not worry about their future. I assured them that no matter what happened to me, I would ensure that they were placed as promised. My only condition remained that they put sincere efforts into learning. I asked them if they had any questions for me.

As I finished speaking, one girl stood up and asked, 'How have you been, sir?' Tears welled up in my eyes. I simply said, 'Carry on,' and left the lab.

The next day, I resumed my professorial routine. We already had an excellent response from the market, with many companies lined up for campus visits.

Support poured in from all directions. We had an event in Bengaluru wherein alumni turned up in good numbers. Each one met me curiously and complimented me, saying they now saw GIM as a happening place. Some confessed that for the first time they felt proud to be alumni of GIM.

One day, around twenty faculty members from a local Goa college came over to express their solidarity with me. I was taken by surprise and thanked them. Teachers from a local school organised a small programme to felicitate and support me. Many civil society groups also visited at my office as well as home to show their backing for me. Three formal public meetings were organised in Goa, in Madgaon, Panjim and Mhapsa, where I informed the audience about the case and its status at the time. Similar meetings took place in many places in my absence in Goa and outside, condemning the police action against me.

My friend Martin Macwan of Navsarjan Gujarat informed me that Dalit organisations in contact with them had demonstrated at 168 locations across the country simultaneously at 11 a.m. in front of the statues of Ambedkar in their localities, protesting my arrest. Invitations to seminars and talks from all over the country resumed. During this period, some organisations declared me as recipient of their prestigious awards. Notably, I received the Professor M. Vaidyanathan Memorial Award in Kerala and the Bodhisattva Award from Spoorthidhama, an impressive institution created by Ambedkarites in Bengaluru. The citation, besides accounting for my professional accomplishments, inter alia, stated:

> His understanding and interpretation of the epistemology has created a paradigm shift in the area and has further resulted in the bettering of the subaltern, stigmatized and socially excluded communities; thus, establishing equality and peace in the Nation, which has paved way for the development of a harmonious civil society. His highly distinguished research and studies have played an instrumental role in the policy making and acted as guidelines for the good governance.

Before the colourful award function in the evening, a meeting of over a hundred activists representing various organisations in Karnataka was organised at Ambedkar Habba (Ambedkar Festival), at Spoorthidhama, a campus in Bedarahalli, Bengaluru dedicated to upholding the values of equality and social justice given by Ambedkar.[11] I was seated behind a table in a crowded hall. The proceedings were conducted in Kannada, and I was just conveyed the gist that the activists individually wanted to express their solidarity with me. I thanked them but wondered what it meant. If they had all converged to support me, why were they saying it in so many voices? Could that not be one? Could they not have a united body? Did they still not understand that their lack of unity enabled the fascist state to lay its hands on me? Fragmented, they risked arrest one by one so that none would be left in the end to express solidarity with anyone. I didn't know if what I said hurt them. I hoped not.

Back at the institute, some faculty colleagues took the initiative to hold an official meeting regarding my situation. They wanted me to be present, but I suggested that they proceed without me and, if needed, call me at the end to provide them further information and answer queries. Accordingly, they conducted the meeting in my absence and, once it concluded, invited me to brief them on the case and address their questions.

The discussion was unexpected, but I explained everything to them – the circumstances leading to the case, the developments that followed, and my current position. I also outlined the broader context, pre-empting many of their concerns.

The following day, the institute officially passed a resolution expressing confidence in me and concern over the harassment I was facing. The resolution was prominently displayed on all notice boards and remained there until my departure from the institute on 24 March 2020.

In the thick of my incrimination by the state, this institute had also honoured me by inviting me to join its board of governors.

With a sword of Damocles hanging over my head, we carried out all our plans undisturbed. Both summer and permanent placements went exceptionally well, surpassing average salary expectations. However, my faculty colleague Hemant Padhiari, who had excellently handled this crucial responsibility, did not live to see me free. Learning of his passing was painful, reconciling with it even more so.

As my arrest became inevitable following the Supreme Court's rejection of my anticipatory bail petition, protests, demonstrations and signature campaigns surged with renewed intensity. University students across India, civil society organisations and alumni networks, including pan-IIM and pan-IIT campaigns, mobilised in large numbers demanding my release.

Amid this growing support, an unsavoury episode left a bitter taste. At my alma mater, the Visvesvaraya National Institute of Technology (VNIT) in Nagpur, a student-led protest and signature campaign was met with fierce resistance from Hindutva-aligned students, escalating into a physical scuffle on campus.

Even more disheartening was the reaction of some of my classmates from IIM Ahmedabad. Anxious about my impending arrest, my younger daughter, Rashmi, herself an alumnus of the institute, wrote to our alumni group urging them to stand in protest. One classmate – whom I once considered reasonable – flatly refused, citing 'national interest', a clear echo of Hindutva propaganda at work. Angry at his response, she retorted on the group that she was ashamed to have passed out of the institute that produced such unthinking simpletons. Upset by it, she advised me to leave the group, which I did without hesitation. Despite the later exposure of the facts surrounding my case, none of them reached out to me – not even after my release.

The polarisation was stark. VNIT's response was somewhat expected, given its reported saffronisation, but IIM Ahmedabad stood in firm solidarity with me. Barring my batch, its alumni, students, faculty, and even the director actively campaigned for my release. The indifference of my own classmates, however, was telling – they didn't even sign the pan-IIM petition. It didn't matter in any tangible way to me, but it revealed just how deeply propaganda had fractured social bonds. And yes, it left a very bitter taste.

5

Theatre of the Absurd

You can put a man in jail, but you can't take away his faith and will.
Uladzimir Mikhalko

It was Saturday evening, 25 January 2020. I was vigorously working since morning on a book I was trying to complete before they took me in. As I was still buried in my books, Rama came in almost shouting that the Centre had transferred our case to the National Investigating Agency (NIA). There was nothing unbelievable any more, but I went out to see it myself on TV. I had a nauseating feeling about the brazenness of the regime.

When the Bhima-Koregaon case was categorised as a scheduled offence by the Pune police, the state government, as per procedure, had to report it to the Centre for review and a decision on whether the NIA should take over the investigations. The Centre also had independent authority to direct the NIA to investigate any scheduled offence. This meant that the Centre had full discretion to override the state police's investigations and transfer the case to the NIA.

In contrast, the legal framework governing the Central Bureau of Investigation (CBI) does not restrict it to a list of scheduled offences, but it cannot investigate cases in any state without the consent of the state government in question. Thus, the issue was not about the Centre's authority to transfer the case from the state police to the NIA, but about the propriety of doing so after one and a half years of investigations and the filing of a charge sheet.

If the Centre had been satisfied with the Pune police's investigations, why did it suddenly hand over the case to the

NIA? The answer was straightforward: politics, the change of government in Maharashtra. The Centre had confidence in the investigations as long as the BJP was in power in the state. But after the BJP's defeat and the formation of a coalition government of the Shiv Sena, Congress (INC) and the Nationalist Congress Party (NCP), that confidence vanished. *The Hindu* called the transfer of the case to the NIA a 'dubious decision' and commented, 'NIA's takeover of Bhima Koregaon probe is a ploy to perpetuate "urban Naxal" narrative.'[1]

In its characteristic hubris, the BJP did not expect it would lose power in the 2019 state assembly elections in Maharashtra. Although it emerged as the single biggest party with 105 seats, it needed the support of its alliance partner, the Shiv Sena, which had won 56 seats. Together, they were well past the majority mark of 145 and could form the government. However, the Shiv Sena declined to support the BJP as, allegedly, the BJP did not keep its pre-poll promise of sharing power and tenure of chief ministership equally with it. In view of the impasse, President's rule was imposed in the state. On 23 November 2019, a bizarre drama took place. The governor of Maharashtra, Bhagat Singh Koshyari, stealthily administered the oath of office to Devendra Fadnavis of the BJP as the chief minister, and Ajit Pawar, who walked over from NCP to support the BJP claiming the allegiance of NCP members of the legislative assembly, as the deputy chief minister at 8 a.m. However, the government collapsed as the makeshift alliance failed to attain the requisite number even after three days of this oath-taking. Again, President's rule was imposed in the state. The crisis was resolved two days later with the Shiv Sena, NCP and INC coming together to form a new alliance, the Maha Vikas Aaghadi (MVA), and forming the government with Uddhav Thackeray as the chief minister.

After the formation of the government, the Bhima-Koregaon case was curiously picked up by the MVA government, especially by its important component, the NCP, seemingly to politically embarrass the BJP. Sharad Pawar, the NCP supremo, went around saying in public meetings that it was a case cooked up by Pune police at the behest of the BJP. He demanded that an SIT be set up under a retired judge to probe the action taken by the

Pune police in the case.² Other prominent leaders of the NCP, such as Jitendra Awhad and Nawab Malik, who were ministers in the MVA government, called it a fake case, a 'conspiracy' of the previous BJP-led government. Malik also called the Bhima-Koregaon violence as 'pre-planned'.³ Surprisingly, the Congress and the Shiv Sena were conspicuous by their silence, indicating either that it was a strategic division of work at play or discord within the government on this matter.

On 21 December 2019, Sharad Pawar issued a statement that his party, a coalition partner in the government, would ask the chief minister to form an SIT to investigate the Bhima-Koregaon case properly.⁴ On 23 January, Maharashtra Home Minister Anil Deshmukh, along with Ajit Pawar, deputy chief minister, reviewed the case with senior officials of the Pune police and the home ministry of Maharashtra. Deshmukh indicated that the government would, within a week, decide whether to drop the case or to set up an SIT to probe it. The next day, that is, 24 January 2020, Sharad Pawar wrote a letter to Chief Minister Uddhav Thackeray seeking constitution of an SIT to probe the Bhima-Koregaon cases.⁵ The very next day the Union ministry of home affairs transferred the case to the NIA.⁶

The decision of the Centre left the Maharashtra government fuming. The home minister, Anil Deshmukh, condemned the Centre's decision to transfer the case to the NIA.⁷ He tweeted that the Centre took the decision after the new Shiv Sena-NCP-Congress government had decided to 'go to the root of the matter'.⁸ NCP chief Sharad Pawar claimed that the Centre's decision to transfer the probe to the NIA was motivated by fears that a fresh investigation could expose the wrongdoings on the part of the BJP-led government. Speaking to reporters the next day, that is, 25 January, Pawar pointed out that the case had been transferred within five hours of his writing to Chief Minister Uddhav Thackeray asking for a probe by an SIT. He also hit out against the labelling of people who spoke out against social injustice as 'urban Naxals'.⁹ It would be interesting to know who in the MVA government might have been providing real-time information to the Centre. Politicians, police, or both?

Given the fact that the Shiv Sena was part of the previous Fadnavis government that developed the Bhima-Koregaon case, it did not share the enthusiasm of the NCP for an SIT investigation.[10] The Congress party in the state, unlike its national leader Rahul Gandhi, who had questioned the arrests, chose to maintain silence on the issue. The bureaucracy and police were anyway complicit. In such a context, the NCP's ploughing a lonely furrow for the SIT appeared quite odd. Sharad Pawar was not a political novice not to know how to get things done if he sincerely believed in what he said. Certainly, speaking around in public and to the press was not the method by which to institute an SIT probe into the case that involved high stakes for the state as well as the deep state. He could have built a consensus internally, within the government and got the state cabinet to decide on it. His actions certainly reflected the realisation that the people expected the new government to expose the truth behind the Bhima-Koregaon case. But the risks of meeting these expectations, the astute politician in Pawar knew, outweighed the gains. Therefore he devised a win-win strategy of pandering to mass sentiment and at the same time creating conditions that would take the case away from the state's ambit.

Sharad Pawar was obviously playing a game, as he mostly does. In 2018, less than forty-eight hours after the violence breaking out at Bhima-Koregaon, Pawar had called it the handiwork of 'outsiders' and said he had learned from some locals that it could be the work of right-wing leaders.[11] He now accused Pune police of plotting it. He kept talking about an SIT, arguing that Section 10 of the NIA Act allowed parallel investigation by the state government. He knew all this would fade away from public memory in due course, as it indeed did.

The drama of the actual transfer of the case began with the NIA moving a Pune court on 30 January for transfer of all records in the case to the special NIA court in Mumbai. Defence lawyers argued that the special court in Pune was not competent to hear the NIA application and that the application should be filed in the Bombay High Court. The state government, which had hitherto showed hostility to transfer of the case, was now lamely opposing the move, saying that the Pune police had ample evidence against the accused in the Elgar Parishad case, and its transfer to the NIA was not tenable.[12] In its reply, it was rather reinforcing the case for its transfer by irreverently stating: 'It is not a case of arrest because of mere dissenting views expressed or difference in the political ideology of the named accused but concerning their link with members of the banned organisation and its activities.' The reply specifically named Gautam Navlakha and me.[13] By then all the noises from the NCP camp had died down.

After the 14 February 2020 decision of the additional sessions court in Pune allowing the NIA application, Uddhav Thackeray on 18 February was still displaying his bravado, saying he would never allow transfer of the Bhima-Koregaon case to the Centre and jeopardise the interests of 'my Dalit brothers'. It was a poor ploy to distance Dalits from our case. In common parlance, our case is referred to as the Elgar Parishad–Bhima-Koregaon case, since the prosecution alleges that the Elgar Parishad event held on 31 December 2017 incited the violence at Bhima-Koregaon the following day. However, there is a separate case pertaining specifically to the riots that occurred on 1 January 2018. That case was never considered for transfer to the Centre or the NIA. Uddhav Thackeray, in a display of pseudo concern for Dalits, attempted to distinguish between the two cases – only to muddy the waters further.

The instance thus exposed the essential anatomy of the case being fully engulfed in pure politics.

6

Surrender during the Pandemic

A political prisoner is someone who is out fighting for his or her people's rights and freedom and is imprisoned for that alone.

Leonard Peltier

THE ONE-MONTH PERIOD GRANTED by the Supreme Court for my obtaining anticipatory bail had long expired during the court proceedings. After the arrest-and-release drama in Pune, we proceeded to appeal the rejection by the sessions court at the Bombay High Court. Each time the hearing took place in the high court, my protection from arrest had to be specifically extended until the next hearing.

There were periods when I was without legal protection, constantly fearing that the police could arrive at any moment. During these times, my wife and I lived under immense tension, anxiously awaiting word from our lawyer about extension of protection to me. On at least two occasions, I had to go into hiding.

The first was at a resort in south Goa, where a journalist friend had arranged for my stay. Apart from the two of us, the resort was filled with foreigners, mostly from various European cities, who gathered there annually for extended stays.

The resort owner, a devout Christian, was deeply moved upon hearing my story from my friend. He was so disturbed that he couldn't sleep that night. The next day, when we reached the resort, he went out of his way to host us, offering us special drinks and elaborate meals. When I went to settle the bill, he refused to accept any payment, saying this was his way of paying tribute to his Jesus. Before we left, he warmly invited me to return with my family once I was free from the case. I promised I would, though in my mind I couldn't help but wonder when that day would come.

Another time I stayed in Madgaon with an old friend who was socially well established. Living like a fugitive, cut off from communication, was an unsettling experience. I couldn't even use the phone. My only solace was his extensive collection of Marathi books, which I immersed myself in during my days in hiding. It was only after my lawyer confirmed that my legal protection had been formalised that I finally returned home to the campus.

Ultimately, on 14 February 2020, the Bombay High Court dismissed my appeal. This was despite a previous order from the Pune Sessions Court, which had ruled that my arrest was illegal and in contempt of the Supreme Court. Undeterred, the Pune police filed an interim application seeking directions for Gautam Navlakha and me (since our applications were linked in the high court) to be physically present at the time of the judgement – presumably so they could arrest us at the court itself. Their move made it clear that they anticipated rejection of our appeal.

Fortunately, the Bombay High Court dismissed their request and granted us four weeks to appeal the judgement at the Supreme Court.

Meanwhile, alarm bells were ringing globally. The World Health Organisation (WHO) confirmed that a novel coronavirus was the cause of a respiratory illness detected in a cluster of people in Wuhan, China. It was reported to WHO on 31 December 2019. On the same day, India also reported cases of respiratory illness in Jaipur. By 11 January 2020, WHO confirmed that the illness was caused by the coronavirus. A month later, the National Institute of Virology (NIV), Pune, identified India's first confirmed case – a twenty-year-old female in Thrissur who had returned from Wuhan. By 3 February, Thrissur's case count had risen to three, all students who had returned from Wuhan.

Throughout February there was no significant rise in transmission. However, on 4 March, twenty-two new cases were reported, including fourteen members of an Italian tourist group. By 15 March, India had 107 confirmed cases.

Our application for anticipatory bail (Gautam Navlakha's and mine) was scheduled for a hearing before a bench of Justices Arun Mishra and M.R. Shah on 16 March 2020. At the time, I was in Mumbai for group discussions and interviews related to selection of students for my programme. Given the circumstances, I had little hope of a favourable judgement. My arrest seemed imminent in Mumbai itself, as soon as the court pronounced its rejection.

Despite the obvious stress, I maintained my composure, ensuring that my team of faculty remained unaware of what might unfold. We were staying at the President Hotel in Cuffe Parade in Mumbai. The previous evening, a few Marathi news portals interviewed me in the hotel, and several friends who were closely following the case came by to meet me.

On the morning of 16 March, my sisters video-called me – almost as though they were bidding me farewell before my arrest. I reassured them, trying to ease their anxiety, and then proceeded to work as usual.

In the midst of the interviews, I received a call informing me that the court had rejected our application. However, in a small relief, we were granted three weeks to surrender. I closed my phone and, without missing a beat, continued with the interviews.

As each day passed, the warnings about the pandemic became more urgent and ominous. Governments worldwide scrambled to bolster their healthcare systems to confront the looming crisis.[1] The Indian government's initial response was limited to thermal screening of passengers arriving from China at seven airports starting 21 January 2020. This was later expanded to twenty airports and included travellers from other affected countries like Thailand, Singapore, Hong Kong, Japan and South Korea. Despite these measures, complacency set in as February saw relatively few cases. However, by March the situation had worsened, prompting the government to issue an advisory urging states to implement social distancing measures until 31 March.

Modi's response was symptomatic of his tendency to convert every crisis into a political spectacle. On 19 March, in his characteristic fashion, he announced a 'janata curfew' for 22

March, urging people to stay home from 9 a.m. to 9 p.m. He also called upon citizens to step on to their balconies or doorways at 5 p.m. to clap, beat metal plates or ring bells in gratitude to our frontline health workers. The exercise, though performative, received an overwhelming response. On campus, we could hear clapping and the banging of thalis from both the hostel complex and some faculty quarters. Across India, people complied. However, the symbolic act was soon overshadowed by chaotic street processions, where crowds gathered in several cities, blowing conch shells, clanging vessels and chanting 'Jai Shri Ram'.

In March 2020, the Tablighi Jamaat, a Muslim sect, held a congregation at its Markaz in Delhi's Nizamuddin, attended by members from around seventy countries. The event occurred weeks before the COVID-19 guidelines restricting social and religious gatherings were issued. It was confined to a building, yet the BJP government seized upon it to fuel Islamophobic propaganda, blaming the Jamaat for spreading the virus in India. Soon hashtags like #CoronaJihad and #TablighiJamatVirus flooded social media. On 3 April, the government blacklisted 950 foreign nationals allegedly involved in the event and announced that some members would be charged under India's National Security Act for violating quarantine.

While Muslims were vilified, the government turned a blind eye to the Kumbh Mela in Haridwar, which took place from 14 January to 30 April 2021 and saw the participation of over 70 lakh Hindu devotees. The government had announced the Kumbh Mela would be held from 1 April to 30 April 2021. Yet it turned a blind eye as pilgrims began arriving as early as January and crowds swelled in March, well before the official start. Even as the WHO raised the alarm about the virus on 11 January 2020, the BJP-led Uttarakhand government proceeded with the event. Chief Minister Tirath Singh Rawat irresponsibly justified it, claiming, 'The flow and blessings of Ma Ganga will ensure that coronavirus does not spread.'[2]

There was no question of following any COVID-19 protocols. Pilgrims, many without masks, packed trains and public transport. It is now well documented that the Kumbh Mela played a critical role in exacerbating India's COVID-19 crisis, triggering a devastating second wave of the pandemic.[3] Several infections across the country were traced to returnees from the event. Modi remained silent throughout, but by 17 April 2021 – far too late – he finally urged that the Kumbh Mela 'should now only be symbolic'. By then, over 5,000 people had tested positive for COVID-19 in the Haridwar Kumbh Mela area between 10 and 17 April.[4]

Although official figures attributed only 6,000–9,000 COVID-19 cases to the Kumbh Mela, independent estimates suggest the true toll ran into tens of thousands, with hundreds of deaths indirectly linked to the event. Sero-surveys in June–July 2021 indicated that 70 per cent to 80 per cent of Haridwar's population had antibodies, pointing to widespread undetected transmission. A post-Kumbh surge was reported in states such as Rajasthan, Maharashtra and Delhi, driven by returning pilgrims. Studies by the All India Institute of Medical Sciences (Delhi) and references by the WHO noted mass gatherings in India as key factors in the Delta variant's global spread. *The Lancet* (July 2021) sharply criticised the Indian government for allowing the Kumbh Mela to proceed despite repeated warnings.

As the pandemic intensified, colleges and institutes across the country shut down, including ours. We decided to suspend the convocation. Rumours were rife that flights might be grounded soon. My wife and I had some urgent work in Mumbai, so we planned a quick trip before that. As we boarded our flight on 24 March 2020, news broke that Modi had declared a nationwide lockdown – yet another abrupt, unplanned decision, reminiscent of demonetisation.

Upon landing in Mumbai, chaos reigned. There were no taxis; we had to call for a vehicle from home. Now we were effectively stranded. The sudden lockdown inconvenienced numerous air travellers like us, leaving us with extended waits just to get our own car. But what about those without private vehicles? And what about the millions of migrant workers stranded in cities, suddenly left without work? With no alternative, they had no choice but to return home. Thousands crowded railway and bus stations in desperation, risking their lives and aggravating the spread of the pandemic.

By the time I surrendered to the NIA, COVID-19 deaths were mounting across the country and the virus had become a terrifying prospect – especially for those with respiratory issues like me. Besides my asthma, I suffered from both cervical and lumbar spondylitis – conditions barely kept under control. As I left our transit home in Rajgruha that day, a haunting thought lingered: I might never return.

In India, the idea of social distancing is a veritable oxymoron. With a population of over 1.3 billion and a density of 464 people per square kilometre – against China's 153 and the United States' mere 36 – physical distancing is nearly impossible. An average Indian family consists of five members, and 40 per cent of all homes, approximately 100 million, have only a single room.

Social distancing was a privilege that only the upper middle class could afford; for the rest, five or six people crammed into a single room was the norm.

The declaration of the lockdown gave our lawyers some hope that our surrender could be postponed until the restrictions were lifted. They moved an application for the same, but the court refused to relent, ordering us to surrender within a week – on or before 14 April.

By this point I had become numb to everything. I was in the midst of completing a book I had committed to a publisher and had been working intensely since the rejection of my quashing petition by the Supreme Court. The second round of legal proceedings, starting from the Pune court and dragging through the high court, had given me some time to work on it. But now I had to conclude it. Additionally, I needed to secure my hard-disk content with a hash value, given the record of seizure of electronic devices of the accused in the case. The police simply took them away, and without taking a hash value that would secure the contents from any post-seizure tampering. I recorded the hash value of my hard disk, removed it from my laptop – which, in any case, belonged to the GIM – and set it aside.

On the evening of 13 April, calls poured in from all over – some expressing sorrow, some literally crying, some offering words of strength. Some people had gathered for meetings and wanted to hear me speak over the phone. I called my siblings, instructing them not to reveal the truth to our mother as she would not be able to bear the shock of my imprisonment. She was used to my frequent foreign tours, so the excuse that flights weren't operating due to the pandemic could serve as a plausible alibi.

At the stroke of midnight, as members of the Ambedkar family, we descended to the room in Rajgruha where Babasaheb's ashes rest, to pay our respects on his birth anniversary. During my years posted in Mumbai, we would mostly travel from our home on Napean Sea Road to Rajgruha to take part in the ritual. But this time was different. After a decade away from the city, I found myself back at Rajgruha – not only to pay my homage but also to surrender to the police as an accused, under the very Constitution supposedly authored by him. The irony was unmistakable. We stood before the urn for a customary prayer. Outside, a police van had already arrived and was parked across the road, likely observing our movements. On the terrace of the first floor, opposite the Buddhist flag, my wife and nephews hoisted a black flag in protest of my impending arrest. After returning to our room, I went to bed and had a sound sleep.

The next morning, calls from friends continued relentlessly. I spoke with my daughters, instructing them to write to me regularly and not to worry. I transmitted all my important contacts to my elder daughter and asked her to handle matters in my absence. I also passed on the manuscript of the book I considered I had completed and asked her to manage the process with the publishers. I thought everything was done. I ate what I believed to be my last lunch at home.

Then, suddenly, I realised I had not yet sent out my 'Open Letter to the People of India', which was still on my computer. I quickly emailed it to my daughters and then to a group of friends, who ensured it was published widely across portals and newspapers.[5]

Here is the full text of the letter:

You will speak out before your turn comes

I am aware this may be completely drowned in the motivated cacophony of the BJP-RSS combine and the subservient media but I still think it may be worth talking to you as I do not know whether I would get another opportunity.

Since August 2018, when the police raided my house in faculty housing complex of Goa Institute of Management, my world turned completely topsy-turvy. Never in my worst dream, could I imagine the things that began happening to me. Although, I was aware that police used to visit the organisers of my lectures, mostly universities, and scare them with enquiries about me, I thought they might be mistaking me for my brother who left family years back [his story is told later in the book]. While I was teaching at IIT Kharagpur, an officer of BSNL phoned, introducing himself as my admirer and well-wisher, informed me that my phone was being tapped. I thanked him but did nothing, not even to change my sim. I was disturbed by these intrusions but comforted myself that it might rather convince Police that I was a normal person and there is no element of illegality in my conduct. The Police generally disliked civil rights activists because they question police. I imagined, it might be due to the fact that I belonged to that tribe. But again, I comforted myself that they would find that I could not perform that role either because of my full-time engagement with my job.

But when I got an early morning phone call from the Director of my institute, informing me that the Police have raided the campus and were looking for me, I was wordless for a few seconds. I had come to Mumbai on official work just a few hours before and my wife had come earlier. When I learned of the arrests, of the persons whose houses were raided that day, I was shaken by the realisation that I escaped their fate just by whiskers. The Police did know my whereabouts and could arrest me even then but for the reasons known only to them, did not do so. They did open our house too, forcibly getting a duplicate key from the security guard, but just video-graphed it and locked it back. Our ordeal began right there.

At the advice of our lawyers, my wife took the next available flight to Goa, and lodged a complaint with Bicholim Police Station that the Police had opened our house in our absence and that we would not be responsible if they had planted anything. She volunteered giving our telephone numbers should the Police want to inquire with us.

Strangely, police had started holding press conferences soon after they embarked on the Maoist story. It was clearly meant to whip up prejudice in public against me and other arrested with the help of obliging media. On 31 August 2018, in one such press conference, a police officer read out a letter purportedly recovered from the computer of previous arrestees, as evidence against me. The letter was clumsily constructed with the information on the academic conference I had attended which was easily available on the website of American University of Paris. Initially I laughed it out but next, decided to file a civil and criminal defamation suit against this officer and sent a letter on 5 September 2018 to the Government of Maharashtra for sanction as per the procedure. There has been no response from the government to date. The press conferences of the police, however, were stopped when High Court reprimanded them.

The RSS hand in the entire case was not hidden. My Marathi friends told me that one of their functionaries, Ramesh Patange, had written an article in their mouthpiece Panchjanya targeting me in April 2015. I was identified as Mayavi Ambedkarwadi along with Arundhati Roy and Gail Omvedt. Mayavi in the Hindu mythology refers to a demon meant to be destroyed. When I was illegally arrested by Pune Police while still under protection of the Supreme Court, a cyber-gang of Hindutva vandalized my Wikimedia page. This page is a public page and for years I was not even aware of it. They firstly deleted all information and only wrote 'he has a Maoist brother . . . his house was raided . . . he was arrested for links with Maoist', etc. Some students later told me that whenever they tried restoring the page, or editing the page, this gang would pounce upon and delete everything and put derogatory content. Ultimately, Wikimedia intervened and the page stabilized with some of their negative content.

There was a media blitzkrieg, reeling off all kinds of canard through RSS' so called Naxal experts. My complaints against the channels and even to the India Broadcasting Foundation, did not receive a simple response. Then in October 2019, the Pegasus story came out that the government had inserted a very pernicious Israeli spyware on my phone, among others. There was a momentary uproar in media but this serious matter also has died still death.

I have been a simple person who has been earning his bread honestly and helping people to the extent possible with my knowledge through writings. I have had an unblemished record of service for nearly five decades to this country in various roles in corporate world, as a teacher, as a civil rights activist and a public intellectual. In my voluminous writings comprising over 30 books, and numerous papers/articles/comments/columns/interviews, published internationally, not an insinuation of support to violence or any subversive movement could be found. But at the far end of my life, I am being charged for the heinous crime under the draconian UAPA.

An individual like me obviously cannot counter the spirited propaganda of the government and its subservient media. The details of the case are strewn across the Net and are enough for any person to see that it is a clumsy and criminal fabrication. A summary note on AIFRTE website may be read. For your benefit I will provide its gist here:

I am implicated on the basis of the five letters among the 13 that the police purportedly recovered from the computers of two arrestees in the case. Nothing has been recovered from me. The letter makes reference to 'Anand', a common name in India, but the police unquestioningly identified it with me. Notwithstanding the form and content of these letters, which were trashed by experts and even by a justice of the Supreme Court, who was the only one in the entire judiciary to have gone into the nature of the evidence. The content does not refer to anything that could be remotely construed as even a simple crime. But taking shelter under the draconian provisions of the UAPA Act, that renders a person defenceless I am being jailed.

The case may be depicted for your understanding as follows: Suddenly, a police posse descends down on your residence and ransacks your house without showing any warrant. At the end, they arrest you and put in the police lockup. In the court, they would say that while investigating a theft (or any other complaint) case in xxx place (substitute any place in India) police recovered a pen drive or a computer from yyy (substitute any name) in which some letters written by a supposed member of some banned organisation were recovered that had a mention of zzz who according to the police is none other than you. They present you as part of deep conspiracy. Suddenly, you find your world turned topsy-turvy: your job gone, family losing house, and media defaming you about which you cannot do a damn thing. Police will produce 'sealed envelopes' to convince judges that there was a prima facie case against you that needs custodial interrogation. No arguments about there being no evidence would be entertained as judges would answer that it would be seen in trial. After custodial interrogation you will be sent to jail. You beg for bail and the courts will reject them as the historical data shows that the average period of incarceration ranged from 4 to 10 years before they got bail or acquitted. And this can happen literally to ANYONE.

In the name of 'nation' such draconian legislations that denude innocent people of their liberties and all constitutional rights are constitutionally validated. The jingoist nation and nationalism have got weaponised by the political class to destroy dissent and polarize people. The mass frenzy has accomplished complete denationalization and inversion of meanings where destroyers of the nation become *deshbhakts* and selfless servers of people become *deshdrohis*. As I see my India being ruined, it is with a feeble hope that I write to you at such a grim moment. Well, I am off to NIA custody and do not know when I shall be able to talk to you again. However, I earnestly hope that you will speak out before your turn comes.

7

Entering the Hellhole

There is no greater hell than to be a prisoner of fear.

Ben Jonson

I WAS NEITHER THRILLED nor nervous at the prospect of going to jail on 14 April 2020, the birth anniversary of Babasaheb Ambedkar, incidentally from his own Rajgruha, where my wife had an apartment, wherein we stayed after coming from Goa. It may be because the Damocles' sword of imminent arrest had hung too long over my head for me to feel its weight. My mind was as empty as the streets of Mumbai, deserted during the lockdown, as I was being driven to the NIA office, escorted by my brother-in-law, Prakash Ambedkar; Kapil Patil, member of the legislative council; my wife; and a nephew. As decided, some activist friends came over to Kemp's Corner to see me off at the NIA office, just about a couple of hundred metres away, but they would not be let into its premises.

The NIA was in a building from which we stayed just about a kilometre away at Nepean Sea Road for seventeen years. It was moreover close to my daughters' school on Peddar Road, and where one of their friends, who often came to our house, stayed. But everything looked Kafkaesque, unfamiliar. Those days, it was not the NIA office. As the police at the gate let us in, the gates were shut behind us, following the police's standard operating procedure. From nowhere a crowd of journalists showed up at the gate with their cameras, trying to catch a distant glimpse of me, shouting out my name for a byte. I turned back and waved at them but was prevented by the cops from even doing that. Still, some people stole a snap of me for the next day's news. The police did not let anyone come up with me into the building except my wife and a lawyer friend, Maharukh Adenwala. We were taken by a lift to the seventh floor to the NIA and seated in what looked like a reception area. The place was unlike a police station, being housed in a modern building, but the air was eerie. Most of the people moving around appeared to be civilians except for some policemen in uniform seated at the entrance of what looked like an office of a government department.

After a while, we were conducted into a big room, the office of the superintendent of police (SP), in-charge of the NIA, and seated in chairs placed according to social distancing protocol because of the pandemic. My lawyer friend informed the SP that I was surrendering as per the order of the Supreme Court, which did not necessarily mean that the NIA should arrest me. The SP did not mince his words. He said he was arresting me and got the paperwork completed. I was taken to a cell which was behind a steel-barred door at the end of the corridor, not dissimilar to the one I had experience of in Pune but much neater and excessively lit by an intense beam from a high-wattage bulb directed from outside and into the cell. I was allowed some clothes and medicines in a backpack, which of course stayed outside the cell. The balance things, which included a book and a notebook, had to be returned with my wife.

After a short while, I was taken to the court escorted by two cops sandwiching me in the seat behind the driver. By now I was used to this police procession. The roads on which I was daily driven to my office looked strange and dreary. Even the people who were part of my defence team looked like strangers playing complementary roles in a Kafkaesque, surrealist drama. One cop in my escort, when left alone with me in the vehicle, whispered to me that it was ironic that they had arrested me on the birth anniversary of Babasaheb Ambedkar and told me that there was quite an unease among the Ambedkarites outside. I asked for details, but by then he saw his colleague coming in and stiffened into official formality. He occasionally appeared during my NIA custody but never made eye contact again.

The other policemen were mostly cordial. One, whose surname indicated he was a Brahmin, was particularly considerate. He inquired about my food preferences, ensured I had hot water for my bath and promptly arranged for my medicines. I couldn't help but contrast the confidence of this Brahmin cop with the apprehension of the Dalit one who had spoken to me in a whisper earlier.

The biggest physical ordeal was sleeping on the floor with a thin bed sheet and another as a cover. Though the SP had agreed in the courtroom with the judge's advice to provide me with a cot, mattress, etc., as I was 'also an officer', the SP went back on his word and informed me through his administrative subordinate that he was unable to provide me a cot nor would permit me to get one from outside. He took shelter under the written order, which obviously did not have directions to provide me with a cot and mattress. However, he instructed his people to get me a cotton mattress, which hardly helped as my real difficulty was bending down to lie on the floor and getting up again to go to the toilet. Every time I went to the toilet, I had to indulge in risky acrobatics to get up. A cop would open the lock, accompany me to the toilet just ten feet away, and artificially stand on guard within that small enclosure, although the lavatory could not be shut and the bathroom was nothing but an open space barely one and half feet wide with a tap just behind a partition separating the wash basins. I wondered if that floor in that modern high-rise was specially modified to be made sadistic enough to become a jail.

I also smiled at the thought of how the law-enforcement machinery shreds the right to dignity enshrined in Article 21 of the Constitution with impunity.

The saving grace was that I was supplied hot water for bathing, obviously instructed by the SP, as nothing moved without his specific permission. I would take a bath in that small space as quickly as possible so that nobody came to the bathroom and caught sight of me in the awkward state I was in. Another great privilege was the permission given to my wife and lawyer to meet me daily at the assigned time for an hour, but in the presence of a cop standing close by. Nothing else was permitted. I once asked a deputy SP, for a blank sheet of paper to keep my notes. He was the one who supposedly did my interrogation. He asked the SP, who declined the request. These irrationalities and humiliations, I realised, were part of the world that I would be living in for I did not know how long.

On the second day, the SP came to me and asked me to deposit my hard disk and mobile phone with the police. I had kept them ready, anticipating this demand. Rama brought them, and my lawyer, while handing them over, insisted upon the hash value being taken. But the SP declined, saying they did not take it. I told him that he should then acknowledge the hash value taken by me. He refused that too. An argument ensued, and he threatened my lawyer, saying he would cancel his meetings with me. It was clearly unlawful as it was my legal right to have my lawyer while I was interrogated as per the norm. But who cares; there appeared no law for the minions of the state. Whether it is an ill-educated policeman or his supposedly well-educated sahab, in the face of legal and rational challenge, they immediately resort to their presumed authority with impunity. Seizure of electronic devices without a hash value was a violation of procedure, which they openly did in our case.

The next day, my lawyer submitted the hash value to the court, as per my request. But the prosecution reportedly kicked up a fuss in the court, saying the lawyer was creating a huge interference in the investigation. Such false representations by the prosecution are a routine matter in courts. And the courts invariably accept the prosecution's word as gospel truth. How could there possibly be interference in an investigation when a lawyer was merely submitting a written argument to the court about what he perceived as a violation of the law? You reconcile in course of time with the asymmetry of the structure, the so-called rule of law. The justice delivery system in India is structurally skewed in favour of the state – it grants the state overwhelming discretion while subjecting the ordinary citizen to endless scrutiny. The state, in turn, aligns itself with the interests of the rich and powerful, leaving the common person with little recourse but to surrender to fate rather than expect fairness.

I lived in that place for eleven days, supposedly for my interrogation. During these days a young doctor from KEM Hospital would come religiously in the morning for my medical check-up. NIA brought the medicines as prescribed by him. My breakfast and lunch were outsourced and one cop was assigned the responsibility to get it in time. It was of reasonable quality and taste. I had a chair to sit on inside the cell but nothing to do. Suddenly, a cop would come and walk me behind him to an officer's room within that small, confined place. On the penultimate day, they took my pictures from all possible angles, then fingerprints on several papers with a stamp pad to colour both my palms violet. All this data is readily available in the Aadhaar database, but the sadistic system would continue with the old ways that entailed harassment of people. Aadhaar was supposed to be a substitute for all identification processes but nowhere had this actually happened. You have to have all kinds of previous paper identities and, above all, Aadhaar. Contrary to its projection as a support, it had become an additional instrument with which to harass people. But while all this is just humiliation and harassment to people like us, it is a question of life and death for the poor in remote areas!

My police custody had perhaps come to an end when the SP came over to my cell and informed me that they would 'deposit' me in a prison. What language! I would be deposited, like luggage! As a matter of fact, that confirmed the way the police handled you, sans feeling, emotion and dignity, as if you were an inanimate object. I was no longer a human. That also perhaps explained why the police infrastructure did not bother about Article 21.

In the court, my lawyers made a last-ditch effort for bail, raising the issue of my asthma, which would put me at risk of COVID-19 infection in jail. The public prosecutor read out some lines from my medical report to the judge, saying I had a minor blockage. It was an old report when my asthma was detected some twenty years ago, which had since worsened. The WHO's January 2020 guidelines clearly recognised the increased vulnerability of individuals with chronic respiratory conditions such as asthma and COPD to severe outcomes from COVID-19.

It emphasised the need for close monitoring of such patients, particularly for acute exacerbations and sudden drops in oxygen saturation, which could indicate life-threatening complications. It did not have a qualification of severity of asthma.

My wife and nephews had come to see me but were not allowed inside the court premises because of COVID-19 restrictions. They were running around to get a glimpse of me. After everything was done and we were parked in the premises for getting the paperwork done, with the SP's permission I was allowed to get the food my wife had brought for me. There was a long wait inside the car, the police sitting and sandwiching me. They were friendly, one of them being the same fellow who had taken care of my food and other needs earlier. The same guys would turn stern in the presence of others. Essentially, they feared each other – that one might bitch about the other. This is the way humane policemen look inhuman. After a long drive, we entered an unwelcoming, antiquated-looking gate that was better suited for a crematorium. Nobody would believe that it was barely a dozen years old – a grim testament to boundless corruption. The irony was stark: a place meant to contain crime stood as a monument to the criminality of unchecked graft.

A short drive and we reached the intimidating structure that was Taloja Central Prison. The vehicle was parked under a nearby tree. The cops went in with the papers and I was left with the driver, who had perhaps waited all along to vent his feelings. He began to abuse Modi and the BJP for tormenting a highly educated person like me. He was a Gujarati, and obviously a Dalit. I was amused, because I was only too familiar with these identitarian arguments. There was no use telling him that the issue was a little more complex than what he thought. For the caste thesis did not fully hold even among us, the BK-accused.

The entire day passed in depositing me at the prison. This is the way the government worked, squandering poor people's resources. It took a three-hour wait before I was ushered in through a small steel door framed in a giant door, called the 'red gate'. It was a well-lit space but still looked like a dark cave. I was kind of enrolled into the jail and directed to the other side, where they uncaringly poured out the contents of my backpack on the platform for *zadati* (search) and announced that the backpack was not allowed in. Later, of course, I would see people carrying very fancy bags to store and carry their things. My problem was mundane; how to carry my things. When I voiced my problem, they offered me a big plastic-coated gunny bag.

This was followed by the personal search, where you are stripped naked and searched thoroughly as the CCTV camera looked on. With this humiliating introduction, the next gate opened to the world that would be mine for I did not know how long.

8

Black Flag over Rajgruha

> Slavery does not merely mean a legalised form of subjection. It means a state of society in which some men are forced to accept from others the purposes which control their conduct.
>
> B.R. Ambedkar

RAMA CAME EVERY DAY to the NIA without fail at the appointed time, as did my lawyer, Nilesh Ukey. On the second day, Rama informed me that news of my arrest was widespread and had sparked some protests. The lockdown had dampened them. She informed me that a controversy was created by some Ambedkarite groups over a black flag hoisted at Rajgruha. Interestingly, Prakash Ambedkar had owned up to it, saying, 'It [my arrest] is a very shocking and unfortunate development. As a mark of protest, I hoisted a black flag at Rajgruha – the residence of Dr B.R. Ambedkar – at Dadar.'[1] Those people, hurt by a black flag on the auspicious day of Babasaheb Ambedkar, seemed unconcerned about the unjust arrest of one of his family members on that very day and from his own house! This verily highlighted the paradoxical nature of the so-called Ambedkarites, who revelled in symbolic gestures while showing little concern over real-life atrocities.

The Ambedkarites seem oblivious of the fact that, on average, over three Dalits are killed and a dozen Dalit women are raped every day in India, as per sarkari statistics.[2] Even when a Dalit atrocity occasionally garners attention, it often fails to stir the community. The heinous atrocity at Khairlanji, where a Dalit mother, her daughter and two young sons were sexually assaulted and brutally murdered, failed to provoke a response from Dalits until after a month, when some unlikely youth came forward and catalysed an agitation among the community. When news of vandalism of an Ambedkar statue broke on 28 November 2006, amid growing resentment over the police handling of the Khairlanji protests, a mob of over 6,000 protesters stopped the Deccan Queen passenger train near Ulhasnagar on 30 November, ordered the passengers to disembark and set five of its bogies on fire.[3] These incidents were not isolated but rather part of a disturbing pattern. The anger was not over the hundreds of youths beaten and locked up in Nagpur, Kamti, Amravati and Yavatmal by police, as our fact-finding revealed, but over vandalism of an Ambedkar statue, one of the hundreds that Mayawati had erected to fortify her core constituency of Jatav/Chamar, quite the way Modi builds temples for his Hindu gods and does all the Hindutva antics for his constituency.

Ambedkarites are often enraged by any perceived disrespect to Ambedkar statues but are seldom provoked by the killings and rapes of their own people. This is not to say that Ambedkar statues are unimportant – they undoubtedly represent the collective identity and aspirations of Dalits. However, their outrage over these symbols should be matched, if not exceeded, by their anger at the violation of their bodies. How can rapes and murders of their own sisters and mothers fail to provoke them if they truly value their dignity? Dalits ought to understand that their obsessive concern for symbolism, particularly in Ambedkar, is cynically exploited by the ruling classes who ignore their material concerns. Unlike any other community, Ambedkarites across India can be manipulated with a single lever of the Ambedkar icon. Therefore it is that all political leaders eyeing Dalit votes sing paeans to Ambedkar in a competitive manner, and any party in power expends any amount of public money on building memorials for him, so that Dalits remain engaged with pilgrimages and forget to look at the actual condition of their lives and community. Under the Modi raj, this has been as glaring as sunlight.

Ambedkarites must know that Babasaheb Ambedkar prided himself on being an iconoclast, a breaker of idols. He is the one who more than anybody else expressed his disapproval of hero worship. His hero was a person who played a vital role in societal growth and renewal; he was 'a scourge and scavenger of society'.[4] And still he was not to be followed blindly, even less worshipped. He was to be sincerely thanked for enabling us to see farther than himself. Ambedkar had even categorically asked people to stop celebrating his jayantis at the public function held to observe his sixtieth birthday. Unfortunately, these truths will never get across to the crowd of zombies who claim to be his followers. Sadly, the Ambedkar icon that should have been a symbol of their liberation has become the instrument of their collective enslavement at the hands of the ruling classes.

As regards the black flag hoisted over Rajgruha to express the family's protest against my arrest, people need to understand in mundane terms that Rajgruha is a private property of the Ambedkar family and no one else can have any claim on it whatsoever. Are the family members not entitled to express their concern at something within their own premises? Those who objected to the black flag over Rajgruha might have been justified in their objection if Rajgruha had been a public memorial. Did they ever ask themselves why Rajgruha is still not a national memorial? Did Ambedkar not deserve one? Is it not their collective unconcern for a concrete object related to Ambedkar that it is not a national memorial? Rajgruha should rather remind them of their collective incompetence that they could not convert it into a public memorial for their Babasaheb!

When I was out of prison, many Ambedkarite Dalits met me and said that people were not protesting my incarceration because they were confused by the silence of Ambedkar scions like Prakash Ambedkar over it. I wasn't entirely convinced, because I knew that Ambedkarites are motivated by the symbolic or abstract Ambedkar that the state reveres. Ambedkarites have internalised the principle of being on the right side of the state. Outrage over insult to the symbolic or abstract Ambedkar in the form of Ambedkar icons does not contradict the state. It is far more economical for the state to manage such a large and potentially volatile mass by keeping them emotionally invested in an abstract ideal than by addressing their basic material needs. This strategy is also more cost-effective than trying to win over an equivalent number of non-Dalits through tangible benefits or policy concessions. Tolerance of violence is out of the question unless it is sponsored by the state itself. This is why Ambedkarites are not seen reflecting concern at the daily rapes and murders of their own people.

I couldn't quite understand why they felt the need to apologise for the lack of protest by Dalits over my arrest. Was it because I happened to be related to the Ambedkar family by marriage? I have never flaunted this association – if anything, I have actively discouraged any reference to it in public. Why then is there an expectation that Prakash Ambedkar should speak for me?

Before me, Sudhir Dhawale and Surendra Gadling – both Dalits and committed Ambedkarites – were arrested in the very first round of detentions. No such concerns were raised on their behalf. And long before them, scores of Dalits fighting for justice were beaten, jailed or even allegedly killed by the state – all met with silence.

As I have explained earlier, collective protest among Dalits is often reserved for symbolic affronts – like damage to Babasaheb Ambedkar's statue or iconography. Why then make an exception for me? In fact, the very act of making an exception betrays the same mindset: that I, too, am being seen not as a person, but as an extension – an object – associated with Babasaheb.

My connection to the Ambedkar family is purely incidental. It is neither a qualification nor an accomplishment. If people truly cared about Babasaheb Ambedkar's ideals and respected his legacy, they would understand that I have never needed such associations to define my worth. In my own right, I have done enough to be considered a rightful legatee of his vision.

I have always acknowledged Babasaheb as a profound source of inspiration in my intellectual journey. I have instinctively imbibed many of his attributes, yet never claimed to be his bhakta. As he mandated, I am not bound to accept every one of his ideas and be a blind follower. Therefore, I am wary of being labelled any '-ist' or '-ite'. My lifelong struggle for justice – for the oppressed and the exploited – has run parallel to, despite being at odds with, my formal profession. And it is this struggle that the state has chosen to criminalise, charging me under its most draconian laws. It's these, not inherited ties, that are my true credentials – ones that Babasaheb Ambedkar would surely have been proud of.

It's not that Ambedkarites haven't protested for me. Dalits, as did many others, protested my arrest and incarceration (see p. 40). I was told that Ambedkarites in Marathwada and some other pockets in the country had also protested in various ways. Their protests might not be at the scale people expected to take place when Ambedkar's own family member is being jailed on obviously false charges. But there is another angle from which to look at the protests. They needed to be seeded and transformed into an abstract concern for the Ambedkar icon. The whole episode had to be translated into one in which disrespect had been accorded to Babasaheb Ambedkar as his grandson-in-law, a member of his family, was being tormented. My own contributions to the cause he espoused his entire life were of no consequence. This issue of 'grandson-in-law' is itself not simple; the deep-seated patriarchal culture of Ambedkarites tends to exclude my wife herself (and for that matter all his great-granddaughters) from the Ambedkar family, making her husband a distant entity!

Beyond this intricate explanation, the question about the silence of Ambedkar scions itself was based on a false if not dishonest premise. While Prakash Ambedkar might not have been politically involved in my case, he did not distance himself from me as a family member, at least until I surrendered. As mentioned earlier, although he did not hoist the black flag at Rajgruha on 14 April 2020 protesting my arrest, he owned up to it when controversy arose.[5] Just a fortnight before the Supreme Court's final verdict, he held a press conference at Maharashtra Sadan in Delhi, expressing the family's concern over my imminent arrest. He told the press that I was being targeted by the BJP government because I was part of the Ambedkar family.[6] He had accompanied me to the NIA office at the time of my surrender and had also come to the court when I was in NIA custody. Therefore, it is false to say that Ambedkarite Dalits did not protest my arrest because Prakash Ambedkar had not.

It is true that after my arrest and incarceration, neither he nor his brothers, who are very much in public life, have uttered a word about me, or even made any inquiries with Rama, their own sister, who was running around everywhere for me all by herself. They may have their own compulsions for what they chose to do and not do, and we ought to respect them.

9

My New Address

A political prisoner is someone who is out fighting for his or her people's rights and freedom and is imprisoned for that alone.

Leonard Peltier

FROM THE GATE OPENING to my new world, a guard conducted me to the nearest ugly structure that looked like an old warehouse, though 'Hospital' was painted on its fascia. The guard presented my papers to a person sitting inside a room that looked like a cage. He muttered some unintelligible things to me and returned the papers to the guard, who swiftly walked me into the nearest big hall and locked the door behind me. Strangely, I was alone in that big hall. Never thereafter did I find it empty as at that time. I did not know what to do. Dusk had fallen and nobody was in sight. I stood at the bars and tried to size up the jail, but not much was visible except for bars everywhere. I turned my sight indoors and surveyed the empty space and the space beyond, which had three lavatories on one side and three compartments with a tap each, supposedly bathrooms, on the other. The whole place was dirty beyond description. None of the compartments, including the lavatories, had doors. There was an LDPE barrel containing water. It was surrounded by muddy dirt, which prevented one from accessing it without dirtying one's feet. The place badly stank. In the hall there was another barrel filled with water, I guessed drinking water. There were two small steel containers. One contained rice and rotis and the other some yellow, watery stuff. With curiosity, I dipped my hand into it to see that was a cabbage subjee. I shuddered at the prospect of eating such food, my fond definition of which is what tastes good. After a short while, a gentlemanly person accompanied by a guard came asking for me. He was a jailer. He inquired whether I needed anything. As he sounded good, I requested him to put me in a better place as I would not survive there. He appeared sympathetic and asked me to bear with it for some time. He sent some cotton blankets to cushion my bedding, but it hardly helped.

I spread the blankets over a dhurrie in the corner opposite the toilet space, placed my clothes on the wire hung across, and again stood listlessly, staring out from the grills. No soul was visible; only some occasional groaning was coming from some distance.

In that deadly solitude, my mind began eddying across the times and spaces I had left behind; my village, school, childhood friends and all that. It paused at those people I had seen behind bars in Wani for the first time. They were underfed, unkempt and miserable. They had become the definition of criminal for me. Will I not look like them to outsiders? They may see me, locked up behind bars or surrounded by guards, as a criminal, nay a terrorist. Indeed, what would the people in my village who loved and respected me so far now think of me. They would have surely known about my arrest, even seen me on television in connection with this episode. There was no way for them to know more than what television news showed and told them, or the newspapers. I did not know if the media reached them at all. If my elite classmates from IIM Ahmedabad could think that there must be something that the police had arrested me for, what could be expected of simple, ill-educated villagers? Many such thoughts fluttered across my mind, like a hazy ribbon in the wind.

People are jailed for committing a crime. What crime did I commit? I do not know. Crime is what crosses the line of law. The SP at NIA had told me that one of my lectures published on the web for free download was found on some Maoist's computer, and this was an instance of my crossing the line of law. Strange logic, but you can't argue with it. I was outraged by his silly logic and simply said that even his computer might have the said lecture because it had registered thousands of downloads. His masked face could not hide his embarrassment. I asked him in what way the line of law is crossed if the stuff is freely downloadable on the net. He did not have an answer.

The simple definition of crime is what the police think it is. By that definition, police are free to arrest you, slap whatever sections they like on you and put you behind bars. Yes, the Constitution gives you the remedy of approaching the courts. But that would take years to settle, whether you committed a crime or not. Until then, you are already reduced to becoming a beggar for bail. You live with the stigma of being a criminal in the society. When a trial takes place, you may get convicted or acquitted by the courts years later. What if you get acquitted? Do you get the years of your unfreedom back? What about your family, which suffered more than you without committing any crime? What about your children, whose future might be jeopardised or compromised because of your incarceration? Does any justice delivered, if it has been delivered at all, address all these issues? How does one's acquittal recompense for the humiliation, the indignities, and the loss of social standing and the disorientation one has suffered? Perhaps there are no answers to all such questions. The only possible answer is that those who are vested with authority to decide your crime – the police, prosecution and judges – should be held accountable. The problem is that they are not. That has given the system the impunity with which it operates.

Even if someone apparently committed a crime, what makes one think that they are entirely responsible for it? After all, crime does not happen in a vacuum. To what extent do extraneous factors share the responsibility for it? What if the law that determines what crime is, is itself flawed? Such a perspective may lead to entirely different conclusions. As a civil rights activist, I was not entirely ignorant of these issues, but mere knowledge of them proved utterly inadequate in the face of having to experience them. Even though I had had ample time to mentally prepare for my imminent arrest, the full weight of what it meant to be inside a jail never quite struck me until it actually happened. The court proceedings – which stretched over twenty months as I pursued quashing and anticipatory bail – had already exposed me to the celebrated myth of the 'rule of law' in this country.

Once imprisoned, the battle for bail could drag on indefinitely. As I write this, two of the co-accused – Surendra Gadling and Mahesh Raut – are already in their eighty-fifth month in jail without trial.

Before I exited my IIMA WhatsApp group, one of my classmates – oddly a lawyer by choice after his MBA, and hailed in the group as a legal luminary – remarked smugly that if I were innocent, the courts would surely grant me relief. I wished he was in Gadling's place.

As I somehow managed to recline against the wall on my dhurrie, many such thoughts whirled in my mind. I never had such blank times in my life ever as I faced since I had surrendered to the NIA. For the last eleven days, I had not written a word as I did not even have paper or pen. I had not read a single page of anything as there was nothing to read. I was now alone in this huge cage meant for perhaps forty-odd people, as marked on the walls.

After a while, the door clanked open and a skeleton of an old man thrusting his chest out as though he too had 56 inches of it, with nothing on him was pushed inside. He murmured something to himself. He did a recce of the toilet side, as I did. He came back, took the plastic mug on the barrel and drank water from the barrel. He exclaimed with a distorted face, 'Shit, it's gutter water.' It didn't take much to make him start off. He was from Vasai, a typical Vasai Catholic. He had been arrested for a murder. He was kept in a lock-up for a week before being shifted here. He said with much pride that his father had been a loco driver during the British times and that he was a mechanic. He asked about me and I vaguely answered that I was from Mumbai and had been brought there in the Bhima-Koregaon case. He did not understand what it was, but did not dig further either.

Extending the conversation, he said I looked *padha likha* and asked me to speak in English with him. He said it in such a way as to demean those who did not speak English. I pleased him by saying I would. He then picked up a sheet, stretched himself out on it and soon fell asleep.

I didn't have any idea of what time it was. I tried to emulate him and straightened myself out, rolled up part of a blanket into a thin roll under my neck and tried to close my eyes in an attempt to sleep, but in vain. The hazy thoughts of earlier still glided across in kaleidoscopic patterns in my head. In a side barrack a man was crying aloud, but it did not disturb me as much as my own thoughts. I might have fallen asleep in the wee hours, because when I heard the guards shouting and clanking their batons against the steel bars in the morning, I found that I had been sleeping.

More than a dozen people had filled the barrack during the night. Soon the breakfast came. It was served through the bars on a melamine plate and a bowl. I asked the server for just tea, but unmindful of me the fellow pushed a bowl full of upma and a glass full of tea towards me. I took a small morsel of the upma in my mouth and asked the boys around whether they wanted it. They happily grabbed it. I tried sipping the tea but could not. I poured it into a drain, washed the glass and returned it.

It was hard passing the time. I did not have anything to read. The adjoining cell housed a man in his thirties. I learned that he belonged to some (gangster) company. The TV placed on a stand was turned towards him by the guards. As I stared blankly out, the man called me by my name, 'Anand Sir, aap TV dekhenge?' I was surprised and asked him how he knew my name. The guards had told him about me. He advised me to try to eat the food served to us and offered me some salt and some masala powder to mix up with the dal and subjee to impart some taste to them. It was my first encounter of experiencing humanity in a supposedly hardened criminal.

The fellow who had cried himself hoarse the entire night was tied to the bars outside and was beaten by guards. He cried in pain but calmed down after some time. I was told that he was 'mental'. Such 'mental cases' would be brought from the circles (a block in a prison; there were five such circles in Taloja besides Hospital, Anda and BC, which also housed prisoners) and lodged in Hospital, one would imagine for treatment. There was no wherewithal to treat them except for a psychiatrist who visited once a week and prescribed some medicines. There were far more serious cases of psychological disorders that I would see later. The jail would keep them in solitary confinement without any treatment.

My day passed listlessly. I did not eat anything at lunch or dinner. I had some dried fruits to chew and tap water to drink from a used mineral water bottle given by an inmate. The jailer visited, and on his own comforted me, saying that something was being done for me.

The next day we were walked in single file to a shed called the 'checking hall'. The prisoners in blue and white striped khadi jail uniforms managed it. They were quite respectful towards me. In the hall they asked us to remove our upper garment and sit on the floor in rows. I was spared as I could not sit like the others. I stood against the wall. Those boys then photographed each person in that condition. The pictures were fed into a laptop and each was assigned an undertrial (UT) number.

Even after the process we waited for nearly an hour before the superintendent of the prison with his battalion of a dozen officers and scores of guards walked in. All shouted in chorus, 'Jai Hind Sir'. The podium was neatly laid out with clean tablecloths. The process began with me standing before the superintendent. He asked me about my health problems and I reeled them off. The gentleman jailer standing behind him whispered to the superintendent something about me and I was asked to stand outside. As I stood outside, I heard sounds of whiplash and agonising cries coming from the hall. Some of the poor chaps who were called after me were whipped with a special device, which was like a thick belt, by hefty guards with full strength. They were whipped as many times as signalled by the superintendent with his fingers.

I had seen those devices neatly arranged on a table. I did not know, however, what they were for. I thought judicial custody was safer than the police custody, where interrogation de facto meant torture. In the former you are directly under the court. But the lawlessness was not any less in judicial custody either. Later I would hear about people being mercilessly beaten by the jail staff to such an extent that they had to be carried out on a stretcher and convalesced for months.

I would see my immediate neighbour, a young Muslim man of twenty-nine, being beaten so much that he was swollen and bled everywhere. That was the mode of prison jurisprudence, where judge, jury and prosecution all merged into the superintendent and where there was no appeal. Like custodial torture, which in law is not permitted but is pervasively practised and is winked at by judges, this mode also is a norm. How else would those well-made whips placed to terrorise poor prisoners be accounted for? The very existence of them in the jail testified to its lawlessness.

After this ritual of indoctrination, we were marched back to our barracks in single file.

Sometime after lunch, which I did not take, Chacha, a kamwalla who served food, came and rolled up my belongings without asking me and ran upstairs with them, saying, '*Saab bulaya hai*' (sahab has called). Around the same time, Arun (Arun Fereira, my co-accused) sent word that he had come to see me using the excuse of seeing the doctor. I barely saw him on my way upstairs as I ran after Chacha. Not knowing where to keep them, Chacha dumped my things in a corner barrack meant for TB patients, and left. I did not know it was a TB barrack, but still dreaded it as it was to be my lasting arrangement. Fortunately, the jailer saw Chacha and asked him to get my things to the cell that was being cleaned up by the kamwallas for me. He himself was overseeing it. A cot with a mattress and two buckets and a mug and a new plate, glass and bowl were arranged for me. It was like a windfall for me. I thanked the jailer for his consideration. In the bargain, all my things, including my toiletries and the dried fruit packets on which I had sustained myself the previous three days, were lost.

The first thing I did was to take a bath after three days and sleep without any dinner that night. All this seemed to suggest the possibility of my survival through the impending ordeal!

Upstairs, there were two barracks at the corner of two sides of a rectangle, one occupied by TB patients and the other by kamwallas and patients brought from the circles. The rest of the floor had cells, half of which one did not know what they were for. The other half of them, some ten, had a bath and lavatory and were meant to house odd numbers of prisoners, that is, one, three and five. The next morning, when the *bandi* was opened, I took a round of the corridor and was first greeted by a man in the cell near mine. I reciprocated. He was sitting on the floor while his father, who was apparently very sick, lay on a cot. He then asked me if I was a Maratha. I was taken aback. I knew that was a way of asking what caste I was. I simply said, '*Hun*', and moved on. But for this encounter, none asked me my caste at the prison.

I was unaware at first, but the inmates in the hospital seemed to see me as someone special simply because I was given an individual cell. Such cells were usually reserved for those affiliated with a 'company', dreaded killers, police officials or politicians. The guards added to the mystery by spinning their own version – that I was the mastermind behind the Bhima-Koregaon case, a 'senior' Maoist leader, as even the charge sheet described me. Whatever the reason, in the given circumstances, the solitary cell was nothing short of a blessing to me. As for the others, it didn't seem to matter to them in the least.

Later, of course, many people in the jail seemed to know my relation with Ambedkar.

I did not know there was a red-ant menace in the hospital. One boy brought four cups cut out of mineral water bottles to place the legs of my cot into, filling them with water to thwart the ants. Such creativity and cordiality abounded in prison. These boys would occasionally come and voluntarily tidy up my cell and go. In return they asked me for some small consumables from the canteen. For some days one of them tried to learn English from me, but he did not continue for long and suddenly one day was transferred out to one of the circles.

Within the prison, the role of the *jababdar* is pivotal. Tasked with maintaining order and overseeing the daily activities, the jababdar ensures sanitation, food distribution, addresses inmates' grievances and implements the jailer's directives. Upon my arrival, the jababdar was a Marathi individual who appeared educated, often interspersing English words into our conversations. He confided that he had previously served as an accounts officer in the Brihanmumbai Municipal Corporation

(BMC) but had been incarcerated for the alleged murder of his wife.

The cells surrounding mine housed individuals with notorious reputations – gangsters, serial killers, those convicted of communal crimes, and even encounter specialists. Their formidable statuses commanded a unique form of respect; even the jababdar approached them with heightened politeness, reflecting the intricate social dynamics within the prison walls.

One of the first things I asked of him was about the procedure for sending and receiving letters. He provided me with my address with my UT number. Postal stamps could be bought from the jail canteen (actually a provision shop, but called canteen because it sold special dishes like chicken or special subjees on Sundays or some festive days) and a prisoner was designated to deal with our incoming and outgoing letters. I immediately got some stationery, envelopes and toiletries from the canteen and wrote my first letters home, which contained individual letters to my daughters.

It was my fifth day in jail, and I still had no communication with my family. I requested the jailer for a phone call; he told me to write an application. That was the first of the countless applications I would go on to write. For even the smallest request, one had to address the superintendent in a tone of supplication – no matter if what you were asking for was your rightful due. The superintendent, of course, was under no obligation to respond, let alone act. It was a one-way street. Often, if an application was inconvenient for the administration, it simply wouldn't be accepted. In that case, it never existed. As a result, prison files remained spotless – untouched by prisoner complaints.

I was thus slowly getting acclimatised with the hellhole that would be my new address for the next thirty-one months.

10

And I Survived COVID-19

> Men do not accept their prophets and slay them, but they love their martyrs and worship those whom they have tortured to death.
>
> Fyodor Dostoevsky

UNLIKE THE FIRST AND second batch of arrestees of June 2018 and October 2018, I had witnessed the coronavirus striking the country from outside prison. Despite the harsh lockdown, the number of cases was increasing at a scary rate. On 14 April, the day of my surrender, the number of confirmed cases had risen to 10,541, with reported recoveries of 1,205 and 358 deaths. In addition to suffering the real incidence of the disease, people suffered in many more ways due to the unpreparedness of the administration and the utter shortage of hospital infrastructure across the country. News of coronavirus deaths began trickling in from everywhere. During the period of my custody at NIA, on the fourth day Rama brought me shocking news of the death of a close friend of mine. I was not sure about the cause of his death, but it was most probably COVID-19. It was terrible for me to reconcile with the fact that Dharmaraj Nimsarkar, someone who knew me from my childhood, was no more in the world. I felt miserable that I could not even phone up his family and convey my feelings.

Dharmaraj was senior to me by two years and was with me right from the village school through the high school at Wani. He treated me with great affection, like a younger brother, and might have been pained by the things that befell me lately. Unlike me, he was always smartly dressed, sociable, smart and communicative, and stood out in his surroundings. Until our times, there had been no one who had brought some prestige to our village. He had a flair for Marathi and a rich aesthetic sense, which effortlessly flowed through in the numerous letters he wrote to me from my engineering days through my job at Indian Oil, until they reduced to a trickle naturally with his increasing responsibilities of family. But still, we remained in close contact. He wrote beautiful poems and made a name among the first generation of Dalit litterateurs. This passion might have overtaken his academic pursuits as he did not seem much interested in studies. I did not know exactly why, but he took a job and was posted at Paras Thermal Station, thereafter at BARC, and ultimately at Bharat Electronics Pune, from where he retired. His writings were regularly published in Marathi periodicals, and they came out in a book form very late. During one of the visits I managed to his house, he affectionately gave me a full set of seven books published by then. I trust he still had much more in store.

After his retirement, he worked for a newspaper with Professor Vilas Wagh, an ardent Ambedkarite social worker and educationist who set up a chain of hostels for poor students around Pune and Dhule, and a publication house called Sugawa Prakashan for progressive literature, mostly in Marathi. Professor Wagh too died during the latter half of my incarceration. The last thing he contacted me for was to write an introduction to a book he had edited. I did send it but did not know what happened to it.

Somehow, I had a strong feeling that I would not survive the jail life. This negativity was probably my way of preparing for the worst. I was more worried about my family – mother, daughters and wife – living away from me. I just wished for their safety.

As it is, we barely lived together as a family. My daughters and wife were quite accustomed to my frequent travels – within the country and abroad. Even on weekends when I was home, I was mostly confined to my study, buried in books and glued to my computer. Once my younger daughter began playing competitive tennis, my wife and she were constantly on the move, travelling across India and later abroad for tournaments. There were stretches when we didn't even know which country they were in at a given moment.

Phones in those days didn't work as cheaply or reliably as they do now. Once, I met with a near-fatal accident on the Nairobi–Mombasa highway in Kenya. For three days, there was no contact with my family, even as the Kenyan government tried reaching them through the Indian High Commission. I vaguely remembered that my wife and daughter had left for a tournament in Malaysia, but I wasn't aware they were to travel to Indonesia afterwards. My elder daughter, then pursuing her MD and often staying with my in-laws in Dadar while we were away, finally managed to call me on the third day – just to confirm that I had survived the accident.

For the twenty-fifth-year reunion of our class at IIM Ahmedabad, we were asked to submit a family photograph. We searched through our albums and realised, to our surprise, that we didn't have a single picture of all of us together. At best, we had photographs featuring two of us at a time. So I sent three separate photographs with the caption: 'This is the closest we come to as a family.' It turned into a bit of a joke among our batch mates.

In the jail, the social distancing was mere compliance drama. The jail was overcrowded to the extent of 170 per cent of its capacity. COVID-19 protocol was imposed in the wearing of masks, and making prisoners stand in circles at a distance of two feet from each other in queues in the office premises and the hospital. It legitimised the doctors' observance of untouchability with prisoner patients. The doctor visiting patients was a comic sight. He came with an orderly, a regular guard so designated and a couple of kamwallas (prisoners) carrying a medicine box and basic tools like an infrared thermometer, sphygmomanometer (to measure blood pressure) and, most important, a big torch, the kind that railway guards carried to signal all clear to the engine driver from the other end of the train. The doctor would focus its beam on the patient and decide the medicines to be administered, which anyway varied little as most people were given the same medicines.

Spaces were created for quarantining entrants to the jail from outside. The quarantine barracks themselves were overcrowded and posed the danger of infecting healthy people if a single person happened to carry the virus. The influx of prisoners was so high that the Taloja prison had to hire a nearby school to accommodate them (see p. 3). The conditions there were reportedly much worse than inside the prison. The people coming from there narrated horrific experiences: a small classroom crammed with thirty-five to forty inmates making social distancing impossible; only three toilets and seven urinals shared among nearly four hundred prisoners leading to rampant bribing of jail staff for access. And this was flaunted as quarantining by the administration.

The prison superintendent saw to it that no case of COVID-19 in the prison was reported outside. That meant he wouldn't send prisoners to an outside hospital even in an emergency, fearing a COVID-19-positive result would expose his false claims. Until the COVID-19 cases outside had reached an alarming level, there was no testing in jail. Only the ritual of the kamwallas taking temperature of inmates with infrared thermometers and checking their pulse rate with fingertip pulse oximeters was observed. All the people who died passed through Hospital, and we counted as many as a dozen deaths in a single month. Surely, none of them were recorded as COVID-19 deaths.

In India, people contracting COVID-19 and dying of their comorbidities were not counted among COVID-19 deaths. The *Times of India* on 10 June 2020 reported Vijay Rupani, chief minister of Gujarat, explaining this:

> As per the guidelines of the ICMR, if a comorbid patient dies then a committee of experts decides the primary and secondary causes of death . . . If that committee identifies the main cause of death as heart attack, then even if the patient was infected, such a death is not counted as being caused by Covid. The same system is followed across the entire country.

It was because of this strategic way of counting deaths that India's death toll from COVID-19 was grossly under-reported, as the later reports would reveal.

Much later, after the second wave of the pandemic, they began swab testing at the prison, initially through some outside agency and then within the prison hospital itself.

In July, I experienced a sudden bout of high fever, vomiting, convulsions and dysentery, which lasted for five days. I was so drained of strength that I couldn't even get out of bed. I couldn't keep down a drop of water, as even a small amount would be violently expelled, causing severe abdominal pain. When I sent word downstairs to the doctor, prisoners working in the hospital came up with a saline stand to my cell. They administered saline and gave me some pills, which I still violently threw up. They had to pierce both my hands in five different places to find the right spot for the needle. There was no nurse, no compounder and no MBBS doctor in the hospital, yet the state continued to claim that it had a well-equipped hospital at the Taloja prison to justify their refusal to send patients to outside hospitals. No doctor visited me, despite my messages through kamwallas. I asked the guards for assistance as I couldn't get out of bed, but there was no response from them. I had sent a message for the jailer, who came on the third day and saw me in my pathetic state. I asked him to send me to an outside hospital immediately. He was sympathetic and said he would try. After some time, he returned to take me to the superintendent.

With great difficulty, I managed to get up from the bed. I was completely drained of energy and unable to walk. The jailer supported me and walked me to the superintendent's office, fortunately just across the road from the prison hospital. The superintendent didn't have the basic courtesy to even offer me a seat. I cut conversation short and simply asked him to send me to an outside hospital immediately. He argued that I did not have COVID-19. I shouted at him with whatever strength I could muster, telling him he was not a doctor and that even if he were I didn't care. I threatened him, saying if news of my illness leaked outside, he would face dire consequences. He did not react and said he would send a doctor to examine me.

The doctor came the next morning with his orderly and a kamwalla, who took my blood pressure and temperature. I told him that it was surely a COVID-19 infection, as I had read about its various manifestations. He kept quiet but did not commit to outside treatment for me. I was in a miserable condition and asked people to send word to my wife. The unofficial communication network in the jail did it. Fortunately, I began to feel better the next day, past the worst of my troubles.

Word had reached my wife of my state of health and she immediately informed the lawyers about my condition. Already, People's Union for Civil Liberties (PUCL) had filed a public interest litigation (PIL) in the Bombay High Court based on reports on the worrisome condition of prisoners in Maharashtra prisons. It was dismissed on 2 July, but not before forcing the prison authorities to make some important concessions around protecting the prisoners during the pandemic. The Bombay High Court directed prison authorities to conduct random testing in jails too, after the state rejected the demand for testing all inmates. When the tests were conducted on a sample of twenty to twenty-five, which included me, many were found with the presence of coronavirus antigens. During the counselling by the chief medical officer (CMO), he simply said to me, '*Tumhala COVID hovun gela*' (you have survived the COVID-19 infection). I asked him, 'What if I had died of it when you fellows refused to send me to an outside hospital?' He had no answer. I, however, knew the answer. He would have simply filled up some shitty forms certifying death due to cardiac arrest, got my body carried out of the jail by the kamwallas in a blanket and closed the chapter, as he had in a dozen cases before.

None died of the coronavirus infection in Taloja jail, it was claimed, and the state flaunted and applauded the superintendent for his excellent control of the pandemic at the prison. Like the ACP in Pune who repeatedly violated the law and even undermined the courts but got an award for investigation, the superintendent of Taloja jail was reportedly honoured for best COVID-19 administration of a jail.

Ever since I arrived at Taloja, I found one of my co-accused, Professor Varavara Rao, an octogenarian, distinguished Telugu poet and one of the founders of Revolutionary Writers' Association, aka Virasam, in poor health. He was admitted to the jail hospital at least three times, each time for a few days, before being sent back to his cell. Once he was lodged in the barrack on my floor in a debilitated condition. He had to be walked to the toilet and bathed by a fellow prisoner. I pleaded with the CMO to arrange for him to be examined by a specialist outside, or at the very least, provide him with a room and care by one of our co-accused. Although the CMO agreed, nothing was done and VV, as he is widely known, was sent back to his cell after a few days.

When Rao fainted in jail in May, he was sent to JJ Hospital, which discharged him after three days, with normal reports, though there was little improvement in his health condition.[1] He was lodged in the jail hospital, and one of our co-accused, Vernon Gonsalves, was assigned to take care of him as he was unable to do anything on his own. Vernon had to attend to Rao's personal hygiene, feed him and move him around in a wheelchair. Rao's family accused the police of getting him discharged from JJ Hospital so they could plead against his bail plea on medical grounds at the NIA Special Court, where a hearing was scheduled for 2 June. The judge accepted the JJ Hospital reports and rejected his bail application ultimately, on 26 June 2020.

Rao continued to show signs of delirium. After voices were raised from various quarters, two former central information commissioners, Shailesh Gandhi and M. Sridhar Acharyulu, wrote to Chief Minister Uddhav Thackeray seeking Rao's release on bail.[2] He was again sent to Sir JJ Hospital on 13 July and admitted in its neurological department.[3] His wife, two daughters and nephew, who travelled from Hyderabad to see him, found him on 15 July in a pathetic condition lying on a urine-soaked bed in the transit yard, completely unattended.[4] He tested positive for coronavirus the next day and was shifted to St George Hospital, the designated COVID-19 hospital. The family made a strong plea that Rao's life may be saved only if 'the Bombay High Court [where an appeal was pending hearing] gives him medical bail, and [he] is shifted to decent private speciality hospital'.[5] On 17 July, the National Human Rights Commission (NHRC), acting on a complaint from the special monitor of the commission, Maja Daruwala, issued notice to the

Chief Secretary and director general of prisons of Maharashtra, seeking a report on Rao's health within two weeks.[6] Following an NHRC notice to the state government asking it to ensure that adequate health facilities were provided to Rao, he was shifted to Nanavati Hospital in Mumbai on 19 July.[7]

He was sent back from Nanavati Hospital on 28 August 2020 to Taloja Prison Hospital, but continued to have serious health issues. His wife filed a writ petition at the Bombay High Court for his bail on medical grounds and for shifting him to Nanavati Hospital immediately in the interim. He was shifted to the hospital on 14 November, as directed by the high court (HC), for treatment at the cost of the state government,[8] and was released on bail for six months on medical grounds on 22 February 2021.[9] The Supreme Court granted him regular bail on 10 August 2022. VV had a miraculous escape from the jaws of death!

The second wave of COVID-19 was deadly, and affected the prison too. Stories of shortages of hospital beds, oxygen and ventilators poured in from all over. We worried for our family members, and they in turn worried for us. Concerned about my precarious health condition, my wife moved a petition for my bail on medical grounds. However, the NIA court rejected the petition. Communication became extremely important. We anxiously awaited our weekly phone *mulaqats*, which invariably extended to ten to fourteen days because of the superintendent's sheer misadministration and sadism. Enough mobile phones were available in the prison to provide even daily mulaqats to each prisoner if the phones were allocated to each circle. However, the prison administration's sadistic attitude made matters worse by forcing batches of prisoners to walk to the mulaqat room, where so-called face-to-face meetings took place across a glass partition, with conversations conducted over phones. As mentioned earlier, until the second wave of the pandemic in India peaked, creating an alarming situation outside, the jail did not have even swab testing facilities to detect COVID-19. When the tests began, they scarcely detected positive cases. It was scary because we were in a closed space, vulnerable to infection if even a single carrier brought in the coronavirus. Daily, dozens of people came in with no effective testing or quarantining. As a result, many inmates did catch the infection, but the severity differed. Most, like me, survived it without any effective treatment. Varavara Rao proved lucky to get treatment in time, but not Father Stan.

11

We Lost Stan

Blessed are ye, when men shall revile you, and persecute you, and shall say all manner of evil against you falsely, for my sake.

Matthew 5:11

I DID NOT REALISE that when I said, 'Don't come back here,' to Stan while seeing him off at the gate of the jail hospital, it would prove ominous.

It was 28 May 2021, and Arun and I drove him in a wheelchair to the gate of the jail hospital, extremely happy over the Bombay High Court order to shift him to the Holy Family Hospital, albeit for only fifteen days. I was quite hopeful that his bail petition, which was being heard, would also be granted during his hospital stay and so he may not be back, quite like VV. Stan tested positive for COVID-19, and two days later he was moved to the intensive care unit. Though he was also being treated for heart-related ailments, the newspapers reported that he was responding very well. The court monitored his health closely and extended his stay till 18 July.[1] Everything appeared to be going well. However, on 3 July, his health deteriorated and he was shifted to the ICU and the next morning put on ventilator support. The next day, that is, 5 July 2021, during the hearing of his bail application, Mihir Desai, his lawyer, announced to the Bombay High Court that Stan had died that morning.

The long journey of Stan from his village in Tamil Nadu to Jharkhand to the Philippines to Bengaluru and then back to Jharkhand and finally in a jail and hospital in Mumbai had come to an end. He had completely dedicated himself to the most dispossessed and marginalised, as a true Jesuit. With his death, he brought the focus back on the fundamental rights of Indian citizens, the legal architecture that curtailed these rights, what it meant for those who worked with communities, at the grassroots, through legal and non-violent means, and the conditions of prisons. In his life and death, Swamy left lessons for India.

I had not heard of Stan before. While at IIT Kharagpur, I often conducted training programmes for managers at the Indian Institute of Coal Management (IICM) in Ranchi. Most evenings, I met friends in town but did not know about Stan or his work at Bagaicha, which was also in Ranchi. The first time I heard of him was when his name appeared in the Bhima-Koregaon case along with mine. When I filed my petition in the Bombay High Court to quash the FIR against me, Stan's petition was also filed, incidentally, also argued by my lawyer, Mihir Desai. I was present in the court when it was first heard. While my case was keenly opposed by the Pune police, in Stan's case they simply told the court that he was just a suspect. Hence his petition was set aside while mine and Gautam Navlakha's were heard further. Stan remained outside during the time of our surrender.

When Varavara Rao was lodged in a cell on the ground floor of the Hospital, along with Vernon Gonsalves and Arun Ferreira as his caretakers, my loneliness ended. Though meetings with them were not allowed, communication was possible. People on the ground floor could come into the courtyard and easily speak with us on the first floor. Important information coming through letters or mulaqats was thus exchanged. Another channel was the kamwallas, who stayed upstairs but worked in the hospital downstairs. Since they could go anywhere, they were easy conduits for transmitting messages.

Stan was arrested on 8 October 2020 and brought to Taloja Hospital during the night of 9 October. As I learned of his arrival downstairs in the morning, I went to see him with the permission of the jailer. He was lying on the floor near the door in the common barrack. When he was woken up by fellow inmates for me, he struggled to get up and was helped by others to rise. He fumbled for his hearing aids and put them on. His face lit up like a child's on hearing my name, and he conveyed all his affection through the grip of his Parkinsonian hands on mine across the bars.

After the meeting, I saw the CMO and pleaded with him to put Stan in a separate cell with caretakers, preferably from among our co-accused, as was done for Varavara Rao. The CMO readily agreed, and the very next day Stan was shifted to a separate cell along with Chacha, the kamwalla. When Varavara Rao was sent to the outside hospital, the jail could have easily placed Vernon and Arun with Stan, but for whatever reasons they sent Vernon back to his circle and thankfully placed Arun with Stan, along with Chacha. Arrested under the Protection of Children from Sexual Offences (POCSO) Act following charges pressed by his step-granddaughter, Chacha had told Arun that he had been trapped. One did not know what the truth was, but Chacha worked very hard in jail, doing all kinds of jobs after jail duties to earn a packet of cigarettes, which he was fond of. Arun and Chacha lived with Stan until he left the prison forever.

Stan had multiple issues in prison due to his health condition. He could not even hold a glass of water steady to drink from. Outside, he told us he used a sipper bottle and straw to drink water, but they were disallowed by the prison staff when he was brought to Taloja. He could not hear without a hearing aid and was unable to speak on the phone during mulaqat. To ensure that his precious minutes were not wasted, Arun would take the phone and communicate with his friend Joe, who was registered with the jail. Fortunately, the guards were humane enough not to object to this.

By the time the sipper issue was communicated to the lawyers and they could file an application on 7 November, already a month had passed. The court nonchalantly asked the NIA to file a reply by 26 November, after seventeen days, comfortably, after the Diwali vacation. For every single matter, the court would mechanically ask for a 'say' from the the same circle superintendent or NIA, or both. Courts often talk about 'application of mind', but I hardly found the judges demonstrating it themselves. Small matters like a sipper and straw requested by a Parkinson's patient should not have been an issue to resolve with arguments. A judge should rather be amazed that such issues are brought to the court at all and summon the jail superintendent to explain matters. But such things are just not done. It is a ritual that on every single application, the respondent party must file a reply.

The NIA responded that it had conducted a personal search of Stan Swamy during his arrest in the presence of independent witnesses and 'no such straw and sipper were found'. The court ruled: 'In view of this contention, the application being devoid of substance deserves to be rejected.' When this matter leaked outside, it created a wave of denunciation and became a metaphor for the insensitivity of the Indian prison system and the state towards an eighty-four-year-old Jesuit dissenter.[2]

Meanwhile, Stan had asked for a full-sleeved sweater, a thin blanket and two pairs of socks. He wrote in a letter to Joe, 'I am sorry to hear that these materials were not accepted at the prison gate and the one who brought them had to take them back not once but three times.' A prisoner would not know about such things until he is informed by a letter or in the next mulaqat, both of which were so uncertain. Letters suffered delays and mulaqats happened with a cycle time exceeding a week, extending sometimes to even two weeks. Stan's defence team had to make another application seeking directions to the jail superintendent to allow Swamy to receive winter wear and a straw and sipper that would be sent to him at his own cost. The court sought a report from the jail superintendent and posted the hearing for 4 December. News of this leaked out and the 'sipper and straw' issue became an international outrage.[3] Ultimately, on 4 December 2020, Stan finally received a straw, a sipper and his winter clothes from the jail staff.[4]

Those days were scary. COVID-19 was at its devastating peak. We often heard of someone dying and occasionally saw a dead body being taken out. There was not even a proper stretcher in the hospital to show respect at least to a dead body. The kamwallas dumped it on a thick jail blanket and carried it by holding the corners. Only after months, when the COVID menace had receded, did we see a formal stretcher being used in the jail.

There was built-in motivation throughout the hierarchy to flaunt excellent management of the pandemic across the country. Despite reports of half-burnt carcasses floating in the Ganga, the government remained in denial mode. The country's entire health infrastructure collapsed under the severe wave of the COVID-19 variant that struck it, but the government did not budge in acknowledging, leave alone trying to rectify matters. Instead, in the wake of the deaths of sixty-three children due to oxygen shortage at Gorakhpur's BRD Medical College hospital, the doctor in charge of the paediatric section, initially hailed for paying out of his own pocket to purchase oxygen cylinders as parents panicked, was blamed. Predictably, he had a Muslim name. Some twenty days later, Dr Kafeel Khan was arrested by the Uttar Pradesh Police Special Task Force, allegedly for his responsibility for the children's deaths. He spent eight months in jail before being granted bail by the Allahabad High Court in April 2018, with the court observing that there was no direct evidence of negligence on his part. Two years after his suspension, arrest and imprisonment, a fifteen-page government probe report confirmed the high court's observations.[5]

Such instances of brazen injustice had become the new norm. Later, when the pandemic subsided and the actual death count began to emerge, India's under-reporting became world news. The WHO claimed that several million COVID-19 deaths had most likely gone unreported, estimating that over 4.7 million people – more than ten times the government figure – had died because of the virus.[6] As usual, the government vehemently denied this until the issue faded from public memory, like hundreds of others.

Even in those crisis-ridden times, we managed to steal little moments of joy. Stan was supposed to be walked in the corridor by Arun, as per the doctor's advice. Besides, both Stan and I were included in the daily monitoring of blood pressure, temperature and oxygen count of prisoners. This provided me a convenient excuse to come down and meet both Arun and Stan every morning, allowing us to spend time together. I would walk with Stan as he recounted stories and expressed his concern for the jail staff. He pitied the kamwalla boys who had to carry heavy metal containers of food three times a day to distribute to inmates. He wondered why the prison administrators hadn't thought of a simple solution like wheeled trolleys. I retorted, saying it went against the very purpose of the prisons. Stan, too innocent to grasp my sarcasm, genuinely believed in humanising the prison system. Besides, there was no ramp provided in the prison so the wheeled trolleys could be plied. The prison, just ten or twelve years old, didn't comply with disability norms.

To my dismay, in the next weekly round Stan stopped the jail superintendent and voiced his suggestion. The contingent of officers and guards must have been stunned by such concern from someone whose own suffering knew no bounds. It was too human a request to be understood by the superintendent, who seemed devoid of empathy and particularly prejudiced against us. When his juniors explained what Stan had said, he simply dismissed it and moved on.

On another occasion, Stan, with childlike glee, was eagerly waiting to disclose something to me. He said, 'Do you know, Anand, I am going to live up to one hundred and eighty-five years.' Never before had we seen him bothered about the charges against him. His only complaint was about being separated from the people he loved. However, the previous evening he had counted the punishment for each charge against him from Arun and did some mental maths to amuse himself with the foolishness of the entire system. His maths was a simple summation of all the sentences the charges entailed, plus his present age. I remarked that if the authorities found out, they might make the sentences run concurrently, denying him even that privilege. He seemed disappointed.

In jail, one of the sadistic methods employed is to keep you constantly on the move. Without notice you might be ordered to shift to another circle or even inside the same circle within minutes. It was used as a disciplining tool. Not pleased with the persistent challenges we BK prisoners posed, there was a move to shift us to different jails in Maharashtra.[7] Fortunately, it was successfully stalled. Sometimes these moves proved to be blessings in disguise, as when some of our co-accused were shifted to the Anda (called so because it was round in shape and egg-like) cell from various circles. Likewise, one day, suddenly, Stan, along with Arun and Chacha, was moved to the first floor of the Hospital where I was lodged, allowing us to meet comfortably during open hours. Walking and chatting with Stan, I learned much about his past.

Stan was born in a village in Tiruchirapalli (Trichy) district in Tamil Nadu. Inspired by the life of Jesuits while studying at St Joseph's School in Trichy, he joined the Madurai Jesuit province and opted for the Jamshedpur province of the Society of Jesus. He graduated from St Xavier's College, Ranchi, and later pursued theological studies along with a master's in sociology in Manila, the Philippines. There he learned from student protests the importance of struggling against power. During his further studies, he befriended a Brazilian Catholic Archbishop, Hélder Câmara, whose work among the poor inspired him greatly. Stan returned to India and worked in Chaibasa, developing a lifelong love for the Adivasis. Except for his tenure as director of the Indian Social Institute (ISI) in Bengaluru, during which he spent some time studying in Belgium, his work was focused on Adivasis. At ISI Bengaluru, he initiated courses in social analysis and community mobilisation.

Even while living in Bengaluru, his love for Chaibasa remained strong. He returned there in the 1990s after his term at ISI ended. He helped revive JOHAR (Jharkhandis Organisation for Human Rights) to strengthen the gram sabhas in the Adivasi villages based on their cultural values and customary practices. With the advent of neoliberal reforms in the 1990s, extractive industries began displacing Adivasis, prompting Stan to establish 'Bagaicha' in Ranchi in 2005 to address these issues. Before his arrest, Swamy had filed petitions highlighting the misuse of the Unlawful Activities (Prevention) Act (UAPA) against Adivasis. Courts often dismissed these pleas, citing 'national security'.[8] He lived in Bagaicha until the NIA took him to Mumbai on 8 October 2021.

On 23 March 2021, Stan filed an application for bail on medical grounds, which was rejected by the NIA court. During the hearing of his appeal, he was summoned on 21 May before a division bench of Justices S.J. Kathawalla and S.P. Tavade of the Bombay High Court via video-conferencing from the Taloja prison. We thought he could make a case for being shifted to an outside hospital. But Stan was in his element and told the court bluntly, when it asked him if he wished to be admitted to JJ Hospital for 'general treatment in order to improve his overall health':

> I have been there twice. I am not for being hospitalised in JJ Hospital. What medicines will that hospital give me? It will not improve; it will keep going. I would rather die here very shortly if things go on as it is . . . I was taken to JJ hospital and there were a lot of people but I had no opportunity to explain what I should be given. There are some medicines which the jail authorities gave me, but my deterioration is more powerful than the tablets they are giving me.

He further told the court, 'The only thing I request is to consider for interim bail. I have been in deteriorating condition. I would rather be in Ranchi. I do not think any of that [hospitalisation] is going to help.'[9]

Both Arun and I were taken aback when he told us about this exchange on his return. Alas, this simple desire of his would go unmet!

Stan richly qualified to be targeted by the state. His work among the Adivasis was multifaceted – he not only associated with PUCL to expose rights violations but also actively participated in protests and sit-ins. Bagaicha, the centre he established, became a hub for Adivasi activists, with Stan serving as an inspirational guide for their struggles. He focused on fighting against unjust displacement, whether it was for the Koel-Karo hydroelectric project, the Netarhat field firing range in Jharkhand, or other projects involving large dams and extractive industries in predominantly Adivasi regions in the state.

Stan drew his inspiration from the historical Jesus of Nazareth, who fought for the oppressed and exploited. For Stan, the Eucharist symbolised a commitment to continue Jesus's unfinished work. He aimed to bring systemic change in society, ensuring dignity and freedom for every individual. This mission led him to join the Adivasis' struggle for land, forest and water by adopting constitutional and legal means to combat displacement and dispossession. He opposed the government's policy of creating land banks to promote investments and initiated a study of undertrials falsely accused of being Maoists. The study revealed that most of the undertrials in Jharkhand were Adivasis with no connection to Maoism. Based on this study, he filed a PIL at the Jharkhand High Court in 2018. His efforts and the ongoing resistance by Adivasis against displacement were not well received by the ruling dispensation.

In a video posted on social media prior to his arrest, Stan had said he was interrogated for fifteen hours by the NIA because of his activism. The state 'wanted to put me out of the way, and one easy way [to do that] was to implicate me in some serious cases'.[10] Stan said he was 'raided twice' by authorities who 'put before me certain extracts, supposedly taken from my computer, extracts which showed Maoists were communicating with each other, and in some extracts even my name was mentioned'. He said the authorities were unable to tell him who sent those emails, who received them, on which date the emails were sent and if there was any sort of signature on the emails. 'So, I just denied and disowned every single extract that was put before me, except one,' which he said was a message from him and the co-founder of the Persecuted Prisoners Solidarity Committee to other human rights organisations in India. That letter explained the purpose of their organisation and requested other groups to join them in their efforts. 'What is happening to me is not something unique and happening to me alone. It is part of a broader process that is taking place all over the country.'

Stan was very childlike. Arun told me that he sang Mundari songs when in a good mood. I prodded him a couple of times, but he just smiled and sang a few lines while walking. He believed that one day 'the revolution' would surely come and exploitation in the world would end. I asked him what he meant by it. He said, 'Rule of the poor.' 'But how can rulers be poor?' I teased him. He would smile. He would then ask me; did I not believe that the revolution should and would come? I said it should but didn't know whether it would. I would tease him, asking where the revolution would come from so we might send her a pickup. He would laugh. Then he would sublimate into the distant world of Chaibasa. How the Adivasis were simple, how outsiders looted them.

I would say that even insiders do not spare them. His Ranchi itself may be evidence of it. This happens with every community. A class layer soon gets formed, which no longer cares for its own that are left behind. As long as people do not liberate themselves from identity traps, this will go on.

I am convinced that if Stan had been released from prison, he would not have died at the time he did. If it wasn't for his Parkinson's, his health was otherwise good for his age. After the cells opened at 3 p.m., he would come out and take rounds of the corridor alone when he was downstairs, visible from my cell. He seemed happier when he moved to the first floor. Now I would be his company on his walks.

Suddenly, we saw him change. Arun mentioned that Stan ate little and wasn't his normal self. Although he never lost his temper, once when Arun and I were trying to converse with him in a lighter vein, he shut us up, saying, 'Both of you get lost.' I sensed something was seriously wrong. His oximeter readings were plummeting, and I notified the doctor and the jailer, requesting that they send him to an outside hospital. Nothing was done for him, even though his oximeter reading slid down to 75, which I thought was dangerously low. I went down and almost shouted at the doctor, saying they would be responsible if something happened to him. Stan's oximeter reading indicated that he had contracted COVID-19. However, when a test was conducted on him in the Hospital on 27 May, we were told that he tested negative. We learned from the newspapers on 30 May that after reaching Holy Family Hospital in Mumbai, he had tested positive, confirming our fears.[11] That was not the first instance; we had heard of many before who tested negative inside the jail but were found infected (positive) when tested outside.

His death created a wave of indignation across the world. The historian Ramachandra Guha called his death 'a case of judicial murder'.[12] The UN Working Group on Arbitrary Detention released an opinion, declaring Swamy's detention arbitrary and his death 'utterly preventable'.[13] The UN Special Rapporteur on the situation of human rights defenders was quoted as saying, 'The death in custody of Indian Catholic priest Stan Swamy, a renowned human rights and social justice advocate for over four decades, will forever remain a stain on India's human rights record.'[14] In his native Tamil Nadu, VCK chief Thol. Thirumavalavan, MP termed his death 'as a murder committed by BJP government with the help of laws'.[15]

We, his co-accused in Taloja jail, also decided to condole his death. The new jail superintendent was considerate enough to not only permit but facilitate a small condolence meeting in his site office. A rare humane gesture in the sadistic world of prisons!

12

The Killing of My Brother

The people who have really made history are the martyrs.
                                            Aleister Crowley

It was 14 November 2021. As usual, I was woken up by the clang of the guards' staff. And as usual, I walked to the other end of the corridor to listen to the morning headlines on TV. The news flashed across the screen – a major police encounter in the Gadchiroli forests. Twenty-six Maoists killed. Among them, a most-wanted Maoist commander.

A shiver ran down my spine. Over the years, every report of a Maoist encounter had triggered the same sinking feeling in me. I switched channels, searching for more details. On an English news channel, the anchor fumbled with our tongue-twisting surname. My worst fears had come true. Though the reporter mentioned that official confirmation was pending, for me it was already certain.

I returned to my cell and collapsed on the cot, crying silently. Images flashed through my mind in a kaleidoscope – scattered memories, fragmented voices, moments long past yet suddenly vivid. I wiped away the lone tear that slipped from my eye and sat up.

Breakfast arrived. I ignored the food, picked up the tumbler of tea and walked back to the TV. Now my brother's face was everywhere. The police narrative had taken over – claims of a prolonged gun battle, a hardened Maoist commander taken down. In earlier times, civil rights groups would have investigated such encounters, exposing staged killings. But those days were gone. Now these very groups were labelled as Maoist fronts, their voices silenced. No one dared question the state's version.

For me, it was the end of a long, lingering nightmare.

Anil. That was the name I had given him. He was my sixth sibling, fifteen years younger than me. But in the school records, thanks to a family friend who worked as a teacher, he became Milind. The name stuck. Maybe because of his serious nature, I had always imagined he would follow in my footsteps. I had kept my old engineering books, my slide rule, my instrument box – hoping he would use them one day.

Whenever I returned home from Nagpur, where I was studying engineering, he and my younger sister would stare at me, their clothes tattered, their eyes filled with wonder. I never saw them growing up; my visits home were too brief. Each time, I would repeat my usual advice: Study well. But I never really knew which class they were in and how they managed to survive and study in Wani.

By the time Milind reached school, I had already moved to Mumbai for work. I had abandoned my studies at IIT Kanpur and was forced to take up a job to support my family. A large part of my salary went home, but it was never enough. My mother took up any work she could find and my father had exhausted all his ideas to make ends meet, at one point even trying his hand as a shopkeeper, but with no shop to run.

A brother next to me found work in the local colliery but never took responsibility for the family. The next one pursued a welding course at an Industrial Training Institute (ITI) after his matriculation, hoping to get a job. For years he found none. By then I was at Indian Oil Corporation (IOC), and through my contacts I helped him secure a job in Baroda. He worked there for a while before returning home.

Milind had just cleared his tenth exams. I was disappointed with his marks but hoped he would improve in his twelfth and get into an engineering college. That was all I could think of – a career in engineering seemed like the only escape from our struggles. But without informing me, he enrolled in an electrician's course at ITI Yavatmal, following his immediate elder brother.

I was disappointed at first, but I understood. Our family's condition was too precarious. Education was a luxury we could barely afford. At the same time that Milind joined ITI, I joined

IIM Ahmedabad. The opportunity cost of the course was enormous – nearly twenty months of salary, plus expenses – but I covered it with my savings. I had accumulated project leave of nine months while I was working on the Salaya–Mathura pipeline project of IOC. In order to avail of it, I needed to keep a lien with the company I worked for. I managed to get study leave with the help of a local politician friend who had a good rapport with Indira Gandhi, the then prime minister. The entire exercise would prove costly in the long run, but I had little option. Even while studying, I regularly sent money to the family so that they did not suffer additional financial strain.

Milind wrote to me regularly, sometimes asking for money, which I always sent. I never let anyone know. He even took money from Mother, though she had so little to give.

At IIM, my classmates were obsessed with securing summer placements with top companies, hoping to land pre-placement offers and high salaries during the final placements. I did not have the luxury of long-term thinking; financial necessity dictated my choices. Rather than chasing corporate offers, I preferred a salary from IOC over a stipend from another company. While others strategised for their future careers, I simply resumed my old job, earning more than the highest stipend offered on campus.

During one visit home, I passed through Yavatmal, hoping to see Milind. Instead, I was shown his room. He wasn't there. He hadn't known I was coming. I stepped inside.

The room was bare. A dark, mud-walled hovel.

I stood in the silence, guilt washing over me. I had tried so hard, but it was never enough. I could not ease my siblings' suffering. I could not pull them out of the life we were born into.

The next I heard about him was that he had completed a karate course and earned a black belt. He began training the youth in our village, which came as a pleasant surprise – none of us in the family had ever paid attention to physical fitness. He had a natural leadership quality, inspiring the village boys to follow him. By the time I graduated from IIM Ahmedabad, he had joined Ballarpur Paper Mills as an apprentice.

During my brief stay at home before leaving for Mumbai for my new job, I observed that he had an impressive grasp of electrical systems – far beyond what was expected of an ITI graduate. His practical skills were equally sharp. I realised he had far greater potential than his job would ever allow him to use, but I didn't know how to help him realise it.

As an apprentice, he soon began organising young workers to fight for their collective rights. After completing his apprenticeship, he secured a job at the Dhoptala mines of Western Coalfields (WCL). His organising work intensified – he travelled by bicycle or on foot to workers' colonies across the WCL area, waging simultaneous struggles against both the management and the established leadership of the All India Trade Union Congress (AITUC). Eventually, he wrested control of the union. Under his leadership, workers launched multiple struggles and achieved significant gains.

Around 1987, he led a major agitation in the WCL area, which led to his termination. A massive protest ensued, and within a year the management was compelled to reinstate him. The coal mines erupted in celebration.

I learned about his activism from his friends when I arrived at Ballarshah station in Chandrapur district, travelling from Chennai, where I was then posted. Milind had sent his comrades, including a man named Nagesh, to receive me. That night I listened to their stories. Nagesh's tale, as narrated by himself and supplemented by others, reminded me of the Buddhist account of Angulimala – the feared murderer who was transformed into an *arhat* by the Buddha.

As the workers' movement gained momentum, the management and police deployed local goons to crush it. One of them was Nagesh, a notorious figure in Sasti Colony, Chandrapur district. At the time, Milind was organising workers under the banner of the Naujawan Bharat Sabha (NBS). On the eve of a strike, and against the advice of his comrades, he decided to meet Nagesh. There was a palpable risk – Nagesh knew Milind was the backbone of the movement – but Milind went anyway. What transpired between them is unknown, but

Nagesh emerged from that meeting a transformed man. He renounced his past, became Milind's devoted follower, and soon rose as a workers' leader himself. Nagesh was hacked to death by another hired goon.

The next morning, my younger brother who was there with me at the time took me to Milind's room. It was as bare as his room in Yavatmal had been, despite his decent salary – coveted among workers. The following day, I left for our village with my younger brother. Milind came to see me briefly. He was his usual self. That was perhaps the last time I saw him.

Over the years, I heard that his visits to the family had become infrequent and brief. My father, however, was immensely proud of him. He had once seen Milind addressing a mammoth public meeting in Chandrapur and often spoke of how inspiring he was. He proudly called him 'Anil bhaiyya'. My mother, deeply attached to him, would fondly call him 'maha Anil' (my Anil).

I continued receiving occasional updates on Milind from my younger brother and Milind's friends. During one May Day celebration, the police attacked workers and leaders of the WCL Mazdoor Sangathan in Sasti village. They arrested twenty-five to thirty activists, including Milind, and charged them with sedition and other offences. Milind spent nearly three months in prison in Chandrapur. I would learn about it only much later.

By then, thousands of unorganised workers in Chandrapur's industrial belt had united under the banner of the Akhil Maharashtra Kamgar Union (AMKU), with Milind among its leadership. Contract workers from industries such as Super Thermal Power Station, Ballarpur Paper Mills, coal mine washeries, cement plants, and the Mineral Exploration Corporation, along with those from the Forest Development Corporation and small-scale industries, all rallied under AMKU. Milind also organised Maharashtra State Transport Corporation (ST) workers across Chandrapur, Gadchiroli, Yavatmal, Wardha and beyond. Under his leadership, they staged a strike and won most of their demands.

There were smaller but significant struggles too – like the installation of a portrait of Dr Ambedkar at a bus depot in

Pandharkawda, an act aimed at instilling confidence in workers before bigger battles.

To disrupt his growing influence, the management transferred him to the newly opened Padmapur colliery, located in Padmapur village, Chandrapur district of Maharashtra. But that didn't deter him. By then he was not just a leader of coal workers but of workers of the Maharashtra State Electricity Board (MSEB) and thousands of casual and contract workers across the Chandrapur–Ballarshah belt and beyond.

My family, fearing I would be disturbed, shielded me from negative news about him. Thus I remained unaware of many of his struggles, his arrests and even his decision to marry – reportedly a spectacle in itself. My only sources were my old schoolmates who still lived in the region. Occasionally, they would call and tell me things they had read in the local newspapers about Milind. But for long stretches there was no news of him.

Eventually, the family grew accustomed to his absences and stopped worrying.

While writing my book on Khairlanji – *Khairlanji: A Strange and Bitter Crop* – and investigating police atrocities against protesting Dalits in Yavatmal and Amravati, I came across several people who confided in me about Milind's key role in seeding those protests. It was also rumoured that he had played a part in organising the action by a mob of women of Kasturba Nagar slum to eliminate the infamous goon Akku Yadav in broad daylight inside the district court premises in Nagpur city on 13 August 2004. Yadav and his gang had allegedly raped over forty women in Kasturba Nagar, extorted money and murdered those who resisted. Despite forty-odd FIRs against him, he remained free due to political links and witness intimidation.[1] The final trigger came when he openly threatened in a court to rape survivors: 'I will come back and do the same to you again.'[2] A mob of 200–300 people, mostly women, from Kasturba Nagar stormed the courtroom, attacked him with stones, chilli powder and knives, and killed him in front of police and judges. Though twenty-seven people including women were arrested, all were acquitted in 2016 due to lack of evidence.[3] The case became a symbol of a failed judiciary and extrajudicial justice in India. It became an international news item, being widely covered by the BBC[4] and the *Guardian*[5] and became the subject matter of several documentaries such as *Death of a Rapist*[6]. Whether the rumours about his key role in organising this action were true or not, one thing was certain – he had an intense hatred for injustice and the courage to confront it, not as a Robin Hood figure but by mobilising the oppressed to fight for themselves collectively.

These memories flashed before my moist eyes in a swirl of emotions.

When my youngest brother Pravin died of falciparum malaria in 2005 – contracted while conducting research in tribal areas for his doctoral work – Milind did not come. When my father passed away in 2014, he was absent. Family weddings, including that of my daughter, whom he dearly loved, were out of the question. Meanwhile, the police kept visiting our home in the village searching for him, but my family shielded me from the harassment, knowing it would disturb me.

Once, when I was posted in Kolkata, Chandrapur police came looking for him. We then stayed in an exclusive building in Alipur, mostly occupied by foreigners except for three flats, two of which belonged to my company and the third one to some relation of the then chief minister Jyoti Basu, who often visited there. I was away on tour and my wife received them. She seated them, offered them tea, and they left, visibly embarrassed. Friends and relatives later told me that plain-clothes policemen surveilled every family event, hoping to catch a glimpse of him.

We learned about his activities mostly through the newspapers or through the state's responses to his work. There was nothing we could do – he had made his choice, and we had full confidence that he would never commit any wrongdoing.

Then came the media onslaught. Newspapers began branding him a Maoist leader, attributing all kinds of crimes to him. Police placed increasing bounties on his head, projecting him as though he were the chief of the Maoist party. It was terrifying even to think about. Every time news of an encounter surfaced, my heart skipped a beat. Life went on. And then, suddenly, our names were implicated in the Elgar Parishad case.

Eventually, they had his head.

The pain was so overwhelming that I could not even weep in silence. My greatest worry was about my mother – how would she bear it? She had shed her blood to feed us. She never learned about my arrest. My family had told her I had gone abroad and was stuck there because of the pandemic. It was a believable lie – she knew I often travelled abroad for long stretches of time. The only difference was that wherever I was, I never failed to call her, especially after my father's death. But the pandemic provided the perfect cover.

When prison mulaqats over the phone began, I decided with Rama that I would use every third call to speak with my mother. It comforted her when I told her I would return once flights resumed. The guards in attendance knew it and cooperated fully to keep my secret. Did she really believe it? I doubt it. But for my sake she pretended to.

I was terrified that she would not survive the shock of seeing Anil's slain body.

The television channels blared news of his death all day, flashing his photos while linking the story to me. I was futilely curious about the details – how the encounter had unfolded, whether the police had suffered casualties. They claimed three policemen were seriously wounded and flown to Nagpur for treatment. But no follow-up reports surfaced. It was meaningless to look for answers, yet I still did. And when the grief swelled unbearably, I silently retreated to my cell at the far end of the barracks and collapsed on my bed.

When they locked the cells at 2 p.m., I wept in silence. Overwhelmed, I had a desperate urge to pour my feelings on to paper. In a state of deep grief and semi-consciousness, I began writing to my illiterate mother.

The next day, Rama came for mulaqat. She briefed me on the terrible news, though it was nothing more than what I already knew. I asked her to seek court permission for me to visit my mother. In the meantime, my lawyers secured approval for me to speak with her over the phone.

When I called, she sounded astonishingly normal. That comforted me, but it also worried me. In her innocence, she had instructed my siblings not to reveal the tragic news to me. That was her nature. So when we spoke, neither of us mentioned the grief we carried. I reassured her not to worry about me and repeated that I would return when flights resumed.

My mother's courage and determination were simply astounding. In our village, women generally laboured harder than the menfolk. Yet, she stood out even among these hard-working women. She always pushed herself beyond limits, undeterred by the consequences to herself. Throughout her life, she survived by eating last – sustaining herself on whatever was left after feeding us.

She was the only unschooled one among her seven siblings, yet her grasp of things was remarkable. She possessed an innate intelligence and a sharp intuition that let her see through people and situations with tremendous clarity and confidence. What set her apart even more was her unflinching hatred of injustice – she never hesitated to confront it, even physically.

One incident is etched deeply in my memory. I must have been in the fourth standard at the village school. Our well was located near the Dalit end of the village, surrounded by farmland owned by a Kunabi family. That family, as we later understood, perhaps wanted to intimidate the Dalits into abandoning the well so they could claim it for irrigating their crops. One evening, two women returning from the well found it contaminated with cattle dung and garbage – clearly a deliberate act. They came straight to our house and told my mother, who had just returned from her day's work.

Without a moment's hesitation, my mother picked up her pitcher and bucket and marched with them to the Kunabis' well. An argument broke out as they confronted the women there. A Kunabi youth came running over and politely offered to draw water for my mother. But she flatly refused. 'Will you be standing here every time Dalit women come to fetch water?' she asked. When some women tried to obstruct them, she pushed them aside. Then, without another word, my mother stepped forward, pushed a Kunabi woman away from the wheel, and drew water herself – followed by the other two Dalit women. In the skirmish, some pitchers were damaged on both sides.

That evening, one of the upper-caste landlords scolded the Kunabi women for allowing 'pollution' of their well. By nightfall, tension hung thick over the village. We sensed that retaliation might be coming. We children prepared in our own way for the ensuing battle – gathering sticks and stones and even sharpening iron rods. A meeting of the Dalit men was called, where some seemed to blame the women for escalating the situation. My mother stood up and defied them: 'Unless our well is cleaned, we will continue to use the Kunabis' well,' she declared.

Sensing the potential for violence, my father went to the Colliery – a nearby settlement that had become a stronghold of Dalit workers. He had once worked in the coal mines, and later, after the mine was closed, in a lime factory. Our family therefore had strong connections with the Colliery community. He informed the local leaders of the situation and arranged for some militant young girls to reach the village in the morning to defend the women, if necessary.

The next morning, the upper-caste landlord stood nearby with some men to intimidate Dalit women. But the Dalit women marched with their pitchers undeterred, accompanied by the young women from the Colliery. They confronted the Kunabis with coiled ropes in their hands. As some Kunabi women stepped forward to block the path, the Colliery girls began spinning their ropes with such speed and force that the others backed away in fear. One by one, the Dalit women filled their pots from the well.

By evening, the police arrived and brought representatives of both communities together to mediate. The police informed the Kunabis that denying Dalits access to water was against the law. Under pressure, they relented and agreed to allow Dalits to use the well until the original one was jointly cleaned. They also consented to the construction of a new common well, located in the Dalit basti.

Some days later, a public meeting was organised in our village where district-level Dalit leaders were invited. As usual, fiery speeches were delivered and slogans were shouted. But by then, the real battle had already been fought – and won too – not by any leader, but by illiterate women who instinctively understood what civil rights meant and had the courage to assert them. It was like Ayyankali's pioneering 'march of freedom' way back in 1893, which challenged the prevailing caste-based restrictions on movement and access to public spaces in Kerala.

History may never record such battles – quiet, local, fierce – but they have likely been fought in millions by nameless, faceless women like my mother. And through them, dignity was reclaimed, one well at a time. That is the true Dalit history – the history that is unrecorded and unsung.

As I returned from the main gate office, where I was taken to make a call, I was overwhelmed by the courage and forbearance of my mother. Even in such a grave moment of grief, she maintained her composure so that I would not get disturbed.

As with Milind's killing, my mother did not let anyone tell me about the deaths of her three siblings – two sisters and a brother – who passed away one after another during the pandemic. They too were very dear to me. I learned of their deaths only after coming out of the jail.

Milind is gone. His memory would haunt us for the rest of our lives.

13

In Lieu of an Ode to Stan

The tyrant dies and his rule is over, the martyr dies and his rule begins.

Soren Kierkegaard

As his first death anniversary approached, in my solitude of the Anda cell, I penned down the following lines on 3 June 2022.

Stan,
It's been almost a year
Since you slipped past the fascist snare,
Evading the clutches of a regime so paranoid
That it failed to incriminate the virus as your accomplice.
Had they their way, they'd slap UAPA on COVID itself
For daring to deny them their prize.
But the echoes of your defiance grew louder,
Voices from all corners rising in solidarity.
Try as they might, they could not label them all
Urban Naxals.
A judge, burdened with guilt
For delaying your bail hearing,
Dared to add his voice to the chorus.
But even he was not spared
By the monkeys of Modi.
Fearing UAPA, he swallowed his words,
And soon, his recusal joined the endless list –
A sinister game played in the courts:
A good judge recusing,
A bad one rejecting,

Ensuring our captivity for the sadistic pleasure
Of the fascist machine.
Good, you are not here
To witness this mockery of justice.

Stan,
You should have stayed a little longer
To receive the Martin Ennals Prize –
A Nobel for human rights,
A slap in the face of a shameless regime
That branded you a dreaded terrorist.
What an irony!
While the world paid you homage,
The state, Goebbels-like, trumpeted its lies,
Oblivious to its disgrace.
After all, terrorism and human rights do not mix –
Like filth and fragrance,
A sinner and a saint,
Police and the people,
A knife and a sipper.
They claimed you conspired to overthrow the state,
As if their fortress of power
Were a soft toy
That could be snatched from the iron grip
Of Modi, Shah and Doval.
And even if it were –
They knew you could not.
Your trembling hands, unable to hold a sipper,
Were suddenly a threat to a nuclear state.
A sipper, deemed a dangerous weapon
By the paranoid deep state,
Denied to you for days
Until it turned into national black humour.
Yet the thick-skinned hippo of power
Felt no shame.

Can empathy for Adivasis,
Compassion for their suffering,

The Cell and the Soul

Anger against injustice –
Be a crime?
Is educating them about their rights,
Urging them to resist plunder
A conspiracy?
A plot against the state?
A state armed to the teeth,
Boasting global power,
Yet planting fabricated evidence
To jail an eighty-four-year-old Parkinson's patient –
As though he were a gangster.
Even the prison walls
Laughed at the absurdity
When you walked through their monstrous gates –
A frail, deaf, ageing priest
Charged as a terrorist.
Surely, a rare sight for any prison in the world!
You must have been a terribly cunning one,
Eluding capture for decades,
Disguised as an austere Jesuit,
Preaching love,
Teaching tribals their rights.
But were you foolish enough
To leave your sinister plans and contacts
Neatly tucked in your computer?
Strange –
But not to a state
That scripts its own fictions.
You believed you could not be jailed
For doing nothing wrong.
They proved you wrong –
Not only jailing you, but killing you
Without a trial.

Before your arrest,
You asked the people:
'What crime have I committed?'
Your crime, Stan,

In Lieu of an Ode to Stan

Was that you took Jesus at his word.
That you left comfort behind
And chose the poorest of lands
As your *karmabhoomi*.
That you stood by them,
Lived their struggles,
Spoke their truths.
That you built 'Bagaicha' – a sanctuary,
A place of hope for the abandoned.
Like Jesus, you became a pariah to the rulers.
Like Jesus, you were crucified.
As Adivasis were branded Maoists,
Dragged into jails,
You raised your voice.
And that was your undoing.
You disrupted their grand design –
To wipe Adivasis off their own land,
Rich with minerals worth trillions.
To sell forests, rivers, mountains,
To corporations and cronies,
With every cog in the machine
 – from the uniformed executioners
to the khaki-clad lawmakers –
rewarded handsomely in blood money.
Unbeknownst to you, Stan,
You did commit a crime.
A crime of faith in the Constitution,
Believing it placed people above power.
A crime of criminal innocence,
Thinking truth alone could challenge tyranny.
A crime of underestimating the state –
Believing that clenched fists
Could shake the fortress of oppression.
Many did rise,
And found themselves in jails.
Just like you.
I remember the first time I saw you –
Lying on the floor of the prison hospital,

A frail old man, struggling to stand,
Yet smiling like a schoolboy.
You reached out,
Grasped my hands through the iron bars,
And we kept meeting –
Until they took you away in a wheelchair.
I told you, 'Don't come back.'
I never thought you would take me
So tragically at my word.
Let the truth be told:
You were murdered.
Institutionally murdered.
And yet – there was no remorse,
No shame,
Only the mechanical shrug of a brutal system.

Stan,
You mocked your incarceration
With an easy smile.
You endured hardship,
But never let it burden others.
You stunned the jailers
By showing concern for fellow prisoners –
A language they could not comprehend.
While you longed to return to your people,
You spoke with a mischievous twinkle,
Joking that you'd live to 185,
Counting your age
And adding the years of punishment against the fabricated charges.
Little did you know,
The state would prove you wrong
By killing you before a trial.
Even in jail,
You sang the songs of Adivasis,
Eyes shining with belief
In a revolution to come –
A revolution not for vengeance,
But for justice.

In Lieu of an Ode to Stan

All you wanted
Was to die among your people.
Yet the fascist brutes
Would not grant you even that.

14

A Broken System

> The bureaucracy considers itself the ultimate aim of the State.
> Karl Marx

One day during the bandi, the jail superintendent, accompanied by his deputy, came rushing to my cell. He was in civilian clothes and wearing slippers – a clear sign that something serious had happened. As he reached my cell, he thrust his cell phone towards me, speaking incoherently and demanding to know what it was about.

It took me a moment to grasp what he was referring to. The screen displayed a message from my wife that had been shared on social media. It read: *Today, I spoke with Anand on a video call.*

The prison's surveillance system was evidently tracking not just us but also our families. The message had instantly made its way up and down the chain of command and now had the superintendent standing in front of me, visibly alarmed.

His superiors had evidently demanded an explanation for how a video call could have been made from the prison when it was strictly prohibited.

Those were the pandemic days, and communication with families was rigidly controlled. We anxiously waited for our turn, which could take anywhere from a week to two weeks – entirely due to the administration's mismanagement.

I firmly denied that I had had a video call with my wife. I suggested that my wife might have misspelled 'audio' as 'video' in her message. I further clarified that, in any case, we prisoners had no control over initiating calls. It was the prison staff who connected us to our registered contact numbers and handed us the phone. I suggested he inquire with his own staff if there had been any violation. After all, the staff maintained a register, and it would clearly show what type of call it was.

Unable to counter these points, the superintendent asked me to accompany him to the mulaqat room. There, he reviewed the register and found that the call was indeed recorded as an 'audio' call. Next, he got my wife on a call, switched the speaker on, and asked me to question her about the message she had put up on social media.

The situation turned almost comic. I asked her about the message, and she explained that she had shared it on a group and didn't know how it ended up on social media. She couldn't even recall what she had written and kept asking me what the issue was. When I specifically asked her, she categorically confirmed that she was referring to an audio call. The concerned guard also confirmed the same.

At this point I was visibly annoyed by the absurdity of the whole exercise. I asked the superintendent if he was finally satisfied or if there was anything else left to investigate. Embarrassed in front of his staff, he mumbled something and instructed the guard to escort me back to my cell.

However, the matter didn't end there. Without informing us, he passed an order suspending the phone facility of the entire BK-accused for a month. This is precisely how the bureaucracy operates. When questioned by his superiors about the supposed violation, instead of reporting his findings – that it wasn't a video call, or that if it had been, it was the staff's mistake – he chose the safer route. By suspending our mulaqats, he would appear 'competent' to his bosses, unmindful of the fact that his act would establish the incompetence of both.

Punitive actions against prisoners are seen as a demonstration of administrative control, while holding staff accountable is often viewed as undermining the system. For the superintendent, punishing prisoners is always the safer option, as we are unlikely to raise our voice against the prison authorities. Even if we do, by the time a court takes up the matter the issue will already have lost its relevance.

It was only after ten days, when our weekly turn for a phone call came and we were not taken to the mulaqat room, that we realised our phone facility had been suspended. I lodged a written protest with the superintendent, but my protest letter was returned through the jailer without any acknowledgement. My co-accused also likely protested this irrational and high-handed decision, but to no avail. Rejecting applications from prisoners is common practice in jail, leaving us without any documentary evidence to support our case.

Being cut off from the outside world for four weeks during the pandemic – when the entire nation was gripped by anxiety – was a harrowing experience. We wanted to approach the court, but how could we do so without any means of communication? Both we and our families endured anxious moments in the absence of any contact. Even vakil mulaqats (meetings with lawyers) were erratic and unreliable. For the first time I felt utterly helpless, facing the superintendent's blatant high-handedness with no remedy in sight. If this was the situation for people like us, I could only imagine the plight of the majority of common prisoners.

Somehow, I managed to send a message to my lawyers, asking them to take the matter to court urgently. They filed a complaint, but the legal process moved at its usual glacial pace. By the time the court could address the issue, the one-month suspension period had already ended and our mulaqats resumed. This is typical of the legal system – complaints often die a silent death, rendered infructuous by procedural delays. How many such complaints have gone unresolved due to the courts' unresponsiveness to prisoners' issues is anyone's guess.

This systemic failure is one of the primary causes of lawlessness in prisons. Even when the issue resolves itself with time, the illegality that caused it remains unaddressed. This emboldens perpetrators to act with impunity, knowing there will be no consequences. Unless state functionaries are held accountable for their wilful violations of the law, there can be no rule of law – nor, by extension, any true democracy.

Making a complaint against jail authorities' blatant violations of the law is almost always an exercise in frustration. Courts typically require a response from the respondents, which is reasonable in principle. However, in urgent matters courts could expedite the process by demanding a response by mail within a day or two, or by summoning the jail superintendent or a representative to appear in court immediately. Instead, the usual practice is to set a hearing for a fortnight later, only to find that no response has been submitted. A reminder is then sent, often met with further delay. By the time the matter is finally heard – if it even reaches that stage – the issue has often lost its relevance.

This is precisely what happened with the one-month suspension of our mulaqats. In cases where the issue persists, such as denial of mosquito nets, courts often side with the prison authorities, accepting their arguments – usually framed around 'security concerns' – ignoring the prisoners' constitutional right to life. There is no recognition of the vast asymmetry of resources between the state and the individual. While the state can commit illegal acts and defend them all the way to the Supreme Court with virtually unlimited resources, an aggrieved citizen is likely to be worn out mid-course.

These systemic flaws have emboldened state functionaries to act with impunity. And tragically, it is the judiciary itself that bears significant responsibility for the erosion of accountability in the state's dealings with its citizens.

Another instance of arbitrariness involved a letter I wrote from prison. In prison, all incoming and outgoing letters were read by the jailers. The stated purpose was to examine them for coded messages or content that, in the jailer's opinion, could endanger the security of the state or prison, or contained false information about prison affairs. This process of 'examination' was meant to involve scanning for specific words rather than fully reading the letters. Moreover, this scrutiny was mandated to occur in the prisoner's presence for both outgoing and incoming letters, ensuring no tampering took place.

However, in practice, jailers often delayed the processing of outgoing letters by one to two days before forwarding them for dispatch. While prisoners could at least follow up with jailers during this period, once the letters left their hands they were left in complete darkness as to whether the letters were actually sent. At times, letters were promptly dispatched; at other times they reportedly languished at the gate for days due to 'staff shortages'.

In our case, it was revealed in a letter from the superintendent himself that our outgoing letters were scanned at his office after being cleared by the jailers, and the scans were forwarded to investigating agencies such as the NIA, the Anti Terrorism Squad (ATS) and anti-Naxalite cells. We were unsure as to whether incoming letters too underwent the same scrutiny.

The requirement of the jailers reading letters in the prisoner's presence was rarely followed. Jailers typically handed the letters to a kamwalla for delivery, bypassing protocol entirely. Outgoing letters followed the reverse route: prisoners handed their letters to kamwallas, who passed them to the *baba*s (the guards) on duty, from whom the jailers collected them for reading. Ideally, my letters – always sent via Speed Post – would, being local, reach their destination the same day and be delivered the next day. While this often happened, there were instances when delivery took three to five days.

On 16 March 2021, I wrote a letter to my wife enclosing two notes for my lawyers, two letters for my daughters and a note for a friend. My wife would scan the enclosed letters and forward them by email. However, this letter did not reach her even after seven days. Over the next week, I repeatedly inquired with the jailer about the delay but received no satisfactory response. On 29 March 2021, I wrote to the superintendent complaining about the unreasonable delay in the dispatch of my letter. Since I was verbally informed that the contents of the letter had raised objections, I volunteered in pointing out in my complaint that Rules 17 and 20 of the Maharashtra Prison Manual, which were being cited to impose these restrictions, had been declared unconstitutional by the courts.

I handed the complaint letter to the jailer in the morning for forwarding to the superintendent. However, it was returned to me unacknowledged in the evening – an act that was blatantly unlawful but had become the norm. Prisoners were made to write applications for every trivial matter, but whether those applications were accepted or even acknowledged remained at the discretion of the superintendent.

Two days later, on 1 April 2021, an office guard came to my cell and delivered an official letter from the superintendent, titled *Samaj Patr* (which loosely translates to 'warning' or 'advice' in Marathi). I was required to acknowledge receipt of this letter. It informed me that two of the notes enclosed in my letter – (i) 'How Elgar Parishad was made a Maoist Conspiracy' and (ii) 'Elgar Parishad Case: On Who Planted Those Letters in Rona Wilson's Computer' – were deemed objectionable under Rules 17 and 20 of Chapter 31 (Facilities to Prisoners) of the Maharashtra Prison Manual.

The superintendent cited two reasons for withholding these notes: (i) their content allegedly created suspicion about the investigations into the Bhima-Koregaon case, and (ii) they were deemed to propagate the ideology of Naxalism. The letter also contained a directive advising me not to disseminate information about a sub judice matter to the media. It concluded by informing me that the withheld letters were being retained in the prison office.

Apart from the content of this communication, what was particularly frustrating was that the superintendent chose to write the letter fifteen days after my persistent follow-ups and written complaint – and even then without formally acknowledging my complaint. On 5 April 2021, I responded with a detailed letter, pointing out that I had submitted my complaint to the jailer and had explained to him, with relevant court judgements, that Rules 17 and 20 of the Maharashtra Prison Manual had been declared unconstitutional way back in 1987. I quoted the relevant portion of the judgement:

> [T]he restrictions imposed on the prisoners to be valid must have relevance either to the maintenance of internal order and discipline in the precincts of the jail or prevention of escape of the prisoner or prevention of transmission of coded message or messages which have potentiality or tendency to give rise to disturbance of public

order or inspiring commission of any illegal activity or defence or reasons of a like nature. Barring such restrictions, we see no reason why the prisoner should be prevented from writing letters containing matters referred to in Rule 20 . . .[1]

The judgement also explicitly addressed the issue of prisoners' right to propagate political opinions:

By reason of the conviction and being lodged in jail, the prisoner does not lose his political right or rights to express views on political matters, so long as such views propagated by the prisoner through letters do not have the potency of inciting violence or is likely to adversely affect maintenance of law and order or public order.[2]

The court had unequivocally struck down Rules 20 and 17(ix), frequently cited by prison authorities to restrict prisoners' correspondence, as unconstitutional:

'In the result, Rule 20 and 17(ix) of the said Rules are struck down as violative of Articles 19(1)(a) and 21 of the Constitution.'[3]

Although the superintendent did not specify which parts of Rule 17 were being invoked, I noted that other relevant parts – namely, 17(x) and 17(xi) – were inapplicable in the case of my letter. I concluded that his reasoning was, therefore, legally untenable.

I also pointed out that the two notes in question were explicitly intended for my lawyers, as they contained technical explanations critical to my defence. His presumption that the notes were meant for the media was both baseless and prejudiced. Moreover, even if they had been intended for the media, such communication was not barred by law. I cited the Supreme Court's judgement in *State of Maharashtra vs Prabhakar Sanzgiri*: 'The appellant [the superintendent of Arthur Road Jail], therefore, acted contrary to law in refusing to send the manuscript book of the detenu out of the jail to his wife for eventual publication.'[4]

I emphasised that merely being lodged in prison did not strip me of my constitutional rights to expression and publication. Similarly, his assertion that my family and sympathisers should not engage with the media regarding the case was wholly unlawful.

To support my argument, I referred to a recent Delhi High Court judgement addressing the publication of opinions on an accused's innocence:

> [T]here is a cardinal difference in attempting to influence formation of an opinion that an accused is not guilty and the State attempting to influence an opinion to the contrary. An expression of an opinion that an accused is not guilty does not destroy the presumption of innocence that must be maintained till an accused is tried and found guilty of an offence. A media campaign to pronounce a person guilty would certainly destroy the presumption of innocence.[5]

I proceeded to dismantle the superintendent's two observations in his *samaj patr*. Regarding his claim that the notes created suspicion about the Bhima-Koregaon investigations, I stated that, as an accused, it was both my right and responsibility to challenge the investigations in defence of my innocence. The aforementioned judgement supported my right to publicly question the fairness of the investigations.

On his second claim that the notes propagated the ideology of Naxalism, I categorically refuted it as baseless and prejudiced. The notes were purely technical in nature, addressing forensic aspects of the case, and bore no connection whatsoever to any ideology. I even offered to provide copies of the relevant judgements for his reference and cautioned him that persisting with withholding my letter would amount to wilful contempt of court.

The superintendent later summoned me to his office, where he awkwardly attempted to defend his actions. Upon my warning that I would escalate the matter, he relented. The next day, he informed me, through the jailer, that the letter had been dispatched – except for the note intended for my friend.

Yet, another instance of the superintendent's unlawful behaviour surfaced in relation to our letters. It was revealed that, beyond being read by jailers, our letters were also scanned in the superintendent's office, saved in a system and forwarded to the NIA, ATS and Anti-Naxalite Cell. The superintendent even issued a samaj patr to three of my co-accused – Ramesh Gaichor, Sudhir Dhawale and Arun Ferreira – based on their correspondence.[6] He wrote to the court, citing the police commissioner and special inspector general (Naxal Virodhi Abhiyan), Nagpur, as finding these letters objectionable. For instance, he flagged Gaichor's poems on Veera Sathidar, Ferreira's article 'Stan's Profound Simplicity' and another article titled '*Patthalgarhi cha Father*' in Dhawale's letter.

This blatant violation of our right to privacy led us to collectively file a complaint with Maharashtra's home minister.[7] The situation escalated further when, in response to a petition filed by my wife and Vernon Gonsalves's wife in the Bombay High Court, the NIA submitted an affidavit detailing the full content of our letters, arguing that they contained 'suspicious content'.[8] This was clear evidence that the NIA was in possession of our private correspondence.

The unauthorised reading of our personal communication with our families and friends violated our fundamental right to privacy. Worse still, many of these letters contained communication with our lawyers, which is legally considered 'privileged'. Such communication is protected by law and cannot be accessed by investigative agencies without proper authorisation. Any attempt to do so is not only unlawful but potentially criminal.

One fine morning I was summoned by the superintendent through the jailer. He showed me on his phone an article in the *Caravan*[9] and asked me what it was. I denied that I had sent it to any publication outside and that the jailer could vouch for it. It was a part of the letter to my daughter which was duly cleared by the jailer. It might have been leaked to the press, I did not know how. The article was as follows:

Economic Goals Cannot Disavow Constitutional Vision: Anand Teltumbde Writes from Prison

Anand Teltumbde

10 March, 2021

Anand Teltumbde, a professor and writer, is currently incarcerated in the Taloja prison in Maharashtra, under the Unlawful Activities (Prevention) Act. He is awaiting trial in what is broadly termed the Bhima Koregaon case.

The ongoing debate on the Narendra Modi government's programme to privatise public sector enterprises, or PSEs, has a certain ring of déjà vu. The proponents of privatisation argue, in support of the government, that [the] private sector has always been more efficient than the public sector. Unbeknownst to them, this argument in its logical extension might lead to a preposterous but valid question: Why not privatise the government itself?

Exemplifying their point, they often say that the United States, which strongly favoured the private sector, grew into a global economic power, whereas the United Kingdom, which favoured the public sector, was driven to bankruptcy by the late 1980s. They conveniently forget that capitalism (read: private capitalism), pushed to its death bed by the great depression of 1929, was rescued by the Keynesian prescription of public investment. This prescription has been largely instrumental for the genesis and spread of [the] public sector across the world. This was brought into disrepute by neoliberal economists only beginning in the 1980s.

Likewise, it is a fact India's Nehruvian tryst with socialism emphasised the commanding role of the public sector in the mixed economy and the licence raj that thrived in its wake. And so, when India began to liberalise in [the] 1980s, the private sector simply zoomed and overtook the public sector in performance. But even in this bland reading of history, one needs to remember that it was not as much Nehru, as it was the Bombay Plan of 1944, prepared by the eight leading capitalists of the country at the time, which proposed huge public investment in basic industries. Politically, the workings of this plan served as a socialist rhetoric for the then government. When one reads about economies of Russia and China 'taking off' after they privatised their PSEs, one should remember that their privatisation success was also due to the infrastructure created by their PSEs. Therefore, such superficial presentation of historical data sans analysis may win the argument but would not help us grasp its true import.

It may be said as an axiom, that an enterprise, if left unencumbered from every regulation and control, will surely be more efficient than the one shackled by them. This would explain the seemingly higher efficiency of the private sector than that of the public sector. But when one reels off selective data on performance to show the purported superiority of the private sector, then one must also account for various tax and non-tax exemptions routinely granted to it, not to mention the huge Non-Performing Assets of the PSU banks, created in large part by private debtors.

In 1995, as a member of the study group for deregulation of India's Oil Industry, I studied the long-term comparative performance of Oil and Natural Gas Corporation, a quintessential PSE, vis-à-vis global oil majors. To the discomfort of the government, our team did not find any significant difference. Again, in the post-liberalisation euphoria, when the government gave more power to the boards of the cash-rich PSEs, the oil companies rushed to form dozens of joint ventures with private partners in the private sector (the PSE equity was restricted to 50 percent). Within a few years, all of these ventures, barring a few, ended up needing huge write-offs. Therefore, there is no conclusive evidence that the private enterprise is intrinsically more efficient than the PSE.

The most important factor, however, is not efficiency but effectiveness – a term conspicuous by its absence in this debate. Even in conventional business management, efficiency is not singularly valorised, without its conjoint parameter effectiveness, which is a measure of fulfilment of the enterprise's goal. The enterprise that makes money in [the] short term but falters on its strategic directions is no good. Likewise, the economy that makes huge leaps in its GDP, may not be good if it fails to provide basic liberties and amenities – health, education and livelihood securities – to its citizens.

Hypothetically, if we hand over the economy to a corporate entity of some repute, to maximise GDP, it would likely take it to unimagined levels. But would this serve our purpose as a nation?

The goal of the economy cannot be divorced from the Constitutional vision as spelt out in its preamble and articles, and most importantly, in the directive principles of state policy. These command the state to 'strive to promote the welfare of the people by securing and protecting as effectively as it may a social order in which justice, social, economic and political, shall inform all the institutions of the national life.' This social order is based on liberty, equality and fraternity and justice, as Babasaheb BR Ambedkar explicated in the Preamble.

While there is no conclusive proof that [the] private sector is more efficient than the public sector, there is no doubt that it can never meet the effectiveness criterion of the economic development of India.

Anand Teltumbde is a writer and activist. He is a senior professor and chair of Big Data Analytics at Goa Institute of Management, and was earlier a professor at IIT Kharagpur. He is currently lodged in Taloja Jail, awaiting trial.

I assured the superintendent that even if I had consciously written the article for publication, it was not unlawful.

He did not have anything to say, but as was his wont, and as in the previous phone episode, he banned not only me but all my co-accused from sending or receiving letters. When our families came to know of this, they had to seek remedy from the court. My wife and Susan Abraham, wife of Vernon Gonsalves, had to file a petition with the Bombay High Court.[10]

There were numerous such instances of brazenly unlawful and high-handed actions by the jail authorities, which would push us to knock at the doors of the courts. The process could take months, rendering the petitions infructuous. It may be an interesting piece of research to know the proportion of such petitions that die still deaths. This process, however, contributes to the impunity of the system vis-à-vis citizens.

15

And Bhola Hanged Himself

Suicide is man's way of telling God, 'You can't fire me – I quit.'
Bill Maher

He was a quintessential prototype of a proletarian prisoner – innocent and illiterate, living in the moment out of sheer obligation to existence.

Around 8 p.m., a commotion broke out in the general ward downstairs. Guards rushed in, followed by hurried movements by others. Something had surely happened – a quarrel, an emergency, or perhaps a death. In jail, everything seems normal, so no one paid much attention.

Soon the news spread: Bhola had hanged himself. The same hushed movements following any death in the prison followed, barely visible through four layers of steel bars. They likely carried his body out wrapped in a bed sheet, as they did with others. And that was it – the abrupt end of a teenage prisoner's story. The next morning the barracks opened, breakfast arrived, and life went on without any sign that tragedy had struck.

I don't know why I felt compelled to write about Bhola's death. I had witnessed over a dozen deaths in the prison before, but none had saddened me like this. Just that morning I had seen him dancing to a song on television, delighting others with his bare, glistening black body and oversized pants sliding precariously at his waist, pulsating to the tune. He often did this on his own, oblivious as to whether anyone was watching.

For most of his stay, he was in a cell two doors away from mine. I noticed him on his first day – a hefty, dark young lad in oversized clothes that barely clung to his body, exposing all

And Bhola Hanged Himself

that they were meant to conceal. He ate poha from a piece of newspaper and drank tea from a torn mineral water bottle, sitting on the floor near the door. I wondered why he hadn't been given prison crockery.

New faces were common in the Hospital, appearing and disappearing with the constant admissions and discharges. People carried their belongings – a bed sheet, a blanket, a bag of clothes and a bucket – when they entered or left. That was the model prisoner. We were exceptions, with books, papers, clothes and canteen goods that required a handcart to move. Bhola had nothing.

He must have been in his teens. He had grown up in a slum dominated by *bhai log*. In any conversation, he ended his sentences with *haan bhai* or *haan na bhai*. My neighbour, a Muslim man arrested under the Maharashtra Control of Organised Crime Act, 1999, was the bhai for many young prisoners, impressing them with tales of his exploits, his legend growing within the prison walls. After dusk and dinner, inmates engaged in pastimes – some sang hymns, praying for an early release, while others gossiped across the cells. Conversations between my neighbour and Bhola were particularly entertaining, Bhola responding with his unwavering *haan bhai* to every command. If asked to neigh like a horse, he would whinny high and loud, earning himself the nickname 'Ghoda'. He never objected. Perhaps that's just how he had learned to exist.

But there was a melancholy side to his life that few noticed. At night he would clutch the iron bars and engage in a long, tearful monologue with his mother – his sobs filling the silence. Such behaviour was labelled 'mental' in jail.

The psychiatrist visiting the Taloja prison for the first time had sought me out, saying he had read my books and followed my case. I asked him about Bhola. He said there were no clinical symptoms of mental illness, though he had given him some medicine to suppress his emotional outbursts.

Bhola would do any job for anyone. Once, he cleaned my toilet and I asked him to take whatever snacks he liked from my bag. Initially he declined, then hesitantly said, '*Aap hi do.*' I gave him a few packets of Haldiram's. Seizing the moment, I asked about his family. He said he had no one except his mother. My guess proved right.

Over time, his story unfolded. He had dropped out of school in the fifth grade and worked as a helper in a garage near Bombay Central railway station in Mumbai, earning around ₹5,000 a month. His mother worked as a maid. His father had died before he was born, and his elder brother too, or so his mother had told him. Now, with him in jail, she was alone.

He didn't know why he had been arrested. One morning, as he joined his friends at their usual gathering spot, a police jeep arrived. Two constables grabbed him by his torn shirt and threw him inside as if he were a sack of grain. 'I asked them what I had done, but I never got an answer,' he said.

They accused him of theft. He spent the night in custody and was given only a single meal of dal and rice late in the afternoon. The next morning he was handed a loaf of bread and tea before being sent to Arthur Road Jail in Mumbai. After three weeks there, he and twenty others were transferred here. He hadn't seen his mother since. He wasn't sure if she even knew he was in jail.

When I asked if he had been taken to a court, he said he didn't know. The jail authorities had taken his thumbprint on some papers during his first week, but no one explained what they were for. Did he want to go home? 'Badly,' he whispered. 'But I don't know how.'

I mentioned this to a police officer lodged in a cell on our floor in a high-profile case. He became friends with me along with an ex-MLA serving under the Prevention of Money Laundering Act, 2002 (PMLA), and joined us for our morning coffee. He rudely dismissed it, saying every criminal made up such stories. He advised me against engaging with 'these lowly people', calling them 'born cheats and criminals'. I recalled the Criminal Tribes Act of 1871 during British colonial rule that branded entire communities as hereditary criminals. The act was repealed way back in 1949 but its legacy still operates with Indian police. This gentleman sincerely believed that the 'lowborn' people are more likely to be criminals than others. It would be futile to prolong such irrational argument. The paradox, however, was that I had seen the same officer call Bhola 'beta' when he needed something cleaned, of course without any remuneration. I didn't argue. I simply picked up my cup of coffee – made by him – and left.

He was the quintessential policeman – ruthless, unquestioning and proud of his killings. He boasted about the number of Muslim criminals he had gunned down. When I asked if he had ever killed a Hindu, he admitted he had – 'a low-caste one'.

He himself wasn't of a high caste; he was something like a Kunabi-Maratha, a historically agrarian community, often considered OBC in Maharashtra. In Western Maharashtra, in the seventeenth and eighteenth centuries, Kunabis who entered the military of Muslim rulers were called Marathas (Marathi-speaking) to distinguish them from others. In course of time, after Shivaji's ascent, this Maratha identity hardened, insinuating Kshatriya varna status, away from Kunabis.[1] But when I pointed out that Kunabis were essentially Shudras, he fiercely refused to accept it. To him, only Scheduled Castes were Shudras. Of course, no one expects police officers to be well informed, as they are drunk with power. But his ignorance was peculiar enough to set him apart. That ignorance might have extended to not suspecting me to be his 'Shudra', obviously.

One day he startled me with a confession: if he had lived in Bhagat Singh's time, he would have been the first to pull the trigger on him. Unsurprisingly, his advice to me was simple – stay away from the lowly inmates in jail.

As a civil rights activist, I knew that thousands of undertrials like Bhola languished in Indian jails, unaware of the charges against them. It was common, especially among those labelled Maoists. Police would round up entire villages of Adivasi men after an insurgency attack, dumping them in prison without evidence. These men didn't understand what they had been accused of; they just accepted their fate languishing in jails.

For the police, arrests meant promotions and cash rewards. In high-profile cases, they would pluck suspects from their 'inventory' to claim swift resolutions of the cases, earning praise from the media and the middle class. The 2006 Mumbai train bomb blasts case, as Abdul Wahid Shaikh has exposed, was just one such example.[2]

Bhola often helped bring my packs of mineral water bought from the canteen upstairs from the ground floor. One day a pack tore and three bottles burst open. Bhola repeatedly begged for my pardon. I asked him to take some canteen snacks from me, but he refused, feeling guilty for causing me a loss. I had to force him to accept them.

Jail has its own ethics. In its microcosm – where accumulation is impossible – humanitarian instincts surface more naturally than in the outside world. Sharing what little one has, helping those in need, is a way of life here.

The next morning I asked my neighbour Abil and others in the general ward if they knew why Bhola had taken his life. Nobody had a clue. Most dismissed him as a 'mental case' and moved on.

But I couldn't.

A strange, unsettling feeling overtook me. I sat down, gripped by an overwhelming urge to write these lines in a single breath.

> Good, Bhola, you rejected this world.
> Though suicide was never your choice –
> It was forced upon you, a compulsion.
> No tears, no mourning, no requiem,
> No one noticed your passing,
> Just as no one had noted your arrival.
> Your proletarian fate was inscribed at birth,
> A destiny beyond your grasp.
> But you avenged their neglect –
> Your final act a defiance,
> Choosing death when life gave you none.
> Monochrome, the colour of void,
> Wrapped you in its silence.
> I don't know where you were born,
> Or how you lived,
> But you told me how they brought you here –
> This hellhole that swallowed you whole.
> You didn't know why you were here,
> Like countless others of your kind.
> The police came, lifted you like debris,
> Dumped you in their vehicle,

And Bhola Hanged Himself

And abandoned you in this abyss.
How simple, how cruel,
This definition of the rule of law,
For the poor in this grand democracy –
Or the 'mother of democracy', as they say now.
There was nothing to know about you.
Your history was carved into your body,
Like Ashoka's edicts on stone,
Or like the cryptic confessions of forgotten kings.
They kept democracy far from your slum,
Littered thorns on your path to school,
Taught you just one refrain:
'Han bhai' – yes, boss –
A submission, a survival.
Jail taught you silence,
Laboured you for a packet of Haldiram or a bidi.
But when dusk fell,
Your agony burst forth,
A lone wail to your unseen mother.
You believed the sea of darkness
Melted the iron bars, carried your cries to her.
A bellyful of grief in a cell full of inmates.
And then, in a moment,
You neighed like a horse,
Danced to Bollywood tunes,
Your dark, bare body writhing to unseen rhythms,
Your oversized pants slipping in reckless abandon.
Laughter erupted,
But no one saw the layers of pain beneath.
The authorities never called you mental,
But you needed care never given.
Your silence was loud,
Your 'han bhais' a camouflage.
People should have known.
Your proletarian fury found rhythm,
Dancing on the jail's flickering TV screen,
Grasping at stolen colours,
Only to have them fade into your pain's dark palette.

What if you had lived?
A life of toil in or out of prison,
Saying 'han bhai' to every master,
Dragged through a cycle of servitude.
What if luck had freed you?
Would it have been luck at all?
Still shackled, still drowning.
I never knew your caste or creed,
But I knew your fate.
If you were Muslim,
You would have died a thousand deaths –
'Han bhai' would not shield you from lynching.
If you were Dalit,
You'd be torn apart,
Privileged in words, damned in reality.
Your body told me what you weren't:
Not an upper-caste Hindu, not a Christian, not anything else.
Just another footnote in a story written at birth.
Your choice:
A life of countless deaths,
Or a death with a full stop.
Neither mattered to a world that moved on,
Unshaken, indifferent.
Unless you had rebelled,
Denied both choices,
And roared: 'Death to you!'
But neither you nor the world was ready for that.
Perhaps we wait for another Bhola –
One who will rise and change it all.

16

The Proximity of Captivity

> Everyone is a prisoner of his own experiences. No one can eliminate prejudices – just recognize them.
>
> Edward R. Murrow

I GOT TO READ Howard Zinn's fascinating book *You Can't Be Neutral on a Moving Train: A Personal History of Our Times* in jail. At one place it said:

> I am convinced that imprisonment is a way of pretending to solve the problem of crime. It does nothing for the victims of crime, but perpetuates the idea of retribution, thus maintaining the endless cycle of violence in our culture. It is a cruel and useless substitute for the elimination of those conditions – poverty, unemployment, homelessness, desperation, racism, greed – which are at the root of most punished crime. The crimes of the rich and powerful go mostly unpunished. It must surely be a tribute to the resilience of the human spirit that even a small number of those men and women in the hell of the prison system survive it and hold on to their humanity.[1]

Prisoners do not come from outer space; they are drawn from the society. But the conditions and constraints imposed upon them show them differently. In jail I can certainly say that the people were more cooperative, more considerate and more proactive in helping each other than outside. The outsiders' perception of a criminal as a rogue, an arrogant, insolent and amoral person, is often belied inside prison. None I met was so. It is hard to believe that they were a danger to the society and hence were locked up here. Like myself!

I recalled my own rhetoric in my *EPW* column on the Aam Aadmi Party (AAP) some years before I myself landed up in prison. The party never problematised the structure of the state and often blamed the people who manned it. They said that if good people are brought to govern, everything would be all right. In the absence of a definition of 'good people', what it meant was people like themselves. I have always been sceptical of this kind of language. People are important as part of the system, but what matters most is the structure – the manner in which the various parts are networked – that largely determines processes within it. People merely operate within this framework. The behaviour of the system is an emergent property of the network itself. One may ask who creates the system. Well, it is people but not with their free will. Even there, they are constrained by the structure within which the system is created. The question may arise: Who creates the structure? Well, it may be people, but again they do not do it with their free will. They do it within the different structure. It is essentially a systems view. My PhD work, done in the 1990s, expounds, using cybernetics theories, how these structures are to be conceived and built to achieve our goals.

In any case, the belief that people are innately good or bad, may be more dangerous than the problem of misgovernance. Nonetheless, we often blame people for everything; and never suspect the system of which they are a minor part. Without wasting so many words, I simply asked where does one find 'good' people – they are all in jails. It was much before the advent of the current autocratic regime that has made it a starker reality!

The people I met in jail were excessively cordial. In the general barrack, people took care of each other as not even family members would. People were often brought to the prison hospital in dilapidated health conditions, resulting mainly from lack of timely treatment. Many a time people had to be literally lifted up and carried about. Skin diseases were common because of the lack of consideration given to personal hygiene in jail. People did not get enough water to bathe, to wash clothes or even their utensils. They did not have enough space because the jail was overcrowded, and they were thus prone to picking up infections from each other. Some have unseemly rashes on their entire body, and some festering wounds. But the people in the jail would unhesitatingly wash them, apply medicine for them and walk them, lending them support. I rarely saw such humane behaviour outside.

The attitude of the outside world was quite reflected in the look and feel of the jail itself. The Taloja jail was barely a little over a decade old but looked as if it was war-ravaged. It was shabby, dilapidated, unpainted and tattered. Sadism and corruption were writ large all over its design, layout and processes. All the buildings leaked profusely during the rainy season and had to be covered with giant-sized heavy-duty plastic sheets. This was a yearly feature executed at the cost of lakhs of rupees, which potentially provided for huge corruption. When I came to the jail, the entire roof of the Hospital was covered with a thick bituminous carpet to keep away the rainwater. Within one year all of that was torn apart by the winds and hanging in shreds, which had to be constantly removed with great difficulty by the kamwallas. Surely, it would have cost a fortune. I wondered what kind of audit condoned such brazenly questionable expenditures. The condition of the roads also mirrored substandard quality of construction and lack of maintenance. The interior of the buildings was to be seen to be believed. In the Hospital, where I lived for the most part of my incarceration, the concrete cover over the reinforcements had fallen off the roof. The heavily corroded reinforcement was precariously holding up the roof slab, which could fall any time, endangering the lives of the inmates. The guards told us that the condition of their living quarters was even worse. The entire roof slab had fallen in one of their houses, just inches away from where the occupant was sleeping. In the Hospital, the kamwalla boys constantly chipped off the loose parts of the roof slab with a hammer lest they should suddenly fall, injuring someone.

Inside the barracks and cells, not an inch of the walls appeared to be straight. They looked like mud walls, leaving crevices to make homes for red ants and lizards. The condition of the wash area reflected full-blown sadism. The floor was broken all over and people had to sleep on it on thin dhurries. It appeared that everything had been deliberately customised to be worse than what was obtained in the worst slums. There was no question of consideration to disabled people. As a public facility, it was supposed to be disabled friendly. Except for a ramp to the mulaqat room, I did not find ramps anywhere. All the structures were two-storeyed and there was no lift or ramp provided for the disabled. It is due to this that the trolleys Father Stan suggested would not have worked even if the jail authorities had accepted his suggestion.

Big food containers had to be carried up the stairs. Water shortage was endemic. Taloja had a water connection, but reportedly its registered demand with the Municipal Corporation was far less than its requirement. As a result, it had to be perennially supplied water by tankers. The piped water supply would be disrupted most times. And the people in the jail would have to carry buckets of water from a pit nearby where water was stored. Even that water was regulated by the guards, and just a bucket or two per person was allowed. People were always to be seen carrying buckets hither and thither. The elderly and physically challenged could not manage this and the younger lot had to fetch water for them. Of course, the jababdar, a designation given to one of the kamwallas on each floor in every circle, looked after the needs of the prisoners. But to carry those buckets upstairs required quite strenuous physical toil. There was no option, however. As per the jail manual, every prisoner had to be provided 135 litres of water per day.[2] But what we got was ten to twenty litres, even if water was released in the taps.

All kinds of services were available against payment, both in cash and kind. There were many poor people around who sought work from the people who lived in individual cells and could pay. Work like toilet cleaning, washing clothes, cleaning and mopping of the cells and any such chores were paid for by the equivalent of canteen materials. Some people worked for bidi bundles and tobacco sachets, which worked as a medium of exchange in the circles. Special services could be bought for cash exchanged outside with the jail staff by relatives. One usually held sufficient stock of canteen materials to feed the needy and to get some work done. A barber service was provided by the jail once a week as scheduled for each circle. Those who could afford it gave the barber some canteen stuff and bidi bundles. Likewise, the maintenance people attending to some tasks for your cell were given some packets of snacks from the canteen or whatever else they wanted. These were legitimate exchanges. But there were big-ticket ones for services to be bought from the jail staff, such as getting sent to outside hospitals, getting phone calls, provision of messaging services, canteen supplies beyond permitted limits, getting home food, and various other liberties, which had hefty price tags running into the thousands.

I met a cross-section of people at the prison, from gangsters to professionals, terrorists, murderers, rapists and scores of undertrials serving for alleged petty crimes. Of course, they were so called after the charges slapped on them by the police. None of them confirmed these official labels for them. No doubt some of them admitted truthfully to what they had done. They had committed a rape or a murder or done some wrong. For example, a retired person from the army, a Punjabi settled in western Maharashtra, came to the barrack and after a couple of days made acquaintance with us, the old residents. He had a rape charge against him. He was very disturbed as he had lost his job with a security agency. When he learned about my background, that I held senior positions in companies, he imagined that I might help him get a job. He admitted that he had had an affair with a lady but suddenly their relationship turned sour and she filed a rape case against him. He was trying to settle with the lady. Indeed, after a few days he went away.

There was a Muslim youth (say, Abdul), originally from Akola but living with his wife and children in Panvel in Navi Mumbai. A bit hot-headed, he had had a quarrel with his wife and left home. He went to sleep under a bridge with some money in his pocket; a goon harassed him and took away his money. In the night, when everybody was asleep, he smashed the head of the goon with a boulder. He then walked to the nearest police station and informed the police truthfully about what had happened. He was arrested and lodged in Taloja jail, where he became a kamwalla in the jail hospital. He excelled as a hospital helper. I heard that using his own experience as a drug addict, he successfully rescued many prisoners from drug addiction beyond any formal hospital processes. Many of them gratefully acknowledged his help while leaving the jail. Beyond his hospital duties, he extended himself to doing all kinds of jobs. I have scarcely seen anyone who worked so sincerely and hard as he did. He cleaned the entire corridor floor twice a day, served food thrice a day, worked in the hospital and did all kinds of chores, bathed people with severe skin problems, applied medicine over their bodies, bandaged their wounds, and so on. He was always seen working, whether it was sun or rain. The jail administration would ask the kamwallas to clean up algae on the floor of the open yard and on the walls of the jail, and he would be there working harder than anyone else. He would climb the walls like Spiderman, stand on a narrow ledge holding on to something precariously with one hand and clean something with the other. The jail staff hardly bothered about the safety aspects; the death of a prisoner has never been consequential in jails.

The entire design of the jail at Taloja was lacking in any safety feature or provision for maintenance. There was no provision for the water tanks at the top to be accessed and therefore they would not be cleaned at all. During my stay of thirty-one months there, I saw them being cleaned only once and was stunned to see how dangerously people managed to reach it, working while standing on the sloping roof. This person simply worked from dawn to dusk, across seasons and irrespective of bandi or no bandi, as though work was what sustained him.

His trial had started while we were in the Hospital. He was quite hopeful that he would get released from the jail as he had already put in more than six years. But the poor fellow was awarded a lifer when I was away in the Anda cell and was transferred to another jail before I came back. I felt terribly sad for him.

There was another skinny fellow, a companion of his, called Chuha by everyone. He too was a Muslim and a very hard worker. He was imprisoned over rape charges and had secured bail. But after his release, he threatened the parents of the girl and was again arrested. He too was transferred to some other jail while I was in Anda.

In my wing, the corner cell was vacant and the one next to it was given to me. The cell next to mine was occupied by a Muslim youth of twenty-nine, a MCOCA-accused, let us call him Abil. He was locked up almost all the time, supposedly because he was unruly. He was unlettered, married, with a small daughter who barely recognised him. He aspired to a career in crime, probably inheriting it from his father. Despite his aspirations, he had very pleasant manners. He proudly narrated his exploits to me and often repeated how, at a young age, he had outsmarted the established *dada*s. He would keep telling me how he had caused the jails to ring alarms. I did not exactly understand what that meant, but guessed it might be a security alarm going off in the wake of some extreme act of violence in the jail. He remained friends with me throughout my stay. He had a knack for communication that captivated all the youngsters who were lodged upstairs; they spent their entire free hours chatting with him, seated at his locked door. All his friends also became friendly with me. He was the first to welcome me when I was sent to the first floor with a very pleasant smile and remained quite helpful to me all through my stay at the jail.

He was a jailbird and knew all the tricks of the trade, including how to bring in mobile phones and drugs hidden in the anus. One day he showed me a phone, the size of which I had never seen outside. On my asking, he said there was always a place where such things could be safely kept. I did not understand what he meant but had to believe him. He once offered to make me tasty dinner and coffee if I could get him a vessel. I was cautioned by many people to keep a distance from him as he might land me in trouble. But I did not find any reason to do that. He explored the possibility with the guards and told me that one of them had agreed to get him a small vessel for ₹2,000. I asked him what would happen if he were caught the next day. Not only would they take the vessel away but they may even punish him. He did not give up on his idea and one day passed me a dabba of dal tadka that he had prepared in his *handi* (stove). It was tasty. He showed me next morning a tin plate bent so as to hold the liquid. His *chullah* was made out of three concrete blocks and the fuel pellets from the newspapers taken from me. Such were the sheer creative ideas illiterates like him conceived and implemented out of necessity. His handi ran for over a month, making coffee for me and occasionally a recooked subjee or dal, until one evening his cell was raided by the jail people who confiscated the entire equipment. Fortunately, he was spared from punishment. While one may not fault the jail for confiscating Abil's handi, what about the well-known handi that our don's assistant ran openly just three cells away?

Once Abil had a quarrel with a guy in his thirties. He was a Dalit from Marathwada and in jail for murder. It became physical and the guards had to run up. While the Dalit man was locked up in his tiny cell next to the TB barrack, Abil was taken out during the bandi and brought back after half an hour, profusely bleeding all over. He had to be helped by the babas to walk. His face was badly swollen and one eye had popped up so much that I feared it was lost. In that condition, they tied him to the door bars inside and locked the cell. He would tell me the next day how all the officers, guards and the superintendent himself had kicked and beaten him on the road with their boots and batons. He said he escaped their clutches and took a boulder, threatening to smash his own head with it. That scared them into stopping and they brought him back. Surprisingly, he recovered fast and became his original self, although the scars near his eye took time to heal. The punishments, no matter how severe, however, failed to deter him from indulging in violent quarrels. I saw him in action at least two times thereafter during my stay and managed to save him from being punished by the jail authorities.

While many, like Abil, admitted to their crimes – some even expressing regret, unlike him – there were a significant number who swore they had been framed by the police. It is possible that all they claimed might not be true, but not everything they said can be discounted either. The police framed them either under public pressure or under pressure to perform or at the instance of someone who paid them bribes in cash or kind. Police usually had an inventory of petty criminals in their areas and often used it to attribute a crime to someone when there was no possibility of catching the actual culprit in time. I met at least one person who fell into this category. He had just accompanied his friend, who had perhaps committed a murder. He was arrested, charged for the murder and dumped in jail. He had already spent more than five years in jail, and had lost his mother while he was inside. He had a married sister but did not know her whereabouts. He worked on stray jobs and hid the scars in his mind. In a melancholy mood, he said he felt like a corpse; he didn't know why he was around. He appeared normal but certainly had psychiatric problems. I felt he could kill himself any time.

And then there were the elites, who were gangsters and serial killers, police officers accused of custodial murders or fake encounters and suchlike. They lived in style, confining themselves to their own company, not mixing with the ordinary prisoners. They would not even allow the ordinary prisoners to trespass into their precincts. They were lodged in cells, ostensibly for security reasons. Perhaps I too fell in the same category.

The most notable person was a guy in his early sixties. With an exceptionally well-built, glistening black body, long, greying hair tied up tightly in a bun, flowing beard and serious demeanour, he looked like a sage from Hindu mythology. He was mostly in his underwear and wore clothes only when he had to go out or during the weekly rounds of the prison superintendent. He wore a no-nonsense, stern look, and was engrossed in his own affairs. He had lots of books neatly kept in boxes made of cardboard packing boxes from the canteen glued with brown tape, neatly stacked in his cell. I never saw him reading but painting was his enduring hobby. He diligently copied pictures for days together using the costliest painting materials. I envied his collection of art books and looked forward to reading them.

Why did he become a criminal? At our first meeting itself he told me that when he was doing his science degree, his father, a businessman, was killed by a gangster. He avenged his death by killing the gangster. He gave up his studies and took over his father's business. That was a pretty brief narrative that he introduced himself with to me. Now, of course, he was settled in Hong Kong. He was arrested in Singapore and extradited. He was in Taloja since that time, for some eight years. Curiously, he was a staunch Hindu, supported the Hindutva of the BJP and hated Muslims. Originally from Kerala, but having been born and brought up in Mumbai, he followed the local Hindu culture and had celebrated the Ganapati festival in a big way. He would always have a couple of 'disciples' around him from the barrack to listen to his sermons as he sat on an improvised stool made out of a paintbox, cushioned with bed sheets, in front of his own cell.

As I passed, I would pause to hear snippets of his sermons. He did not mind it and rather initially relished my addition to his audience. Once I found him narrating a typical Hindutva canard against Muslims as to how they would, one day, outnumber the Hindus and make India a Muslim country. They need to be resisted in time, etc. I foolishly intervened, saying that it was not true. While it was true that their population growth had been higher than that of all other communities, the differential was of such a magnitude that just to come on par with the Hindu population would take them nearly a thousand years. It may take them even longer because lately their population growth rate had been decelerating and closing up with that of other communities. He vehemently disagreed and said that Muslims were already 33 per cent of the population. I corrected him, saying it was not 33 per cent, it was 13 per cent; to be precise, 14.23 per cent as per the last census. He was agitated: 'No, no, you are wrong,' he said, and went inside to get a book to refute me. After a couple of minutes he came out somewhat composed and said, 'Yes, you seem to be right.' His face paled at being proven wrong before his disciples. Obviously, he had not liked my poking my nose into his affairs. It had to dissipate, and after a few days it did. For some months we did not talk.

He related with very few people, just a couple of them, and scared most others. When two PMLA-accused brothers, owners of a business house, came to one of the cells on our floor, they became his closest company. He variously facilitated them with his relations with the jail administration and even shared home food with them when they were not officially granted their own.

As a don, he liked obliging people with his generosity. He had a reputation for philanthropy in terms of arranging a lawyer for someone, or paying up bond amounts for people's release. Of course, that had to be a select few. For instance, he was said to have arranged a lawyer for Abdul's appeal in the Bombay High Court against his life sentence. The jail canteen sold special subjee, chicken, fruits, sweets, etc., on most Sundays and during festive seasons. While those who got money orders from home bought these goodies for themselves, this don bought them for all those who did not.

All his activities were managed by his help, paradoxically a Muslim man, staunchly anti-BJP and anti-Modi. Wheatish-complexioned, lanky, with long hair and somewhat effeminate in his mannerisms, he hailed from Alibaug and was a backhoe operator in some construction company. I guess he too had a murder charge on him. He wrote satire in Marathi against Modi and Shah calling them Billa and Ranga, an infamous pair of kidnappers and murderers in the Geeta and Sanjay Chopra case in Delhi in 1978, who were hanged for their crime. This lanky prisoner managed the affairs of the don and looked after his needs. He would distribute currency notes of ₹500 each to the guards every month. I did not know whether it was to all the guards or only those who were on Hospital duty. Of course, the officers might have been paid separately as they all behaved obligingly with him. He showed me his handi arrangement where he made coffee for the don and his friends during the daytime and for the guards during the night. At times he would send me too a cup of coffee through those guards. Likewise, when they got some good subjee, etc., he would invariably share it with me, of course, not without approval from the don. This happened even when I was not on speaking terms with him.

He always sent some eatables to Stan when he lived downstairs as he said that he had been asked by his teacher in his convent school to take care of Stan. This is a typical profile of dons, criminal otherwise but quite humane to the people who were not in conflict with them. They would show a big heart in sharing with people whom they considered poor and helpless to earn themselves a good name. It is the same ethics that informs the conduct of Indian politicians, who are the legitimised versions of the criminal dons.

Next to the don's help was a person in his fifties, famous in the world of crime and, of course, in the Taloja prison. He buried himself in law books as he fought his case in court in person. He was always in high spirits and would share his proud moments in the courts against the much acclaimed public prosecutor Ujwal Nikam. I had not heard about him before coming to the jail but he appeared to be well known. There was a book written on his exploits by a journalist and even a television serial based on his story. He showed me the book and shared some extracts of his complaint filed against the author. He told me he had a business in Barcelona, which was managed by his wife. He had court orders for everything from a shaving kit to business-style clothes, leather bags, belt and shoes, umbrella, etc., ordinarily unimaginable in the jail. Whenever he went to the court, he was attired like a business executive. He would tell me how, before the pandemic struck, he used to have court visits frequently so as to be able to carry his soiled clothes to get them laundered outside and get his laundered clothes in. He would treat his guards at decent restaurants, including at the Taj, and have all kinds of fun before returning to the jail. During my meetings with him I realised how RTI (Right to Information) was being most effectively used in jail. He had piles of RTI applications and the corresponding responses on all kinds of issues, neatly arranged in files, which he used effectively to tame the jail authorities. The jail staff generally kept their distance from him and never dared to cross him. Talking to these gentlemen, I became convinced that Indian laws worked better for hard-core criminals than for ordinary citizens. Whenever I sat with him, I was captivated by his legal exploits. He never explicitly denied the crimes attributed to him, but instead explained how he would dismantle each charge. Our friend, the police officer, however, remained unimpressed and insisted he would not escape the gallows.

Next to him lived a young man in his late thirties. Built like a wrestler, he was a typical Marathi from the rural Pune belt. He roamed around in the jail wearing a well-pressed, spotless white, half-sleeved kurta, pyjamas, a Gandhi cap, a napkin and a well-oiled, twirled moustache in a style reminiscent of a village Patil. He was called Bhau by most of the people there, including the guards. He had a makeshift place of worship in a corner of his cell, with pictures of assorted gods, where he sat in a *sanskari* style and prayed in the mornings and evenings, reciting some Marathi hymns accompanied by clapping. He had a help in one boy, and on his transfer a person who was known as Mama, who would collect his food, wash his clothes and clean up his cell. He would eat his food in a perfect, Hindu way, neatly sitting with folded legs, taking the food on his plate, doing a namaskar and then eating it. His claim to fame, the people who had been in Yerwada jail during his times told me, was his killing of Qateel Siddiqui, an alleged Indian Mujahideen terrorist suspected in the German bakery blast case in Pune. It was a sensational murder as it took place in a high-security Anda cell, and was done by strangling the victim using the drawstrings from a pair of Bermuda pants with the help of another inmate. He had a well-oiled network among the guards, who functioned as his communication medium. He would help me too in an emergency. We would walk in the corridor together and gossip in a lighter vein about Hindutva, he justifying and I ridiculing it. Once I told him about how Hindutvawadis' bête noire Aurangzeb had been wantonly vilified. Of course, he did not know anything of history, leave alone Aurangzeb; he knew little about even Shivaji, beyond the hearsay. He wanted to read about Aurangzeb and took a book by Audrey Truschke from me. After a few days he returned it saying, 'All your English people write anything.' When I asked him what he had read in it, he admitted he could not understand English. True to his breed, he had very dirty ideas about women – that they are available for a price. While watching Marathi movies on television, he would tell me the price per night each one charged. He was acquitted in most of the cases slapped against him, which numbered more than fifteen, and was confident that he would get out soon. He would rather discuss with me which political party he should join after getting out of the jail. I told him that as a Kunabi farmer he should work for his class and not do the bidding of a Brahmanical party like the BJP. He was taken aback.

After my coming to the first floor, two persons, both brothers, were added to the elite club. They were arrested in an infamous case of alleged defrauding of seventeen banks in a multi-crore scam. They tied up with the don to get home food as their request for it had been rejected by the court. As they settled, things changed briskly. Every evening, they would walk to the telephone room and have relaxed conversations with their families. The don mediated their access to the jail authorities, and money took care of the rest.

Each floor of the Hospital had a television set, closer to the common barrack. They noticed that the television set on our floor did not have a USB port to play movies from a pen drive. A few days later a new TV set had replaced it. I learned that they donated a dozen sets to the prison so they could get one for us. Some replaced the old ones in the jail but some were allegedly embezzled by the staff. Whatever the truth, it was certain that our TV set had been replaced by one with a USB port. They would ask me my preferences, and to my dismay the next day call me to watch those movies. We (I and the elder of the two brothers had a chair permitted by the court) would carry our chairs there, some their improvised stools made of inverted empty paint-dabbas and the rest of the inmates would sit on the floor and watch the movie in style. This went on for months, until we had exhausted most of our favourite movies.

And then came the brothers' hospitalisations. The younger brother was hospitalised in a top-notch hospital for months, followed by the older brother too, in KEM hospital in Mumbai. There used to be a board in the front gate office displaying the names of prisoners who were admitted in outside hospitals for anyone to see. While people like us had to fight in the courts to be taken to outside hospitals as outpatients for serious health issues, here were the wealthy prisoners getting ensconced in private hospitals for months together. It was reported in the papers that they were running their businesses from the hospital rooms.

It is a common feature of prisons in India that if you have money you can buy your comforts. Subrata Roy, the controversial founder and chairman of Sahara Group, alleged to have defrauded 30 million investors of ₹24,000 crore between 2008 and 2011, was lodged in Tihar Jail in an air-conditioned office with video-conferencing facility and staff, to conduct business meetings, provided with many more facilities including air hostesses visiting and staying with him for hours as alleged by former Tihar Jail Public Relations Officer Sunil Gupta. Subrata Roy may not be the only high-profile inmate to receive special privileges. Scores of businessmen and politicians who go to jail usually get special privileges.[3]

Wealthy people of his ilk variously enjoyed these perks, some with a wink from the judiciary and some from the jail administration. While I was once not allowed to receive food brought from my wife at JJ Hospital, I have enjoyed lavish feasts when I was visited by undertrial or convicted gangsters at the hospital. They had no particular ailment; at the hospital, not only their family members but their gang members too could sit the entire day and feast. While returning in the vehicle, I saw my fellow prisoner distributing ₹1,000 each to the guards and ₹2,000 to the officer. This went on everywhere.

A prominent builder from Pune, who had a well-cultivated network across all political parties in Maharashtra and had earned the moniker of 'Pune's king of good times', was arrested by the CBI in May 2022 and by the Enforcement Directorate (ED) in June 2022 in the infamous Yes Bank-Dewan Housing Finance Corporation Ltd (DHFL) loan fraud case. While in judicial custody, Avinash Bhosale was admitted to St George Hospital in October 2022, that is, less than five months after his arrest.[4] On my release, when my wife and I went to see my mother-in-law who was admitted in a VIP room in the same hospital in December 2022, Bhosale was occupying the adjacent VIP room. We saw him and his minions being served by the hospital staff at a table specially laid out on the lawns for his lunch. There were no guards in sight. After a year, when a court-directed committee of eight experts opined against the need for his continued hospitalisation, the court entertained his argument that his treating doctor's opinion be considered in the matter. Expectedly, St George Hospital gave a contrary opinion, saying that his 'psychiatric condition of increased suicidal thoughts and panic attacks' suggested continued hospitalisation.[5] The special court judge bought the latter opinion, saying that 'mere contention of the CBI for discharging the accused without suggesting any remedies in the event of his health damage likely to take place if the accused is abruptly directed to be discharged against St George's doctor's opinion would be likely to create an unusual situation'.[6] As a matter of fact, the CBI has no medical expertise to suggest a remedy; the court-directed committee of eight experts verily had already suggested one in their report saying 'his health can be monitored through visits to the hospital from jail',[7] which was just a sixteen-minute drive away. Bhosale continued to enjoy his royal stay in the VIP suite of St George Hospital, with the front lawns being specially done up for his parties, as we observed during our several visits to the adjacent VIP suit when my mother-in-law was again hospitalised. Ultimately, Bhosale was released on bail by the Bombay High Court in May 2024 in the CBI case and in August 2024 in the ED case from his VIP room in St George Hospital.

Contrast it with the struggle my co-accused and I had to wage for simple out-patient visits to outside hospitals. Contrast it with the plight of Professor Varavara Rao, one of our co-accused, who, while seriously ill was admitted in JJ Hospital and was kept in a transit ward lying unconscious on a urine-soaked bed sheet, with no attendant. When spotted in that condition by his family members, who wanted to change the bed sheet, they were rudely disallowed. And contrast it with the story of Stan Swamy, who had to die because of the delay in his hospitalisation.

The constitutional rights of equality and non-discrimination are observed more in their violation than otherwise. Nowhere does one realise that India is a plutocracy more than in the precincts of institutions that are tasked to maintain law and order.

17

Jai Bhim Syndrome

Unlike a drop of water which loses its identity when it joins the ocean, man does not lose his being in the society in which he lives. Man's life is independent. He is born not for the development of the society alone, but for the development of his self.

B.R. Ambedkar

O NE DAY, I HAD a call from the ground floor saying that someone had come to meet me downstairs.

This was common practice, even if not officially permitted. We, on the first floor, were not supposed to go downstairs. The official rule was that if we had any health issues, we were to inform the guard – who was not always present – and he would arrange for a doctor or medicines to be brought up. It was irrational, but that's how jails function.

In reality, the kamwalla boys would shout out my name whenever someone from the circles came looking for me. The visitor would use the pretext of seeing a doctor at the hospital and, in the process, meet people like me. Being lodged in the Hospital block, I was, in a way, better positioned to meet my co-accused and others than if I had been placed elsewhere.

This particular call was one of the earliest I got, when I was still new at the jail. As I descended, curiously looking for the person or persons who had summoned me, three men suddenly leaped forward, trying to touch my feet – right in front of the guard's table. I was taken aback. I managed to stop them and simply responded to their '*Jai Bhim*'.

Their leader was a tall, fair-skinned man in his early thirties, a long-time inmate, apparently involved in some gang activities. His long hair was tied in a tight bun, and he carried himself with remarkable élan. Like a typical Ambedkarite, he spoke as though we were already living in Dalit Raj. He praised me excessively for challenging the upper castes and declared that we would eventually triumph. According to him, the upper castes were scared – so much so that they had jailed an intellectual like me. I didn't know how to respond to his hyperbole, so I tried to steer the conversation towards their location and cases.

The guards seemed familiar with them and even otherwise were generally softer on gang members. The leader assured me that if I needed anything I could pass a message to him through any guard. He continued to meet me whenever he came to the hospital, always speaking with the same hubris.

One day, during one of his visits, he said he had a question for me. As is my wont, I welcomed it.

'Why do you write "Ambedkar" and not "Dr Babasaheb Ambedkar"?'

I was momentarily taken aback – not because I hadn't heard this before, but because such a canard had spread so widely that even a prisoner like him had picked it up. It was a testament to the intensity and reach of the propaganda against me by the so-called Ambedkarites, not unconnected with the police.

For a few seconds I didn't know what to say. I was sure he had never actually read any of my books. So I asked him, tactfully, where he had found me writing only 'Ambedkar' and not 'Dr Babasaheb Ambedkar'. He said honestly that he had heard people say it.

Then I explained myself. I told him that I wrote primarily in English to facilitate translation for activists in other states. Most of my work was published by reputable publishers. In any standard academic writing, great figures are introduced with their full title the first time, but later referred to by their last name for readability. For instance, Mahatma Gandhi is introduced as such initially, but then simply becomes Gandhi. Karl Marx may be mentioned for the first time but then becomes simply Marx. Likewise, I, or for that matter, all other writers, may write Babasaheb Ambedkar but thereafter it is simply Ambedkar.

This was not an act of disrespect. Many serious authors explicitly state that they will use a shorter name after the full version appears once. I too followed this norm in writing my papers, articles and books – first writing 'Dr Babasaheb Ambedkar' and then simply 'Ambedkar'. The practice is not uniquely applied to Ambedkar. Leaders across history – Gandhi, Nehru, Lenin, Marx, Mandela – are all referred to without honorifics in scholarly writing.

Fortunately, he didn't retort with something like, 'How dare you compare Babasaheb to Marx?' – though I knew that such a reaction wasn't far-fetched.

I continued. Karl Marx received his PhD in 1841, over eighty years before Babasaheb Ambedkar did. Yet, no one calls him Dr Marx. Why? Because such a prefix, rather than adding honour, actually diminishes the stature of a thinker in relation to his intellectual legacy. Marx is considered an epoch-making philosopher and a revolutionary thinker – an intellectual stature far beyond the scope of any academic degree. Degrees, after all, are routinely conferred on hundreds of thousands of people every year. Referring to him as Dr Marx risks inadvertently reducing his legacy to the level of these multitudes. The same holds true for Babasaheb Ambedkar. He stands uniquely in history as someone who not only confronted the deeply entrenched problem of caste but also dedicated his life to the emancipation of millions relegated to subhuman status. To call him Dr Ambedkar is to lower him to the mundane register of Tom, Dick and Harry. Some names signify more than credentials – they embody struggles, histories and civilisational turning points.

Fortunately, again, he did not counter me with 'Babasaheb is beyond comparison!' though that, too, seemed inevitable.

I went on. Most of India's leaders in Babasaheb's time were barristers. Back then, some used titles – like 'Barrister Jaykar' – but many did not. Gandhi, Nehru and several others were barristers, but we don't refer to them that way today. Why? Because they outgrew the title, and because the trend faded.

Even today, most PhD holders – including myself – do not prefix 'Dr' to their names. It does not diminish their stature. Honorifics like Mahatma, Babasaheb, Lokmanya are used sparingly and are avoided in serious writing. Gandhi is simply Gandhi. Tilak is simply Tilak. These additions, rather than bringing objectivity, often distort it.

I wasn't sure if he fully understood, but he let it go. Before leaving, he told me to take care of my health – I was, after all, 'valuable to the community'. I simply thanked him.

The problem is, you cannot counter these irrationalities with rational arguments. It's much like dealing with Modi bhakts today – you cannot communicate beyond telling them what they want to hear. Babasaheb Ambedkar stands apart among history's great figures for explicitly warning against bhakti. In his seminal final speech to the Constituent Assembly on 25 November 1949, he prophetically warned:

> This caution is far more necessary in the case of India than in the case of any other country. For in India, Bhakti or what may be called the path of devotion or hero-worship, plays a part in its politics unequalled in magnitude by the part it plays in the politics of any other country in the world. Bhakti in religion may be a road to the salvation of the soul. But in politics, Bhakti or hero-worship is a sure road to degradation and to eventual dictatorship.[1]

This is not the only time he spoke against this tendency among followers to become Bhakts. His speech 'Ranade, Gandhi and Jinnah', delivered in 1943 at the Gokhale Institute of Politics and Economics, Pune, is replete with such disapproval of the Bhakti and hero worship:

> [T]here is idolatory in politics. Heroes and hero-worship is a hard if unfortunate, fact in India's political life. I agree that heroworship is demoralizing for the devotee and dangerous to the country. ... For in these days, with the Press in hand, it is easy to manufacture Great Men. ... we ought to be more cautious in our worship of Great Men.

It is ironic that those who flout his advice so often flaunt themselves as devoted Ambedkarites. Expectedly, there were many Dalits in the jail, and they all seemed to know me. Some guards and officers too – some openly identified as Dalit, others didn't. *Jai Bhim, Sir* served as a kind of identity marker.

There were positive experiences, but also negative ones.

One of my early experiences involved food. One day, a kamwalla brought a bowl of special subjee for me, saying a certain guard had sent it from Bisi (the jail kitchen – why it was called that, I never got a clear explanation even from the jailers).

The prisoners in the four consecutive cells across from mine were long-term inmates with well-established connections with the jail staff. They received home-cooked food, but this privilege had been suspended during the pandemic. That didn't mean they ate regular jail food. There was always a special meal prepared for the jail staff and for prisoners who could afford hefty bribes.

Our don – a well-connected prisoner – generously paid off the jail staff and secured these extra privileges. He received special food from Bisi, which he shared with his friends in neighbouring cells.

One of them began sending a portion of this food to me. Who would refuse such a boon? But one day I asked about the source – partly out of curiosity, partly with the thought of formalising it as a replacement for the home-cooked food that my wife was struggling to get court permission for.

His response was immediate: 'Just enjoy it if something comes your way. Don't ask questions.' Then he revealed that a certain baba – a guard in Bisi – was sending the extra subjee for me. I saw it as a blessing. The special subjee made the otherwise unpalatable jail food tolerable. And so, for days, I received it regularly. Then, suddenly, it stopped. That is the nature of jail life – the only certainty is uncertainty.

The flip side of this arrangement, however, was corruption. The ingredients for these special meals were siphoned off from the regular rations meant for prisoners, which led to a sharp decline in the quality of the common food served to everyone. After stoppage of this practice, expectedly the quality of the regular meals had a noticeable improvement but soon it returned to its usual dismal state. They might have discovered another way of stealing the prisoner community's share.

Such was the rhythm of life behind bars.

My benefactor had been transferred out from Bisi and had begun working Hospital duty, introducing himself with a loud *Jai Bhim*. He was a braggart, often drunk, and claimed that even the superintendent feared him because he was an Ambedkarite with ministerial connections. There is a fine line between boasting and lying, and he constantly crossed it. His stories were always grandiose and filled with fabrications.

Once, after a month-long absence on his part, I casually asked if he had been on leave. His response was hilarious – he claimed he had travelled to Hong Kong and Germany, where his relatives hosted him and he only had to buy tickets to get there. When I asked how he had obtained a German visa, he spiralled into further lies, oblivious as to how transparent they were. This was not an isolated incident; every interaction with him involved some outlandish tale meant to enhance his stature.

Many babas in jail served as conduits for private messages from prisoners to their families – for a fee. This service, though widely known to exist, was essential, as mulaqats were infrequent, sometimes occurring only once every seven to fifteen days. The COVID-19 pandemic heightened the need for it. Unlike jails in other states where prisoners were allowed brief daily phone calls, Maharashtra's jails lacked such facilities. Some babas transmitted messages out of goodwill, but most charged for the service.

This baba initially helped me twice but later abandoned me at a crucial moment, offering weak excuses. When I mentioned this to Bhau, he revealed that the baba had stopped helping me because he expected to be paid. I told Bhau that I would have gladly paid him if he had simply asked. The next day, Bhau informed me that the baba wanted ₹20,000. That night, when he came in drunk, I confronted him. I told him that while he could have asked for money, he had instead deceived me. He now demanded ₹15,000. When I pointed out that he had only charged Bhau ₹2000, he justified it by saying that Bhau was an 'old fellow'. I was neither surprised nor outraged – just saddened by the moral degeneration of those who called themselves Ambedkarites. These men saw me not merely as a community member but as part of Ambedkar's family, yet their concern for Ambedkar was only skin-deep.

Then there was this Dalit jailer from Marathwada. Before meeting him, I had heard about him from Varavara Rao, who described him as a staunch Ambedkarite. The left liberals, in the absence of a nuanced understanding of the Dalit universe, often go by politically right thumb-rules: Ambedkarism is radicalism and Ambedkarites are potentially aligned with revolutionary ideology. Varavara Rao, knowing that he was an Ambedkarite, took him as a radical person. When my jailer – also a Dalit and a genuinely decent man – first introduced him to me, he was overly reverent, muttering praise under his breath while glancing sideways to make sure no one was listening. I felt pretty embarrassed.

Before he was assigned relieving duty as the jailer of the Hospital, he would occasionally drop by my cell during the night and check in on me. His concern felt genuine, and I naturally appreciated it. But once he took over at the Hospital, he changed. It was him I had entrusted with a letter to my wife along with letters to my daughters and notes to the lawyer and a friend – which ended up getting me into trouble and earned me a samaj patr from the superintendent. Instead of clearing or returning the letter, this so-called Ambedkarite had taken it straight to the superintendent – something no other jailer had done. I have already described the ordeal that followed in chapter 14. It exposed the back-stabbing nature of this self-proclaimed Ambedkarite jailer. I never expected special treatment from him, but just that he perform his duties impartially. His actions inconvenienced my family and created unnecessary trouble for me. Perhaps he later felt guilty, as he never met my gaze again.

I tried to understand why some Ambedkarite officers behaved this way. Generalisation is risky, but many seem deeply insecure. They go out of their way to prove their loyalty to their superiors, demonstrably toeing the official line. Their gestures of community solidarity often mask an internalised guilt held at a safe distance.

Ideologically, two major currents define Ambedkarite thought – statism and anti-communism. The first arises from the belief that Ambedkar wrote the Constitution; the state operates under this Constitution and therefore one must support the state. Any wrongdoing by the state is blamed not on its structure but on the 'Manuwadi' attitude of bureaucrats. The second stems from historical tensions between Ambedkar and the communists.

Initially, some Ambedkarite officers sympathised with me, assuming the 'Manuwadi' establishment was unfairly targeting an Ambedkar family member. However, when confronted with unfamiliar narratives, they were easily swayed by state propaganda.

I sensed this ideological bias clearly when my brother was killed in a police encounter. Four or five days later, during a night shift, this jailer came over and asked me if he was my 'real' brother. When I confirmed it, he seemed genuinely shocked. His disbelief was not because of his alleged encounter-death but because he assumed no Dalit could be a communist. To him, Dalits were only supposed to be Ambedkarites – never anything else.

There were a few honourable exceptions – individuals who did not flaunt their identity but silently helped others. There was one such officer, who right through my stay maintained cordial relations with me while still being upright when it came to his duties. There were a few more; they simply performed their duties without bias, standing upright in their principles. That is what Ambedkarites are supposed to be. Babasaheb Ambedkar expected them to safeguard the interests of those vulnerable to caste discrimination – not to practise reverse discrimination, but to uphold justice for all.

Many of them, particularly the one I admired most, as I was told, had risen from the ranks. In contrast, the officer who raised an issue over my letter was a direct recruit, and being so could be expected to possess greater confidence and knowledge. Yet, on both counts he faltered miserably. The difference between the two was striking: the former, satisfied with his own rise, sought to assist others within his capacity, embodying a spirit of camaraderie. The latter, however, was driven by ambition and prioritised the earning of approbation from his superiors by demonstrating unwavering loyalty to the establishment.

On my first birthday in prison, I received close to two hundred letters. For nearly twenty days an average of five to ten letters arrived daily, most from abroad. The jailers, who routinely read all incoming letters, were both amused and curious. They often asked me about the countries mentioned and whether I knew the senders. They had never seen anything like it. Perhaps there was a campaign outside – among students and human rights organisations – urging people worldwide to write to me. There was no definitive way to confirm this. Many of them had done the same to others among my co-accused.

Around the same time, I received two or three handwritten notes and a striking pencil drawing of Buddha from a prisoner in another circle. It was his way of sending greetings. I did not know him then, but I was impressed by his artwork and the thoughtful content of his notes. His friends had delivered them to me. Much later, I met him at the Hospital. He was young, spirited and courageous, incarcerated on murder-related charges. His struggle in prison revolved around asserting his Ambedkarite identity.

While in the Kalyan jail, he told me, he had organised the Ambedkarite prisoners and arranged for Ambedkar Jayanti celebrations – an act of defiance in a space where Hindu festivals like Ganeshotsav were openly celebrated with official permission. This led to a confrontation with the administration, which escalated into violence. The superintendent called in outside police, who brutally assaulted the Ambedkarite prisoners. As the supposed 'ringleader', he was singled out for particularly severe beatings. He was so badly injured that he had to be transferred to the Taloja jail on a stretcher and spent months recovering in his barrack.

It was a blatant caste atrocity. Yet, despite his influence – he appeared to have some clout in the community – it did not stir any reaction in Ambedkarite circles outside. This is the peculiar contradiction of Ambedkarite politics: no amount of violence against their own people seems to provoke outrage, but symbolic issues – abstract icons and identities – become immediate rallying cries.

Months later, when he finally recovered, his spirit remained unbroken. He resumed his activism, once again challenging the jail administration for discriminating against Ambedkarite prisoners and favouring Hindu prisoners. He stood out in my memory for two reasons: first, his unwavering courage, and second, his letter in which he declared his sole mission in life – to achieve *Bauddhamay Bharat* (Buddhist India), Babasaheb Ambedkar's unfulfilled dream.

I wondered how he envisioned bringing it to reality. More importantly, what would it mean? Would it create a just society for all? Would it ensure equality? Would it free Dalits from their suffering? Would it abolish oppressive systems and institutions – capitalism, police and prisons? History offered no promising answers.

Buddhist-majority countries like Myanmar, Sri Lanka and Thailand have been just as violent as any other, discriminating against non-Buddhists, much like India does against Muslims. Institutionalised religion, regardless of its tenets, functions in ways that contradict its moral philosophy. Yet, identity wields such power that it blinds people to these contradictions. It intoxicates them, leading them to sublimate their struggles into an imagined utopia, ignoring the very real injustices of the present.

He was just another innocent victim of this illusion.

18

Thou Shalt Not Speak

The hate of men will pass, and dictators die, and the power they took from the people will return to the people. And so long as men die, liberty will never perish.

Charlie Chaplin in *Great Dictator*

One evening, without warning, we were informed that we would be shifted out of the Hospital as the authorities intended to convert the entire floor into a quarantine ward. The very next day, they moved us to Anda, the high-security prison.

Most of the BK-accused were already housed there. On the positive side, I would have an independent room again, much like in the Hospital. The next morning, the jailer came and asked us to pack up once more. In jail, transfers are always instantaneous. The kamwalla boys packed my belongings within ten minutes and carried them on a trolley to the Anda.

The cell assigned to me was fortunately next to Ramesh's. Ramesh was a co-accused in the BK case. The room was better than the one I had in Hospital, but it lacked a cot and mattress, which made sleeping on the floor a challenge because of my spondylitis. When I approached the superintendent, he explained that cots couldn't be provided in Anda but allowed me to get a cotton mattress from home. Until it arrived, I had to make do with a sheet on the floor.

Apart from lacking a cot and mattress, the Anda cell was superior in many ways to my earlier cell. It was generally reserved for high-profile prisoners, such as PMLA undertrials and some bomb-blast accused. Seven of us BK-accused were housed there, although we were scattered across different quadrants and floors. Anda was better maintained, free from the red-ant menace, and served better food than Hospital or the circles. It was, in essence, a 'showpiece' area – visitors to the jail were typically brought to Anda.

The canteen system in Anda was more organised. Each inmate had a transaction book, and a computerised bill was issued every fortnight for purchases. Such transparency was absent in Hospital. There was no bill nor any account. Movement within Anda was restricted to one's quadrant, as it was to one's floor in the circles or the Hospital. After the bandi was open, you met a larger number of people in the other circles; in Anda, it was limited to your own quadrant, which had some thirteen cells. It mattered only to those who were alone in a quadrant, like Abu Jundal, an accused in the 26/11 attack on Mumbai. He was held alone in some quadrant during my times in Anda.

In the Anda barracks, life maintained a semblance of routine despite the discomfort of having to sleep without a mattress. My co-accused were more accessible, and we devised creative methods to communicate, shouting across floors or seizing brief moments during daily activities. For instance, due to my asthma, I was officially permitted to use a steam inhaler each morning and evening. On my way to the office downstairs, where the steamer was kept, I made it a point to see as many of my co-accused as possible. Later, Gautam obtained court permission for a forty-five-minute morning walk within the jail premises. Before and after the walk, he would often visit our quadrant for a brief chat, standing at the locked gate.

Evenings, after the bandi at 6 p.m., offered moments of solace amid the gloom of imprisonment. Sudhir would passionately sing, in his high pitch, Sahir Ludhianvi's fiery lyrics: *'Sar jhukane se kuch nahi hota, sar uthao to koi baat bane.'* Sagar, from the first floor, would follow with Habib Jalib's rebellious *'Aise dastoor ko, subah-e-benoor ko, mai nahi maanta.'* Occasionally, Surendra on the ground floor would join in with Kabir's *'Nadiya dubi nav me, are baap re baap,'* inspiring Ramesh to sing *'Mera rang de basanti chola.*' These impromptu performances were a feast for the soul in an otherwise bleak environment.

Our quadrant housed four prisoners: Ramesh, me, a notorious don and a nineteen-year-old named Pralay (name changed). The don, a moderately built, unassuming Kannadiga man, was a well-known figure in the world of crime. He regaled us with tales of his escapades, such as surviving police shootings in broad daylight near Dockyard Road in Mumbai city. Despite owning a better house in Bandra, he chose to reside in Dharavi, where he wielded significant influence. He claimed to have ploughed in money to build a school in his native village and helped many needy people. He proudly named all the politicians he was pally with. He often spoke of hosting rooftop parties in Anda before restrictions tightened, the increased security being attributed to a shooting incident in Taloja involving another 26/11 accused.

The don's influence extended within the prison walls. Guards treated him with deference, and he often shared his abundant canteen supplies – fruits, drinks and syrups – with us and the jail staff. While we struggled to manage our purchases within the limited monthly allowance of ₹4,500 (also supporting inmates who depended on us), the don and other affluent prisoners enjoyed unlimited supplies through a 40:60 ratio arrangement. This unofficial system allowed inmates to obtain any amount of goods from the canteen provided they paid 150 per cent of the items' value. The specifics of these transactions were unclear, but it was commonly believed that monetary exchanges occurred outside the prison in cash. It is not that such things only happened in Taloja; they happened in all jails in the country.

Consequently, we had access to an abundance of seasonal fruits from the canteen. Pralay and Ramesh would prepare them, and we would sit together to enjoy the feast. During summer, the canteen offered various drinks, ice creams and ice slabs. Thanks to the don, we had a plentiful supply of them. In the evenings, we would prepare drinks with freshly acquired ice and socialise with the babas and some of the don's friends. On Sundays and special occasions, the canteen provided special meals – mostly non-vegetarian dishes – and the don ensured ample distribution to those unable to afford them. Whenever he went outside, whether to court or the hospital, which was quite frequent, he would bring food for us. Typically, external food was prohibited at the gate, but individuals like the don faced no such restrictions.

Once he accompanied me to JJ hospital. As we boarded the police vehicle, he handed some telephone numbers to the police guard, who casually made the calls, relaying messages on his behalf. He asked if I wanted to send a message to my wife or relatives. My wife was aware of my visit and had planned to come to the hospital. He assured me that he had arranged everything for our meeting, including food and other necessities, and I should feel free to enjoy them. However, I had no such requirements. While he had little to do at the hospital, he busied himself meeting his acquaintances. After my medical check-up, Rama and I had ample time together until he was ready to leave, well past dusk. During the return journey, he discreetly handed two ₹500 notes to each of the guards and double that amount to the officer seated in front. They nonchalantly pocketed the money.

This narrative underscores the hierarchical dynamics and informal economies that exist within the prison system, where influence and resources can significantly alter one's experience behind bars.

Pralay was an intriguing figure in the barracks. Hailing from an educated middle-class family, with a father who worked as a small-time journalist, he had found himself pushed into a life of crime at an early age. He was accused of kidnapping a girl, though he claimed she was his consenting girlfriend. Remarkably, Pralay chose to argue his own case, arming himself with legal knowledge drawn from books and case laws. Despite being brainwashed by RSS ideology, like many of his kind outside, he was sharp, disciplined and meticulous. His cell was always immaculately tidy, reflecting his organised nature. While he frequently debated with Ramesh on any issue, he showed a measure of respect towards me, perhaps due to difference in our age.

The Anda barracks offered better canteen food than most other sections of the prison, a fact that initially puzzled me.

However, I eventually understood the reasoning: Anda served as a demonstration piece, a controlled environment intended to impress visitors. Any guest brought to this section of the jail would observe a more orderly and less oppressive environment, and even if they spoke to an inmate, they were unlikely to hear much negativity about the routine conditions. For example, while the prison hospital provided a mere 400 grams of chicken when one placed a one-kilo order, the canteen delivered exactly one kilo of chicken to Anda inmates. We had an extra influence of the don, which fetched us three to four kilos against a two-kilo order. As the don and Pralay were vegetarians, Ramesh and I would have plentiful chicken for lunch and dinner.

Our days passed with small yet significant amusements. Feeding sparrows with biscuit crumbs, sharing fruits and walking in the limited corridor were ways we found to occupy ourselves. Ramesh even befriended a stray cat, which he named Satta (power). Satta soon became a companion to all, lounging on chairs, leaping on to laps, or playfully interrupting reading and writing sessions.

This peace, however, seemed to offend the sadistic logic of the jail system. The new superintendent had a particular reputation for sadism; he took pleasure in inventing new ways to keep prisoners on edge and in a state of constant uncertainty. One of his first moves was to appoint a jailer to the Anda barrack who was perpetually at odds with the inmates. He tried to impose arbitrary rules, only to be met with resistance.

Pralay, in particular, had frequent tussles with the jail authorities, often armed with information he obtained through RTI applications. He had accused the jail of several irregularities and once went on a hunger strike. During the superintendent's weekly round, Pralay refused to stand up in deference, as was the norm, and defiantly bore the wrath of the accompanying officers. An ordinary prisoner would have been beaten black and blue, but the officers were restrained by Pralay's resolve. Eventually, some compromise was reached, and Pralay ended his fast. This method of satyagraha seemed to work: if you held your ground on moral principles, it tended to disarm the adversary. Or was it the fear of exposure of misdeeds the escalation entailed that pressured the authorities to retreat?

The next major disruption to our fragile peace was the sudden confiscation of all our mosquito nets. Taloja is a malaria-prone zone, and most people in the Anda barrack, as well as those kept in individual cells in the Hospital, had mosquito nets. It was out of the question for others, cramped together in overcrowded barracks. These nets were either provided by the jail authorities or permitted by the superintendent to be brought in from outside. Yet, without any warning, the superintendent abruptly ordered all mosquito nets to be seized. One evening, a battalion of jailers stormed our cells and took them away, except those that had court permission. The very fact that the court had permitted a mosquito net should have been sufficient to validate the use of mosquito nets by others. But the logic wouldn't work in jail.

The confiscation of mosquito nets was emblematic of the oppressive nature of the state apparatus, exposing prisoners to severe health risks and violating their fundamental right to life. The tragic death of Stan Swamy was a stark reminder of how such neglect could have fatal consequences. Furthermore, the decision was not only inhumane but also arbitrary. The mosquito nets in question had been previously allowed by the prison authorities, with some even supplied directly by the administration. The nets could not have been smuggled in, and their confiscation was entirely unjustifiable.

Despite significant resistance to their decision, the jail administration stood firm. Another layer of absurdity lay in the argument that mosquito nets were the personal property of prisoners. How could the authorities seize belongings that were privately owned? They claimed the nets would be 'deposited in the store' and returned upon the prisoners' release, but this was merely a hollow assurance. For example, when I later demanded my backpack, it had conveniently disappeared – a common occurrence, as such items were often pilfered by prison staff.

During the initial raid I was spared, perhaps under the assumption that I had a court order. Around the same time, a court order granting me provision of a cot arrived, and I was transferred back to the Hospital ward, where cots were provided. The earlier claim that Hospital had been vacated for quarantine purpose proved to be a subterfuge; it was never used for such a purpose. The jail administration seemed to derive a perverse satisfaction from disrupting the lives of prisoners. After a few months, they began moving people back into Hospital. When I was transferred, two jailers followed me and demanded my mosquito net. I handed it over without resistance, remarking that their actions would be challenged in court – a statement we all knew carried little weight.

Frustrated by this high-handedness, I filed a petition in court against the superintendent's actions. My co-accused, Gautam Navlakha, along with a few others, also submitted similar petitions. However, the court exhibited no urgency or seriousness in addressing the health risks posed by the prison administration's unreasonable decision. Instead, it extended the timeline for the authorities to submit their response, allowing the matter to languish.

During the controversy, an undertrial prisoner dramatically brought a plastic bottle filled with dead mosquitoes to the sessions court to emphasise the severity of the mosquito menace. The jail authorities were embarrassed but more concerned about how the bottle had bypassed security checks than about the actual issue. The court, unfortunately, did not press the matter further.

The prison officials presented a litany of unconvincing arguments. They claimed that mosquito nets hindered their ability to monitor inmates at night and that the ropes and nails used to hang the nets could be weaponised. This 'security threat' argument, a sacrosanct excuse state institutions used, went unchallenged by the court. The officials failed to provide any historical data to support their claims; neither did the court demand clarity on whether specific rules prohibited the use of mosquito nets. Ironically, all known suicides in the jail had been committed using bed sheets provided by the prison. By the same logic, would the authorities ban bed sheets next? If a prisoner were determined to end his life, he could resort to countless other methods, including smashing his head against the steel bars. Should the entire cobweb of steel in the jail be removed too?

The claim that mosquito nets obstructed visibility inside the barracks was equally ridiculous. The ropes and nails posed no credible threat. Rationally, the pressing question remained: Who would be held accountable if a prisoner contracted malaria and died? This was particularly pertinent given the well-documented risks of the prison's malaria-prone location.

Predictably, the court refrained from asking inconvenient questions of the state functionary. It ignored the immediate threat to prisoners' lives and, when it finally delivered a decision, it was to dismiss our petition, thereby validating the superintendent's ego-driven and sadistic actions. The court concluded that prisoners could use mosquito repellent creams available in the jail canteen – an impractical and dismissive solution to a serious issue. Mosquito repellent creams have clear limitations in terms of duration of protection, coverage and effectiveness. They can also cause skin irritation or other health issues with regular use, and their recurring cost makes them less accessible. They simply cannot substitute the mosquito net, which provides a physical barrier against mosquitoes – especially crucial in high-risk, vector-borne disease environments. From both public health and human rights perspectives, mosquito nets are not just practical but essential wherever their use is feasible. But none of this mattered to the court. This episode was yet another reminder of the systemic apathy towards the rights and dignity of the incarcerated.

In response to the confiscation of mosquito nets, one of our co-accused, Sagar Gorkhe, went on an indefinite hunger strike in the Anda cell. He expanded his protest to include other long-pending grievances with the jail administration. His demands included:

1 Urgent provision of mosquito nets and medical treatment for all the Elgar Parishad case accused, along with action against jail officials for their negligence.
2 An immediate halt to the illegal scanning of letters sent to and from prisoners, especially those accused in the Elgar Parishad

case, and the cessation of violations of prisoners' right to privacy.
3. An end to the artificial shortage of water in the prison and the inhumane practice of selling water to prisoners through the canteen. The administration should provide the mandated 135 litres of water per person per day instead of just one bucket (15 litres), and action should be taken against those responsible for the shortage.
4. Construction of permanent sheds for visitors with adequate seating, drinking water, fans, toilets, and a token system for them.
5. Implementation of phone facilities for prisoners, similar to systems in Gujarat, Telangana, Delhi and other states.

In a bold move, Sagar also lodged a police complaint at the Kharghar police station, accusing jail officials of theft for forcibly confiscating his mosquito net, which had cost him ₹620. He also addressed a letter to Maharashtra's home minister, Dilip Walse Patil, comparing the conditions in Taloja jail to a torture camp.

In solidarity with Sagar's hunger strike, all of us, the Bhima-Koregaon accused, observed a fast on 21 May 2022.

During this period, the jail superintendent publicly cited a circular issued by the prison department prohibiting phone calls for prisoners charged with terrorism or Maoist links, claiming he was simply adhering to its directives. This resolution, dated 25 March 2021, was presented by the government in the Bombay High Court during a hearing concerning Gautam Navlakha. The resolution outlines that inmates booked under special acts like the UAPA are prohibited from accessing telephonic communication facilities, such as coin box phones, in prisons, including Taloja. The rationale provided is that these restrictions apply to undertrials facing charges of terrorism or conspiring against the nation, state and government.[1] It just showed the degree of impunity that such utterly unlawful, irrational and inhuman decisions could be taken by the state, and worse, could be placed before the constitutional court.

On the fifth day of Sagar's hunger strike, Kapil Patil, a noted social worker and member of the Legislative Council from the Lok Bharati party, visited Taloja jail and mediated between the superintendent and Sagar. The superintendent, U.T. Pawar, explained to Patil that the removal of mosquito nets was a preventive action taken after a suicide attempt by a prisoner. He alleged that the ropes and nails required for mosquito nets could be used by prisoners to harm themselves or others. Pawar assured Patil that mosquito repellents would be provided free of cost to all prisoners. The superintendent assured resolution of Sagar's other demands. On this assurance – and Patil's promise to follow up with the home minister and raise the matter in the assembly – Sagar ended his hunger strike.[2]

However, none of his demands were actually fulfilled.

The mosquito net issue eventually reached the court, where the jail administration defended its decision and secured a favourable order legitimising the prohibition of mosquito nets. Despite the superintendent's promise, mosquito repellent cream continued to be sold in the canteen, making it accessible only to prisoners who could afford it, leaving others to fend for themselves. There was no concrete commitment or proof that the illegal scanning of letters and their transmission to NIA/ATS had ceased.

While the water supply temporarily improved, it soon reverted to the previous inadequate provision of a couple of buckets per prisoner, far short of the 135 litres per person per day mandated by the jail manual. The construction of a shed for visitors, which was likely budgeted for and already in progress, was completed. However, it lacked many of the requested facilities, such as proper seating, drinking water and fans. As for the phone facility, no immediate change occurred. It seems the decision to implement phone access for all prisoners in Maharashtra was taken at the apex level, independent of our protests, and it remains an unfulfilled promise at Taloja jail.

19

POCSO's Dalit Victims

You can't blame gravity for falling in love.
Albert Einstein

I WAS STUNNED TO find that most of the undertrials under the POCSO Act, 2012 belonged to the poor strata of low castes, Muslims and other such minority communities. They were tacitly loathed and looked down upon in jail and were usually only whispered about.

Yes, there exists a kind of hierarchy of crimes and, consequently, a corresponding hierarchy of accused individuals, who are accorded varying levels of respect or contempt in prison. At the top of this hierarchy are the gangsters, who command the highest respect among inmates. This is often because they provide direct assistance to many prisoners, offering them what they cannot otherwise afford, and exert influence over the prison administration to secure favours. Even their associates or minions take pride in their connection to them, especially if the person is a notable don, much the way individuals outside prison take pride in their association with politicians.

Next in the hierarchy are those accused of murder, who often flaunt their 'accomplishments' as markers of their potential to rise within the criminal world, possibly even to become a don. Following them are those accused of crimes like robbery and attempted murder, who occupy the middle tier in this informal social structure. At the bottom are those involved in petty offences such as theft, who are generally viewed with disdain.

The accused in sexual crimes, including those under the POCSO Act, face particular contempt. This idea comes from conservative belief systems that see women as inherently weak, passive and in need of male protection. In such frameworks, a woman is not viewed as an autonomous individual but as someone whose honour is tied to the men in her family – father, brother, husband. So when a crime like sexual violence occurs, it is not treated primarily as a violation of the woman's rights or dignity but as a blow to the family's or community's honour. This shifts the focus from justice for the woman to restoring patriarchal pride. This stigma often isolates these accused individuals, leaving them vulnerable to severe alienation and psychiatric disorders.

Another emerging category is that of corporate criminals and politicians accused under the PMLA. These individuals inspire a mix of awe and resentment for their wealth, power and social status, which often set them apart from the ordinary inmates.

Yet another distinct group includes those accused of terrorism or linked with organisations like the CPI (Maoist), frequently charged under the UAPA. These individuals, often labelled 'anti-nationals', could more appropriately be termed 'political prisoners', as was the practice during colonial times. Despite the state's branding of them as anti-nationals, they tend to be respected as 'good' or principled people by common prisoners, much the way political prisoners were viewed with admiration during British rule.

The phenomenon of a disproportionately high incidence of POCSO-accused individuals among Dalit and Muslim prisoners was clearly observable, but lacked supporting data. Mahesh Raut, one of our co-accused, took up this critical task. Mahesh, the youngest among us (the BK-16), was just thirty-one when he was arrested in the first batch. Hailing from Gadchiroli, a backward district in Maharashtra, Mahesh had completed his post-graduation from the Tata Institute of Social Sciences, Mumbai, and was a recipient of the prestigious Prime Minister's Rural Development (PMRD) fellowship. Exceptionally sociable and brimming with energy, Mahesh was well regarded in jail by both inmates and staff. His creativity was evident in his meticulously crafted drawings and greeting cards, but his idea to conduct a survey in jail was particularly innovative. He saw the potential for this survey to address the 'POCSO puzzle', which had remained elusive. Recognising its significance, I encouraged him to carry it forward, envisioning its potential for an academic paper. Mahesh carefully designed the survey methodology, keeping in mind the constraints the jail imposed. His approach included one-on-one interviews to gather structured and unstructured data, group discussions and data from charge sheets. For intensive interviews, he focused on a sample of eighty-eight prisoners aged eighteen to twenty-five, selected randomly.

The survey uncovered valuable insights into the inmates' socio-economic backgrounds, the charges against them, their access to legal aid and the status of their trials. It also provided a series of compelling case studies, one of which Mahesh shared with me.

Sagar, a twenty-one-year-old Dalit youth, was arrested and charged under the POCSO Act for kidnapping and sexual assault. Before his arrest, Sagar lived with his mother and two younger brothers. His father, a contractual municipal sweeper, had been rendered jobless after an accident, and another mishap years later claimed his life. To support the family, Sagar's mother took up manual sweeping work while Sagar worked odd jobs, most recently at a car wash. During this period, Sagar fell in love with Poorva, a seventeen-year-old girl from a higher caste and better-off family. When Poorva's family discovered their relationship, they verbally and physically abused her. One evening, Poorva fled to Sagar's home. Upon returning from work, Sagar and his mother found her waiting. Aware of the legal implications of their ages, Sagar's mother advised Poorva to return home the next morning, accompanied by Sagar. However, they were met with hostility. Poorva's family assaulted Sagar, confined him and called the police. Sagar was arrested. His family was devastated. Sagar's mother sold the household items and a mobile phone to hire a lawyer for his bail. Overwhelmed by guilt and the burden placed on his family, Sagar confided in a fellow prisoner. Tragically, he took his own life that night.

Mahesh's survey revealed several striking patterns. A staggering 94 per cent of prisoners in the Taloja jail were undertrials, much higher than the national average of 77.1 per cent, as per the National Criminal Records Bureau (NCRB) 2021 report. Among them, over 80 per cent had not yet faced trial, with many languishing in jail for years. On average, prisoners had been incarcerated for 21.68 months, with more than half having spent over a year in jail. In terms of charges, prisoners in the age group of eighteen to twenty-five saw POCSO cases constituting 20 per cent, on a par with theft-related cases and higher than robbery cases. The prison population was largely composed of marginalised communities, with 43 per cent being OBC, 29.3 per cent Muslim and other minorities, 13.6 per cent Scheduled Castes, and 5.8 per cent Scheduled Tribes. Socio-economic data revealed that a majority of the inmates came from disadvantaged backgrounds, with 77 per cent starting work before turning eighteen and 78 per cent not having passed class ten. The harsh realities of their lives were further underscored by the fact that 36 per cent had lost one parent, 15 per cent had lost both, and more than half came from families earning less than ₹20,000 per month.

Among the POCSO cases in the eighteen to twenty-five age group, Mahesh's findings highlighted that over half involved consensual relationships. Around 70 per cent of these relationships were either inter-caste or inter-religious, with the young men often from the lower castes or minority communities and the young women or girls from the higher castes or the Hindu majority. Family opposition to these relationships, often accompanied by violence, frequently led to FIRs and incarceration. The relationship between Sagar and Poorva was consensual, but it was criminalised solely because of their socio-economic backgrounds. Romantic relationships are a natural part of adolescent development, shaping self-esteem, independence and ideas of love. However, in India, such relationships are often stigmatised, particularly when they cross the boundaries of caste, religion or socio-economic status. The POCSO Act, though intended to protect children from abuse, has unintentionally criminalised consensual teenage relationships and disproportionately impacted the marginalised communities.

Historically, the age of consent in India has been inconsistent, varying across periods and jurisdictions. Before the POCSO Act, the Indian Penal Code (IPC) set the legal age of consent for girls at sixteen years. It was raised to eighteen after the Criminal Law (Amendment) Act, 2013, which followed the Nirbhaya gang-rape case. While the POCSO Act is gender-neutral in its framework, its implementation often disregards this neutrality, with young men or boys being disproportionately prosecuted. This survey and its findings underscore the urgent need to reform the POCSO Act. Laws designed to protect children should not inadvertently criminalise young people's consensual relationships, especially those involving people from marginalised backgrounds. A more nuanced understanding of adolescent relationships is necessary to ensure justice and prevent tragedies like Sagar's.

The high incidence of POCSO cases among men belonging to marginalised communities such as Dalits and Muslims underscores the intersection of caste, class and gender biases in the implementation of laws in India. Here are the chief reasons for the pattern that one sees in POCSO cases:

- **Caste and power dynamics:** The entrenched social hierarchies in India often dictate that lower-caste men, particularly Dalits, are criminalised for relationships with upper-caste women or girls. These cases are less about the legal violation in question and more about the preservation of caste honour and power structures. Inter-caste or inter-community relationships, even when consensual, are seen as transgressions by upper-caste families, leading to the misuse of legal provisions to penalise marginalised groups.
- **Economic and social vulnerability:** Dalits and Muslims, being economically and socially disadvantaged, are more vulnerable to being framed in such cases. They lack the resources and social capital to defend themselves, unlike their upper-caste counterparts, who often escape scrutiny or legal repercussions.

- **Low number of upper-caste accused:** Upper-caste individuals accused under the POCSO Act are a rarity. This is not because such individuals do not engage in similar behaviour but due to the privileges of caste and class that they have. Upper-caste families often have the means to suppress accusations or to manipulate legal proceedings to protect their interests.

The misuse of the POCSO Act to uphold caste hierarchies and patriarchal norms highlights the urgent need for systemic reforms. While the Act is crucial for protecting children from abuse, its enforcement must be sensitive to the sociocultural context and free from biases that disproportionately criminalise the marginalised. A more nuanced approach, backed by research and caste-disaggregated data, is essential to ensure justice and fairness in its application.

Sexual behaviour, like any human behaviour, is influenced by both individual traits and external circumstances. While innate sexual tendencies are neurologically ingrained, environmental factors significantly amplify or suppress these tendencies. The lack of formal sex education for children and the unrestricted availability of pornographic material on the Internet fuel their fantasies, often leading them to explore sexuality on their own terms. While it is desirable to introduce proper sex education and curb the illegal distribution of explicit sexual content with the help of experts, it is evident that both goals are far from being adequately addressed. This raises an essential question: Why should the sexual behaviour of children, particularly consensual acts among adolescents, be criminalised?

The POCSO Act, which is increasingly used to target boys and young men, has three detrimental consequences for society. First, it reinforces outdated societal values that valorise parental control over children, stigmatises premarital sex and often seeks to mask it under the guise of early marriage, especially in cases of adolescent pregnancies. This legal and cultural conflation of sex and marriage perpetuates regressive norms. Second, it denies adolescents their basic right to shape their own lives, curbing their initiative and creativity while forcing their conformity to oppressive customs and traditions. This contributes to a growing pool of reactionaries, with only a few exceptions rebelling against such restrictions. Third, and most alarmingly, it exacerbates systemic biases by disproportionately criminalising youths from marginalised communities, such as Dalits and Muslims.

Why do boys and young men from these disadvantaged groups dominate POCSO cases, despite the law being gender-neutral? Sexual exploration is arguably more prevalent among the affluent and upper-caste sections of society because of their greater exposure to modern values, access to private spaces, and access to resources to navigate the consequences of sexual activity. Yet individuals from these groups are rarely implicated under the Act. Instead, the accused often belong to lower castes or minority communities, while the complainant tends to be from upper-caste or majority communities. The reverse scenario is almost unheard of. This disparity stems from deeply entrenched caste hierarchies, patriarchal norms and power dynamics that treat girls as bearers of family honour – a concept that tolerates upward mobility through marriage but fiercely resists downward alliances, especially with people from lower castes or minorities.

The societal acceptance of girls marrying into higher castes contrasts with the vehement rejection of their marrying into lower castes, and reflects the persistence of caste-based discrimination. Such practices aim to preserve social status and caste purity, reinforcing family honour, lineage and tradition. Higher-caste families see inter-caste marriages as a threat to their cultural hegemony, while marriages into higher castes are often celebrated as a means to enhance their social prestige. This power dynamic perpetuates inequality, with upper castes maintaining their dominance over the social, economic and political landscape.

By criminalising inter-caste and inter-community relationships among adolescents, the POCSO Act inadvertently reinforces the caste system. Reformers advocating the annihilation of caste have long championed inter-caste marriages as a potent means to dissolve caste consciousness. Romantic relationships formed during adolescence, if allowed to flourish naturally, can challenge these divisive boundaries. Instead, the POCSO Act has been weaponised to terrorise young people into confining their relationships within caste lines, thereby upholding the very social hierarchies it should challenge.

This brings us to a troubling observation: despite enactment of the POCSO Act, cases of child sexual abuse (CSA) continue to rise nationwide. A significant contributing factor is the inclusion of consensual sexual activity among adolescents under the Act's ambit. Teenagers exploring their sexuality in their late adolescence often fall under the purview of juvenile justice, as the law does not recognise their capacity to give consent. The rigid age restrictions fail to capture the nuanced reality of adolescent romantic relationships. In cases involving same-sex couples, especially in conservative societies, the idea of mutual consent is often ignored or invalidated altogether. Instead of recognising the relationship as legitimate, authorities – police, families or even courts – tend to view it as immoral, unnatural or criminal. As a result, even if both individuals are consenting adults, their relationship may be treated as coercive or abusive or as evidence of mental illness or 'influence'. This denial of consent stems from deep-rooted homophobia and a refusal to acknowledge LGBTQ+ relationships as valid or equal. Despite the Supreme Court's 2018 decision in *Navtej Singh Johar v. Union of India*, which decriminalised consensual same-sex relations, societal and institutional resistance persists.[1] It is also crucial to acknowledge the possibility of coercion or manipulation, especially of younger teens or children by older adolescents engaging in 'grooming' tactics to obtain consent. Therefore, any consideration of close-in-age exemptions must carefully examine the dynamics of consent and the potential for exploitation.

While the POCSO Act is undeniably a landmark legislation in protecting children from sexual exploitation, it requires significant contextual adaptation to align with the sociocultural realities of the current times and safeguard adolescents' sexual rights. Punitive measures against adolescents involved in consensual sexual activity are counterproductive, as they criminalise normal developmental processes. In cases of romantic relationships, investigations must be gender-neutral and avoid the presumption that girls are always victims. The principles of restorative justice outlined in the Juvenile Justice (Care and Protection of Children) Act, 2015 should be prioritised in such cases.

Comprehensive research is urgently needed to address these gaps and inform more effective policy decisions. The goal should be to protect children from genuine harm without undermining their rights, agency and capacity for personal growth.

20

Abolish Prisons?

> Mass incarceration is not a solution to unemployment, nor is it a solution to the vast array of social problems that are hidden away in a rapidly growing network of prisons and jails. However, the great majority of people have been tricked into believing in the efficacy of imprisonment, even though the historical record clearly demonstrates that prisons do not work.
>
> Angela Davis

ANGELA DAVIS'S WORDS QUOTED above resonate deeply with my experiences in prison, where I had the opportunity to interact with a diverse cross-section of people. These encounters, coupled with my observations of the prison system, have convinced me that incarceration is an ineffective solution to crime in society. When analysed through the lens of cost-benefit, prisons falter significantly, leading to the conclusion that society may benefit from abolishing or significantly minimizing them. Yet, the government seems to believe otherwise. For instance, the Maharashtra government recently announced the construction of fourteen additional jails to house 15,000 inmates. Similar trends can be observed across other states.

A majority of the inmates I interacted with seemed trapped in a cycle of crime and incarceration, largely due to the lack of viable alternatives for them outside. Many referred to prison as their 'second home'. I recall a young man who, during a hospital visit, promised me he would never return to jail. Others around us laughed, predicting his return within three months – a prophecy that sadly came true. I saw him again at the prison gate a few months later, laughing at the inevitability of his situation.

At the extreme end of this spectrum were the gangsters and seasoned criminals who treated prison as a temporary interruption in their 'business' operations. These individuals often wielded significant power and used their wealth to secure luxuries while behind bars. One such prisoner lamented not the imprisonment itself but the financial losses incurred from interrupted extortion schemes. Political prisoners and offenders under the PMLA exhibited little fear of incarceration. For the first, prison was a badge of ideological commitment, and for the second a minor inconvenience compared to their amassed wealth, which often allowed them to navigate the system with ease.

Even among inmates convicted of heinous crimes like murder, most justified their actions and expressed regret only over being caught. Genuine remorse was a rarity among rapists, dacoits and thieves. This spectrum of attitudes among prisoners underscores the ineffectiveness of the prison system in achieving its stated objectives.

The modern prison system, though relatively recent, traces its roots to ancient practices. While detention centres existed as early as 1000 BCE, the concept of prisons as statutes focused on rehabilitation and incarceration emerged only a few centuries ago. Contemporary prison philosophy encompasses objectives like retribution, deterrence, incapacitation and rehabilitation, all aimed at maintaining societal order. However, the effectiveness of these goals remains debatable.

Retribution – the idea of justice as vengeance – focuses on punishment rather than addressing the root causes of crime. Similarly, deterrence aims to prevent crime through fear of punishment. However, several studies – Loughran et al.[1], Nagin et al.[2], Bales and Piquero[3], Villettaz et al.[4], Drago[5] and several reports from criminal justice organisations such as National Institute of Justice (NIJ)[6] and the Pew Charitable Trusts[7] – reveal that incarceration has little impact on recidivism. Research consistently shows that the certainty of being caught, rather than the severity of punishment, is more effective in preventing crime.

Incapacitation, which removes offenders from society, offers only a temporary solution, as it fails to address the conditions that lead to criminal behaviour. Upon release, many criminals return to the same environments and circumstances, perpetuating cycles of crime.

Rehabilitation, the most progressive goal, emphasises preparation of offenders for reintegration into society through education and skill-building. Yet, rehabilitation programmes are often underfunded and undervalued. Norway's nature-integrated rehabilitation model[8] offers a promising alternative, as do initiatives like the Menendez brothers' beautification project in a California prison.[9]

Despite the philosophical underpinnings of the prison system, its practical outcomes are far from satisfactory. India, for instance, houses over 5.5 lakh prisoners in its 1,400 jails, with nearly 80 per cent awaiting trial for more than three years.[10] These individuals, many of whom could contribute productively to society, are instead kept in jail at a significant cost to the exchequer. Their families suffer economically and emotionally, while an entire ecosystem of police, courts and lawyers thrives on this parasitic system. Whose interests does this system truly serve? The answer is clear: the entrenched classes who rely on it to safeguard their privileges and maintain the status quo.

From a human rights perspective, prisons appear as instruments of external control designed to regulate behaviour in a society that fails to provide the basic necessities of life – healthcare, education and livelihood security. If these fundamental needs were met, much of the space for crime would disappear, reducing the need for prisons. Instead, our systems, poorly designed and rooted in retribution, perpetuate cycles of alienation and violence.

Despite being rebranded as 'reformation centres' since the Universal Declaration of Human Rights (UDHR) in 1948, prisons across the world continue to function as punitive institutions. They forcibly isolate individuals, strip them of their liberty and subject them to undesirable conditions. This alienates the innocent among the inmates while hardening the criminals among them. The ethic of retribution embedded in imprisonment allows the state to morally justify its violence while erasing the humanity of prisoners.

The societal acceptance of prisons stems from the belief that they ensure safety and deter crime. Yet, evidence suggests the opposite. Harsh penalties often fail to reform individuals, instead reinforcing cycles of crime and alienation. The historical evolution of prisons, from those of ancient Egypt to modern-day systems, reflects changing philosophies but also exposes enduring flaws. Institutions like the Indian Penal Code (1860) and subsequent reforms have failed to address these systemic issues effectively.

The criminogenic nature of capitalism further compounds the problem. By fostering inequality, exploitation and poverty, capitalism creates the conditions for crime, while the state's law-and-order apparatus protects the interests of the ruling class. The case of Abdul, a poor Muslim youth driven to desperation, highlights the systemic injustices that criminalise the marginalised while perpetuating structural inequalities.

It is imperative to rethink their role and prioritise approaches that address the root causes of crime, such as inequality and lack of opportunity. By fostering self-regulating systems that nurture societal balance, we can move closer to a justice system that not only punishes but transforms offenders into constructive members of the society.

The call for alternatives to prisons is gaining momentum. The most radical proposition, championed by international civil society groups and activists, is the abolition of prisons altogether. The movement for abolition of prisons advocates for the dismantling of the prison-industrial complex and the replacement of punitive systems with transformative justice models. Rooted in critiques of systemic racism, economic inequality and the ineffectiveness of incarceration in reducing crime, the movement calls for addressing the root causes of criminal behaviour, such as poverty, lack of education and social inequities.

The movement has influenced criminal justice policies in several countries.

Despite its growing influence, the abolitionist movement faces significant challenges, including public perceptions of safety, entrenched political interests and the economic dependence of some communities on prisons.[11] While wholesale abolition of the prison system may seem impractical for some time, the slogan inspires us to explore non-carceral solutions to the current hellish conditions of incarceration. It advocates for reducing or eliminating the prison system and replacing it with frameworks of rehabilitation and education that do not centre on punishment or institutionalisation. Technology can play a pivotal role in developing such alternatives. There have been several examples of such reforms.

One inspiring example is Finland's successful experiment with 'open prisons'.[12] Finland, once known for its high incarceration rate, realised that imprisonment was not the solution to social problems. Guided by research and free from political interference, Finnish civil servants re-examined the criminal justice system and drafted progressive policies. This reform, part of broader penal changes initiated in the 1930s, sought to humanise the justice system. Open prisons emerged as an offshoot of these reforms, focusing on reducing recidivism through humane treatment and support for inmates.

Open prisons differ significantly from traditional high-security facilities. With minimal security measures – no walls, no fences – they resemble a small high school campus. Inmates live in dormitory-style accommodations, can work or study during the day, and are often allowed to leave the premises for employment, education or family visits. They cook their own meals, manage their laundry, have cell phones and bank accounts, and even order takeout. This system mirrors life outside prison as closely as possible, preparing inmates for reintegration into society. Today, Finland operates several such facilities, and their success is evident in the country's low incarceration and recidivism rates, among the lowest in the world. Research indicates that the sense of normality and responsibility in open prisons significantly aids inmates' reintegration into society.

Other countries have also implemented radical prison reforms with notable success. The Netherlands has successfully implemented radical prison reforms, such as electronic monitoring, community service and rehabilitation programmes to reduce the number of people in prison. As a result of these reforms, the prison population has been steadily declining in the Netherlands since 2006, leading to the closure of many prisons.[13] The Netherlands experienced an extended period of decarceration from 1947 to 1974. Their prisons have so much extra room that they take in prisoners from other countries. In fact, 19.1 per cent of their prisoners are foreigners.[14] Not only can prisons in the Netherlands house all of their prisoners comfortably, but they can also help out with overcrowding in other countries.[15]

Norway's prison system, known for its humane and rehabilitative approach, prioritises education, vocational training and personal development opportunities in prisons like Halden and Bastøy, aiming to reduce recidivism and facilitate successful reintegration of their inmates into society.[16] In the 1990s, Norway faced a recidivism crisis, with 70 per cent of released prisoners reoffending within two years – a rate similar to that of the US today. At the time, Norway's punitive prison system, modelled on deterrence through harsh sentences, was ineffective, leading to high crime rates, prison violence and escapes. Recognising the system's failure, Norway implemented bold reforms, transforming its prisons into a global model. These changes drastically reduced recidivism and improved prison safety and peace, inspiring some US states to adopt similar approaches.[17] Before Norway's prison reforms in the 1990s, the country's recidivism rate was in the range of 60–70 per cent. Today, Norway's recidivism rate based on re-conviction within two years is 20 per cent, the lowest in the world.[18]

Sweden has implemented several alternatives to incarceration to reduce reliance on prisons, including probation, community service and electronic monitoring (EM). Probation allows offenders to serve conditional custodial sentences under supervision within the community, while community service provides a constructive way to serve penalties. Sweden's 'Intensive Supervision with EM' uses ankle bracelets with GPS/RF tracking to enforce home detention for select offenders, supervised by probation officers. It's a cost-effective alternative to prison, allowing work/rehab while ensuring compliance via real-time alerts. Studies show it reduces recidivism compared to short jail terms.[19] These measures aim to address public concerns about safety and fairness while avoiding the counterproductive effects of imprisonment on resocialisation and reoffending.[20]

The results of these initiatives have been significant. Sweden has maintained a low incarceration rate, and these alternatives have contributed to a steady reduction in the prison population. This, in turn, has led to the closure of several prisons. By emphasising rehabilitation over punitive measures, Sweden has achieved a balanced approach to justice while reducing recidivism rates.[21]

Denmark operates open prisons similar to Finland's. Denmark operates a unique system of open prisons, which prioritise rehabilitation and reintegration of prisoners into society. Open prisons are less restrictive, allowing inmates to engage in work, education and family visits while serving their sentences. The approach focuses on treating inmates with dignity and providing them opportunities to address the root causes of their criminal behaviour, such as unemployment, lack of education or substance abuse.[22]

This rehabilitative approach has led to a significant reduction in recidivism rates, as inmates are better prepared to reintegrate into society upon their release. Moreover, the emphasis on non-custodial alternatives and the reduced reliance on long-term incarceration have contributed to a decline in Denmark's prison population, allowing the country to close or repurpose several prison facilities over time.[23]

Denmark's penal system demonstrates that a humane and reintegrative approach can improve public safety and reduce the societal costs of imprisonment by focusing on rehabilitation, education, and community support for released individuals.[24]

Germany integrates therapeutic approaches into its prisons, focusing on psychological counselling, addiction treatment and skill development programmes aimed at rehabilitating inmates.[25] Again, these measures prioritise addressing the root causes of criminal behaviour, such as mental health issues, substance abuse and lack of employable skills. Prisons in Germany emphasise resocialisation, where inmates are prepared for reintegration into society through vocational training and education programmes. Studies suggest that this approach has contributed to lower recidivism rates compared to more punitive systems. Additionally, the focus on rehabilitation over punishment has allowed Germany to maintain a stable prison population and improve post-release outcomes for offenders.[26]

Portugal's prison system has undergone a remarkable transformation since the country decriminalised the possession and use of drugs in 2001. Under this approach, drug use is treated as a public health issue rather than as a criminal offence. Individuals found in possession of small quantities of drugs are referred to health and social services rather than prosecuted. This shift has drastically reduced drug-related crime, addiction rates and the prison population.[27]

The results have been profound: Portugal has one of the lowest rates of drug-related deaths in Europe and significantly reduced HIV infection rates among drug users. Furthermore, the decriminalisation policy has lightened the burden on the prison system by reducing the incarceration of non-violent drug offenders, contributing to a decline in the overall prison population. This policy is often cited as a global model for balancing public health and criminal justice priorities.[28]

Switzerland's prison system places significant emphasis on restorative justice and community-based sentences. This approach focuses on repairing the harm caused by crime rather than solely punishing offenders. Offenders are encouraged to actively participate in the justice process, including making amends to their victims and contributing positively to the community. Community-based sentences, such as probation and supervised work programmes, are used extensively to avoid incarceration when possible.[29]

The results of this approach have been noteworthy. Switzerland has achieved a relatively low recidivism rate compared to other countries and has reduced the need for expanding its prison system. By integrating offenders back into society and addressing the root causes of criminal behaviour, Switzerland has been able to focus resources on rehabilitation and social reintegration, further decreasing long-term reliance on incarceration.[30]

New Zealand's prison system has taken steps to incorporate Māori cultural practices into the rehabilitation programme for offenders, recognising the over-representation of Māori people in the prison population. Initiatives such as *Te Whare Tirohanga Māori* (Māori focus units) and *Whānau Ora* (family-based approaches) aim to address the root causes of crime by reconnecting Māori prisoners with their cultural heritage, values and traditions. These programmes emphasise *whanaungatanga* (kinship), *tikanga Māori* (customs), and the involvement of *whānau* (family) in the rehabilitation process.[31]

The results of these initiatives have shown promise. Participants in Māori-focused programmes often report improved self-esteem, stronger connections to their cultural identity and better reintegration outcomes upon release. While challenges remain in addressing systemic inequities, these culturally aligned approaches have contributed to reducing recidivism among Māori offenders and fostering a more inclusive justice system.[32]

These examples illustrate that radical prison reforms emphasising rehabilitation, humane treatment and alternatives to incarceration can yield remarkable outcomes: lower recidivism rates, reduced prison populations, and improved public safety.

Several countries are moving towards abolition of imprisonment or minimal incarceration. For instance, Costa Rica has adopted restorative justice principles, focusing on reconciliation between offenders and victims. In El Salvador, activists and policymakers are advocating for the abolition of overcrowded and inhumane prison systems, though implementation remains a challenge. Aboriginal Justice Initiatives in Canada and Australia prioritise indigenous-led systems, such as healing circles, to replace incarceration with community-based reconciliation. Meanwhile, Scotland has introduced measures to reduce incarceration for minor offences by focusing on community sentencing in which minor offenders have to complete community works without payment instead of jail time. It is operated as Community Payback Orders (CPOs), introduced in 2011 along with EM.

These approaches reflect a growing global shift towards restorative justice, rehabilitation and non-custodial alternatives. This trend is often motivated by concerns about overcrowding, costs, human rights, and the ineffectiveness of punitive systems in reducing recidivism. However, the success of such radical models largely depends on societal values, political will and the broader context of criminal justice reform.

Will India, gripped by power-hungry politicians who have weaponised the prison system to suppress dissent and sequester opponents, ever consider such reforms? Of prison reforms, Howard Zinn has said: 'Prisons cannot be reformed, any more than slavery can be reformed. They have to be abolished. And yet, they will not be abolished until society is changed, until people *think* differently about punishment, about law, about crime, about violence, about property, about human beings.'

The task appears to be formidable!

21

A Nation of Anti-Nationals

> I look upon myself as a person. Nationalism is an infantile disease. It is the measles of mankind.
>
> Albert Einstein

IT WAS THE MORNING of 13 September 2020, a morning as colourless as ever, when I woke up with a thudding sound of guards' truncheons. I walked up to the TV unconsciously to get another dose of horror. The saga of the Delhi riots that took place in February 2020 was unfolding. Fifty-three people had been killed, two-thirds of them Muslim.[1] Following the riots, thousands were arrested. But most were released by the courts, which criticised the police for a lopsided investigation.[2]

It was widely known that BJP leaders had incited the violence.[3] A report titled 'Manufacturing Evidence: How the Police Is Framing and Arresting Constitutional Rights Defenders in India', published by the Polis Project, claimed to have evidence of Delhi cops 'leading, participating and encouraging targeted violence against Muslim residents of the region during the violence'; there were 'open threats on the lives of anti-Citizenship Amendment Act (CAA) protestors, including on Muslim women, physical attacks and assault by the police, seen openly with armed perpetrators'.[4] Multiple complaints were filed against Kapil Mishra and other BJP leaders for their incendiary speeches that had incited the violence, but no FIR was registered. When Justice Dr S. Muralidhar had questioned the Delhi police on their inaction and refusal to acknowledge these speeches as criminal, he was transferred from the High Court of Delhi to the High Court of Punjab and Haryana overnight.[5]

Television news channels announced Umar Khalid's arrest with an air of triumph; the arrest underscoring yet another instance of draconian laws being weaponised against dissent in India. Already, police had arrested at least eighteen Muslims, including student leaders, who were booked under the UAPA, alleging a 'larger conspiracy' by them to incite religious tensions – a claim widely dismissed by legal and human rights experts.

I knew Umar as an activist of the Democratic Students' Union (DSU) at Jawaharlal Nehru University (JNU), pursuing his doctoral research on the Adivasis of Jharkhand. His arrest, like many others, was based on allegations that he incited communal violence through his speeches in February 2020. The case bore a striking resemblance to the Bhima-Koregaon incident, where those who made speeches during the Elgar Parishad were accused of inciting violence the following day. Notably, Umar had been named in the initial FIR in the Bhima-Koregaon case alongside Jignesh Mevani[6] before a second FIR shifted the narrative and ensnared a wider group of activists.

Umar was no stranger to state repression or public controversy. In 2016, he, along with Kanhaiya Kumar, then the JNU Students' Union president, and fellow DSU member Anirban Bhattacharya, was arrested on charges of criminal conspiracy for organising an allegedly 'anti-national' event.[7] The event, held on 9 February 2016, was a commemoration of Afzal Guru, who was executed for his alleged involvement in the 2001 Parliament attacks. Guru's hanging was criticised by many as politically motivated and procedurally flawed. Even Gopal Subramaniam, the public prosecutor in Guru's case, described it as a violation of the rule of law.[8] The students' decision to commemorate Guru was rooted in JNU's culture of open debate, but it became the target of a manufactured controversy.

The BJP, which came to power in 2014 under Narendra Modi, a long-time propagandist for the RSS, began systematically dismantling democratic institutions and stifling dissent. The BJP's student wing, the Akhil Bharatiya Vidyarthi Parishad (ABVP), emboldened by state patronage, filed a complaint against the event. The JNU administration, aligned with the government's agenda to 'cleanse' campuses of leftist ideologies, withdrew permission for the programme. The event proceeded nonetheless, sparking a controversy over the alleged 'anti-national' slogans that were used. Mainstream media channels, particularly Zee News, aired doctored videos, claiming students shouted slogans like *'Bharat ki barbadi'* (Destruction of India).[9] The subsequent resignation of a Zee News producer over the channel's biased coverage revealed that these allegations were fabricated.[10]

The JNU administration's response was swift and authoritarian. It formed a high-level enquiry committee (HLEC) to investigate the event, and arrests followed shortly thereafter. Kanhaiya Kumar was detained, sparking nationwide protests and condemnation from human rights organisations, academics and political leaders. Umar Khalid and Anirban Bhattacharya eventually surrendered after days in hiding. Forensic analysis later confirmed that the videos aired by media channels on the event were doctored, but this revelation did little to deter the government from pursuing its agenda. The Modi regime, driven by a Goebbels-like zeal for propaganda, ignored the truth in favour of perpetuating a narrative that framed dissenters as enemies of the nation.

The entire episode encapsulates the dangerous trajectory of India under Modi's rule, where dissent is conflated with sedition and democracy is hollowed out under the guise of nationalism. Umar Khalid's ordeal is emblematic of the state's broader strategy to silence critical voices, delegitimise political opposition and manufacture consent for its authoritarian agenda. It is a grim reminder that in Modi's 'New India', truth is irrelevant, and those who challenge the status quo are branded as threats to the nation.

The HLEC identified twenty-one students as guilty and awarded them various punishments, including fines.[11] When the appellate authority – the vice chancellor – upheld the punishments but reduced the fines, the students went on an indefinite fast that lasted for sixteen days. Subsequently, the students moved the Delhi High Court, which stayed the punishments until the case was decided.

The issue even found its way to Parliament. The JNU administration, in its draft reply to the Parliament Secretariat dated 28 April, claimed that the Truth Lab had authenticated the videos, based on which twenty-one students were incriminated for indulging in 'anti-national activities'. This assertion was a blatant lie, knowingly persisted with nearly two months after the Truth Lab had exposed that the videos were doctored.[12] Yet the Sangh Parivar, Modi's staunch supporters and the *godi media* continue to propagate this falsehood without a hint of shame. They coined the term *tukde-tukde gang*, grounded in the fabricated slogan *'Bharat tere tukde honge'*, alleged to have been used by the students but which was never uttered.[13]

This strategy of manufacturing lies has had deadly consequences, as seen in the tragic case of Rohith Vemula, a research scholar at Hyderabad Central University. Rohith's persecution began when the Ambedkar Students' Association (ASA), of which he was a part, protested the hanging of Yakub Memon – a controversial act many considered unlawful. ASA also opposed the hooliganism of the ABVP, which had disrupted the screening of the documentary *Muzaffarnagar Abhi Baqi Hai* at Delhi's Kirori Mal College. In retaliation, the ABVP president called ASA students 'goons' on Facebook. When ASA members confronted him, he allegedly apologised in the presence of a university security officer. However, the next day, the ABVP president sought treatment for appendicitis at a private hospital and falsely claimed he had been attacked by ASA members. The university doctor contradicted this claim, but the fabricated narrative of ASA's 'violence' persisted.

This falsehood led to the expulsion of Rohith and four other ASA members from their hostel, which eventually drove Rohith to take his own life.[14] No action was taken against the ABVP president or the BJP politicians who had maligned the ASA as 'anti-national', nor against the biased university administration. Instead, the BJP government vilified Rohith posthumously. The one-man Roopanwal Commission, formed after the protests subsided, went out of its way to declare that Rohith was not a Dalit, dismissed his suicide as unrelated to the university's actions and even accused him of fabricating his caste certificate.[15] These claims ignored well-established legal precedents that recognised Dalit status for children raised by single Dalit mothers after separating from non-Dalit fathers. Despite clear evidence to the contrary, the BJP's narrative prevailed, shielding those responsible for Rohith's death.

Similarly, the judiciary and media failed to hold Hindutva goons accountable for the violence unleashed against Kanhaiya Kumar, then president of JNU students' union. While in custody, Kanhaiya was attacked by BJP-linked lawyers and their accomplices within the Patiala House Court premises. A sting operation by *India Today* revealed that these attacks were premeditated. Lawyers like Vikram Singh Chauhan, Yashpal Singh and Om Sharma proudly admitted to orchestrating the assault, with support from police officials.[16] Chauhan even boasted about bringing in outsiders, specifically to attack 'anti-nationals'. Despite video evidence and public confessions, no action was taken against these individuals.[17]

All three arrested JNU students, along with five others, were eventually granted bail in August 2016. These events marked the beginning of a sinister trend of branding dissenters as 'anti-national'. From the Ambedkar Periyar Study Circle (APSC) at IIT Madras to ASA at Hyderabad Central University and the students of JNU, critics of the Modi regime were systematically vilified and punished.

Since Modi's BJP assumed power in 2014, the list of 'anti-nationals' has grown exponentially.[18] Watching TV in jail, it became clear that anyone who challenged the BJP's line was quickly branded as such. This conflation of government opposition with anti-nationalism effectively labels the 60 per cent of Indians who did not vote for the BJP as 'anti-nationals', transforming India into a 'nation of anti-nationals'.[19]

Umar Khalid's targeting is the latest chapter in this grim saga. His crime? Leading peaceful protests against the CAA, 2019. The Act, which discriminates based on religion, violates the secular principles enshrined in India's Constitution. It provides fast-tracked citizenship to six non-Muslim communities from Pakistan, Afghanistan and Bangladesh while excluding Muslims. Although the Act's constitutionality is under challenge in the Supreme Court, delays render it a de facto reality, emblematic of the 'fait accompli' jurisprudence thriving in Modi's 'New India'.

The protests against the CAA began on 11 December 2019, sparking nationwide dissent. On 15 December, Delhi police violently stormed Jamia Millia Islamia University, brutally assaulting students with batons and tear gas. The police did not spare the library, washrooms, or even the female students. Over 200 students were injured.[20] This act of state-sponsored violence triggered the historic Shaheen Bagh protests, led by the mothers of Jamia students.[21] The peaceful sit-in inspired similar protests nationwide, demonstrating remarkable democratic resilience despite the BJP's relentless vilification of protesters.

In Modi's India, standing up for justice makes you an 'anti-national', deserving of incarceration. These labels and narratives are the tools of an authoritarian regime, silencing dissent and consolidating power under the guise of nationalism.

During the campaigns for the Delhi Legislative Assembly elections in February 2020, BJP leaders resorted to venomous hate speeches to polarise the electorate. On 23 January 2020, Kapil Mishra, a former AAP leader who had joined the BJP, tweeted that the contest on 8 February would be an 'India-Pakistan face-off', adding, 'Mini Pakistans are being created in Delhi.'[22] BJP MP from West Delhi, Parvesh Sahib Singh Verma, in an interview on 28 January declared ominously, 'These people will enter your houses, rape your sisters and daughters, kill them. There's still time today. Tomorrow, Modiji and Amit Shah won't be there to save you.'[23] Anurag Thakur, the then minister of state for finance, incited violence during a rally in Rithala on 27 January, chanting, *'Desh ke gaddaron ko, goli maaro saalon ko'* (Shoot the traitors of the country) in Amit Shah's presence.[24] Prime Minister Modi himself, in a speech on 3 February, stated, 'We can't leave Delhi to such anarchy.'[25] Only people of Delhi can stop this. Every vote given to the BJP can do this,' subtly but pointedly signalling confrontation with the protesters.[26]

The riots erupted on 23 February, immediately following Kapil Mishra's provocative ultimatum to the Delhi police to clear the protest sites or face consequences. The violence fuelled by these incendiary remarks ravaged parts of the city until 29 February. The riots left fifty-five dead, two-thirds of them Muslim, as mentioned earlier, with waves of bloodshed and destruction of property. Delhi police played a blatantly partisan role, openly aiding Hindu rioters while targeting Muslims.

Since Narendra Modi's ascent to power in 2014, the term 'anti-national' has been weaponised against opposition figures, activists and dissenters. By consolidating control over state apparatuses, Modi's regime has moved to assert its grip over civil society, creating a climate of fear and compliance. With bureaucratic and institutional support dominated by upper-caste sympathisers aligned with RSS ideology, the state machinery has eagerly followed the government's signals, shedding professional ethics and embracing partisanship. The 'anti-national' narrative became a tool with which to silence dissent. Muslims, Dalits, tribal people and intellectuals are conveniently branded as 'urban Naxals' or anti-nationals, allowing the regime to suppress opposing voices under the guise of nationalism.

The British-era sedition law, once wielded against freedom fighters like B.G. Tilak and Mahatma Gandhi, has been resurrected as a tool of repression. Gandhi famously called it the 'prince among the political sections of the Indian Penal Code designed to suppress liberty'. Independent India, however, failed to abolish this draconian law, leaving it vulnerable to misuse. Under Modi's regime, sedition cases have skyrocketed. Of the 405 sedition cases filed in the last decade, 95 per cent were filed post 2014. Data shows a 28 per cent rise in sedition cases filed annually between 2014 and 2020 from the previous decade. Of these, 149 were for 'critical' remarks against Modi and 144 for remarks against Uttar Pradesh Chief Minister Yogi Adityanath.

Nationalism has always served authoritarian leaders as a tool to consolidate their power, legitimise their rule and suppress dissent. By defining national identity in exclusionary terms, authoritarian regimes foster a sense of 'us versus them', uniting a majority against perceived enemies – whether minorities, dissenters or foreign powers. In India, 'Hindutva nationalism' has emerged as a potent force under Modi, marginalising minorities and stifling democracy. Policies and rhetoric targeting specific groups – based on religion, caste or ideology – undermine the principles of unity and equality that true nationalism should uphold. Instead, this form of nationalism prioritises the interests of a narrow religious and cultural majority at the expense of others, eroding social cohesion.

The concept of nationalism, born in a bygone era, has become a weapon in the hands of power-hungry politicians. In today's interconnected world, its utility is increasingly questionable. Millions continue to die in wars, riots and acts of terror justified in the name of nationalism. Enormous resources are wasted in these futile power struggles, while humanity faces common challenges that require collective action. It is time to question the relevance of nationalism itself. Instead of clinging to outdated boundaries and divisions, humanity must embrace a future defined by solidarity and cooperation. A global movement of people declaring themselves 'anti-national' could disarm authoritarian regimes of their most potent weapon – fear. Only by transcending the artificial constructs of nationalism can we hope to build a world that prioritises humanity over narrow, exclusionary identities.

India's vast arsenal of draconian laws paints a strikingly contradictory picture of its democracy. Appendix 2 provides a representative list of these draconian laws, which, though significant, cannot be considered exhaustive. Enacted in the name of 'security', these laws ostensibly aim to safeguard the nation from threats. However, their sheer number and expansive scope – spanning Central and state levels – suggest a deeper and more troubling reality: a pervasive distrust by the ruling dispensation of its own people. Implicit in the frequent invocation of such laws is the notion that a significant portion of the population poses a threat to the state, which logically translates to branding them as anti-national. This portrayal not only undermines the fabric of democracy but also raises profound questions about the state's relationship with its citizens.

Under the Modi regime, since 2014, the application of these draconian laws has intensified. Laws like the UAPA, the National Security Act (NSA), and various state-specific legislations have been used with alarming frequency to silence dissent, criminalise protest and target marginalised communities. Critics, journalists, academics and activists – many of whom have devoted their lives to social justice – have been labelled anti-national and subjected to prolonged incarceration without trial. The misuse of these laws, often devoid of due process, illustrates a broader strategy to equate disagreement with disloyalty, dissent with sedition and resistance with rebellion.

The prevalence and aggressive use of these laws give rise to a chilling paradox: India, often hailed as the world's largest democracy, appears to view a significant portion of its populace as adversaries. The government's relentless narrative of internal threats – be it from activists, students, farmers or even comedians – has weaponised the term 'anti-national', eroding the space for dialogue and democratic participation. What this narrative effectively conveys is a deep-seated insecurity on the part of the state. Instead of addressing the structural inequalities and grievances that lead to social unrest, the government resorts to oppressive legal frameworks to suppress voices of opposition.

The notion of India as a 'country of anti-nationals' is a grim reflection of this mindset. The irony is stark: those who question the government's actions or seek to hold it accountable are branded as enemies of the nation, while those who perpetuate divisive ideologies are celebrated as patriots. This inversion of values undermines the principles of justice, equality and freedom enshrined in the Constitution. It also risks alienating vast sections of the population, deepening social divisions and fostering a culture of fear and suspicion.

Ultimately, the rampant use of draconian laws underlines a critical failing of governance: the inability – or unwillingness – to engage with dissent constructively. By criminalising opposition and perpetuating the myth of an 'anti-national' populace, the state not only weakens the foundations of democracy but also undermines its own legitimacy. A truly secure and thriving nation cannot be built by stifling its people; it must be forged through inclusivity, dialogue and the recognition that dissent is not a threat but an essential component of democracy.

22

Of Labels and Labelling

> If anything is certain, it is that I myself am not a Marxist.
>
> Karl Marx[1]

ONE DAY, AS WE sat in the corridor eating our breakfast, Ramesh hesitantly brought something up. He said there was gossip doing the rounds in Dalit circles outside that I wasn't really an Ambedkarite.

I smiled. 'Oh, I too have heard it,' I said. 'Didn't they also say I was a Marxist? It's amusing – in Ambedkarite circles I'm a Marxist, and in Marxist circles I'm an Ambedkarite!'

'There's another funny thing,' I added, holding up the newspaper I was reading. It carried a report on me, referring to me as a 'Dalit intellectual'. That wasn't the first time. Almost every journalistic piece on me begins with that adjective *Dalit*. As if it's inseparable from who I am. As if it sums me up.

It got to the ridiculous point where a news report about my company described me as a 'Dalit manager' – and this, mind you, was written by someone often seen in Mumbai's so-called progressive circles. I was so annoyed I felt like tearing into him, but I held back, choosing discretion over reaction.

These are journalists – supposedly progressive, society's conscience-keepers. Most of them come from upper-caste, middle-class backgrounds, educated in elite schools. If even they can't resist the urge to slot me with a caste label – as if it's automatic, subconscious – then what hope is there for the rest of society?

It never seems to occur to them to ask a simple question: Do they ever write 'Brahmin intellectual' for anyone? Or 'Bania scholar'? No? Then why me?

It's not like I ever hid my caste – when it was relevant, I acknowledged it. But I've never needed to lean on it. I've never relied on reservations or any special support. I've always stood on my own scholarly merit – and I've had the confidence to take on anyone on that basis.

Ironically, there's nothing particularly 'Dalit' in the conventional sense about my life or career. So how did this label get stuck to me?

I think it all began with my association with the Ambedkar family. Babasaheb Ambedkar, until he became a universal icon, was always belittled as merely a 'Dalit leader' or something of the sort. Even after emerging as the greatest icon in modern Indian history, his caste never left society's subconscious. It still clings to him – and by extension to those of us associated with his legacy.

As for the Ambedkarite and Marxist labels prevalent among activist circles, they need serious thinking as they have huge implications for the emancipatory movement in India.

It is one of the many ironies of our time that those who should stand shoulder to shoulder in struggle remain estranged. Ambedkarites and Marxists, both born out of the long twentieth century's yearning for justice, now appear to inhabit separate worlds – walled off by suspicion, dogma and an almost theological need for purity. Despite the right wing's unrelenting assault, they seldom reach for each other. I have often wondered: Have they forgotten that their fundamental goal is the same – the annihilation of oppression, exploitation?

All my life, I have urged these two traditions to reflect, to reckon with their limitations, to draw strength from one another. But instead, they have chosen sectarian solitude. Each fears dilution. Each suspects betrayal in the other's embrace.

And yet, history gives us glimpses of another possibility. When the two did come together – even momentarily – the impact was tangible. In the anti-Khoti movement,[2] in the working-class strike of 1938,[3] in the land satyagraha of 1959,[4] their joint action shook the ruling class. But the actors themselves failed to see the historic potential of such alignments. Even when Dalits fought in

Marxist-led struggles – across Telangana, Tamil Nadu, Kerala – they rarely saw themselves as Ambedkarites. Nor were they seen as such. A moment passed, ungrasped.

As for myself, I have never been comfortable with labels. Marxist, Ambedkarite – these names are often thrust upon me, sometimes with admiration, more often with scorn. But I have resisted them all. I am neither. I prefer not to belong.

This insistence on ideological purity – the obsession with neat categories – is, ironically, deeply Brahmanical in spirit. The very thing both Ambedkar and Marx stood against. Did Ambedkar ever call himself an Ambedkarite? Did Marx declare himself a Marxist? Both were restless minds, drawing from many sources, always questioning.

Ambedkar named his intellectual ancestors: Buddha, Kabir, Phule. But he never deified them. His Buddhism was a rationalist reinvention, rejected by traditionalists who titled his work *Ambedkar and His Dhamma* to mark its deviation. In truth, the thinker who shaped him most profoundly was perhaps John Dewey. It was Dewey who taught him pragmatism, constitutionalism, a nuanced view of state and society. And yet, Ambedkar never called himself a Deweyist.

Marx, too, stood on the shoulders of many: Hegel, Feuerbach, the British political economists, the French revolutionaries. He was shaped as much by the failures of 1848 as by the hope of 1871. But he never froze his thought into a final doctrine.

Why then must I? My life has drawn upon many wells.

I grew up in a fog of stories about Ambedkar. Tales of him reading under street lamps, mastering the law, becoming one of the world's great minds – these were passed down orally, in hushed admiration. They gave me a dream. They gave me ambition. That I became a scholar myself owes much to the aura of Babasaheb that surrounded my childhood.

But other influences entered early. When I topped my class in the third standard, I was awarded a small Marathi book: a biography of Stalin. I read it with fascination. Suddenly, the world looked different. The questions I had timidly asked my mother – why are we so poor? why don't we have what others do?

– found sharper, deeper answers. Exploitation. Class. Revolution. Socialism. The ideas lit up my mind.

We had nothing. No land. No cattle. Not even a proper home. My mother could only promise, 'When you grow up, you'll have it all.' But this little book offered something more than promises – it gave reasons, and with them, a sense of agency. I could instantly relate to the book – I had seen my father slog away in a lime factory while the owner lounged nearby, soaking in the blast of an air cooler.

Soon, I was devouring anything I could find. My uncle would bring me more books from the small taluka stall. In the school library, I found a booklet on Bhagat Singh. That was another turning point. I was gripped by his clarity, stunned by his fearlessness. His refusal to beg for mercy before the noose etched itself deep in my imagination. He became my childhood hero – and remains a beacon even today.

This was my formation: Ambedkar, Stalin, Bhagat Singh. Many added to the list as I grew. In them, I found a fierce commitment to justice, an intolerance for subjugation and a refusal to bow. Why should I now reduce this composite inheritance to a single ism?

Indeed, I believe that is the tragedy of our political thought – the fetish for isms. They promise coherence but impose rigidity. They are born of moments but claim eternity. They exhaust themselves in self-preservation. They become museums of thought rather than laboratories.

Worse still, they presume the world remains unchanged. But the world changes constantly. Any thinker who matters speaks to a historical context. And if their thought is to live, it must be reread, revised, reimagined. Marx himself evolved throughout his life. The Marx of *The German Ideology* is not the Marx of *Capital*. Scholars rightly speak of a 'young Marx' and a 'mature Marx'. Yet Marxists today chant formulae like catechism.

When Marx turned his gaze towards Asia, he proposed the Asiatic Mode of Production – a fragile category that signalled a more complex history, not reducible to European schemas. It was an admission that he did not know it all. One can only imagine how he might have thought in our world – of financial derivatives, digital capital, big data, artificial intelligence and data surveillance. He would have revised. He would have rethought. But many who claim his legacy do not.

I have always reserved the right to learn, to unlearn, to change. That is not inconsistency. That is the humility knowledge demands. I will not be boxed into any doctrine, least of all by those who neither understand the ideas they profess nor the lives they claim to represent.

For me, identity is a living thing. It must breathe. And if I must be true to those who shaped me – Ambedkar, Bhagat Singh, Marx – I must carry forward their restlessness. I must refuse closure. I must keep walking.

Speaking of these two – Marx and Ambedkar – I've often felt that neither of them ever imagined they'd one day be packaged into neat little isms by their followers. If anything, Marx offers a comprehensive framework – a system of thought that seeks to understand the world in its entirety, only so it can be changed for the better. There's a method, a structure, a coherence to Marx.

But Ambedkar? I always found it difficult to see him through the same lens. He didn't subscribe to any grand theory of history or revolution. He didn't carry an ideological blueprint in his pocket. He responded to the world as it confronted him – with fierce clarity, moral urgency and a practical mind. If anything, he was a constitutionalist, a pragmatist, someone who thought through problems contextually, not dogmatically. Which is why it always feels odd to me when people try to cast him into a fixed ideological mould. As if Ambedkarism was a doctrine he himself professed. It wasn't. It came later – mostly from the need to locate him in a tradition. But Ambedkar was, above all, a thinker in motion.

Still millions speak of Ambedkarism as though it was self-evident.

A few tried to define it. Raosaheb Kasbe was probably the first. His attempt to define Ambedkarism as a social science that aims to reorganise the world into a socialist society grounded in democracy and the principles of liberty, equality, and fraternity through *Dhamma* is commendable – but conceptually muddled. The terms socialism, democracy and Dhamma are anything but precise. What Kasbe offers is less a coherent ideology than a visionary aspiration, shaped more by affective resonance than analytical clarity.

Each of these terms carries contested meanings. Socialism, for instance, spans from Marx's scientific socialism to Nehruvian state capitalism and Ambedkar's own formulation of state socialism. Ironically, the same Ambedkarites who celebrate him as a free-market visionary and Dalit capitalist would find Kasbe's socialist framing jarring. Democracy, too, is fraught. Ambedkar's parliamentary vision produced a parasitic political class that often silences rather than amplifies the people's voice. His ideal democracy was inseparable from social and economic democracy, without which political democracy, he warned, would collapse. As for Dhamma, Ambedkar distinguished it from *Dharma*, seeing the former as a code of righteous conduct focused on transforming the world, not explaining its origins. Yet, this distinction is debatable – Pali Dhamma is merely the vernacular rendering of Sanskrit Dharma, and few if any religions pursue cosmological origins in the scientific sense.

Kasbe rightly notes that the term Ambedkarism emerged posthumously, yet avoids its historical genesis: the ideological rift within the Republican Party of India (RPI) in the late 1950s. The 'correct' faction identified constitutionalism as Ambedkar's legacy, disavowing the 'incorrect' faction's agitational methods as communist-influenced. Thus, Ambedkarism was born not merely as a tribute but in direct opposition to Marxism. This binary persisted into the Dalit Panthers' split and remains visible today, amplified by the rise of a Dalit middle class, electoral competition and neoliberal opportunity structures – encouraged, often subtly, by the state.

Attempts to define Ambedkarism since have only added to the confusion. Sada Karhade once described Ambedkar as combining Buddha's peace with Marx's revolution, suggesting a fusion of Buddhism and Marxism. But he stopped short of offering a coherent synthesis. More recently, Suraj Yengde's *Loksatta* piece proposed a tree of Ambedkarism with social and spiritual branches sprouting into utopia, caste capitalism, rebellion, literature and internationalism – a formulation I found incoherent, even contradictory. If, as Yengde claims, no one has defined Ambedkarism, it may explain why the term is so casually flaunted, as if its meaning were self-evident.

Ambedkar's emphasis on religion stands out among modern thinkers. After the Mahad debacle, his call to reject Hinduism carried an implicit political threat – that Dalits could convert to Islam, shifting the electoral balance. Later, his language shifted from political to moral: Dhamma as the ethical glue of society. But this raises questions. If Dhamma is to maintain moral order, why does one need a Constitution or a state? As I argued in my first book, Ambedkar saw society as needing a two-tiered control system: internal moral regulation (through Dhamma) and external legal compulsion (via the state). Both, however, are historical constructs, not eternal truths.

My discomfort with Ambedkarism goes beyond these conceptual ambiguities. Isms serve to forge identities – but often insidiously so. They divide humanity into competing tribes, fuelling sectarianism. There are two types of isms: ideological (liberalism, socialism, fascism) and eponymous (Marxism, Gandhism, Ambedkarism). The former, though broad, emerge from historical movements with identifiable doctrines. The latter are rooted in personality cults, often weaponised by followers to assert sectarian difference. While innocuous among elites, these labels are divisive among oppressed classes. Ambedkarism, rather than unifying Dalits, has sometimes deepened intra-Dalit fissures by turning Ambedkar into a sub-caste icon. It has also stood in the way of class solidarity, positioning itself against class-based ideologies.

Such identity-based isms foster ideological inertia. They presume that faithfully following a great figure's thought is sufficient to resolve contemporary issues. But any thinker's ideas are products of their historical moment. Even in science, foundational theories evolve – Newton gave way to Einstein not by negation but by expansion. In politics, too, reverence must give way to reinterpretation. To canonise a figure into an ism is to risk turning a dynamic legacy into dogma.

Until the last century, these isms still held some weight – perhaps even meaning. The world seemed relatively stable, and the ideas of great men appeared timeless because the world they addressed remained largely unchanged across generations. But that's no longer the case. Technological advancement has radically accelerated the pace of change. What once took a thousand years now happens in a few decades; what took centuries is now compressed into mere years.

In such a rapidly evolving world, no single ism – however profound – can claim to be a comprehensive guide to action. The world is simply moving too fast, splintering too unpredictably. At best, the ideas of the past form a kind of repertoire, a database of experience and insight from which we can draw. They are resources, not road maps.

The road itself? That, we must build ourselves – often on the fly, responding as we go, improvising.

Epilogue

Walking Out of Taloja

Life without liberty is like a body without spirit.

Khalil Gibran

On 18 November 2022, I received an unexpected call from a baba for a mulaqat at around 2 p.m. Those fleeting ten to fifteen minutes of conversation with a loved one, separated by a dirty glass barrier and speaking through a phone amid noise on both sides, were moments prisoners lived for. I hurriedly put on my shirt, rushed down the stairs and waited to be escorted to the mulaqat room. Unlike ordinary prisoners, we, the Bhima-Koregaon accused, were labelled 'dreaded anti-national terrorists' and had to be accompanied by an officer. Ordinary prisoners could be herded by a baba or even walk about unescorted. But our status also came with a peculiar privilege: while the others stood under the blazing sun, waiting for their names to be called, we were taken straight inside to await our visitors.

That day, as usual, there was no coordination between the registration desk and the mulaqat room, separated by some 300 metres. I stood there for nearly forty minutes, repeatedly prodding the baba to call my wife. Finally, Rama appeared on the other side of the glass. By now familiar with the process, she signed the register and grabbed the phone at the slot I signalled. She had come straight from Bombay High Court and told me that I had been granted bail. Oddly, I didn't react. After having navigated the legal labyrinth since 2018, I had trained myself to accept events with equanimity. Rama added that the NIA had requested time to appeal to the Supreme Court and had been granted seven days. But nothing would feel real to me until it actually happened.

And then it did. Incidentally, the day the hearing of NIA's appeal was to be heard happened to be the date for our production too before the Special NIA Court. As we reached the court, I saw Rashmi, my daughter, who had come from Singapore where she worked, ready with cash, in anticipation of a positive outcome from the Supreme Court. Rama, in her anxiety, had flown to Delhi to attend the Supreme Court proceedings. As the hearing at the Supreme Court began, our lawyers in Mumbai court huddled by the windows to catch a signal on their phones, following the proceedings online. I sat quietly in a corner in the veranda of the court, somehow believing my premonitions that the Supreme Court would confirm the grant of bail. It was an irrational hunch, but it persisted. After fierce arguments, the court adjourned for lunch. There was palpable tension on the faces of those who had listened to the arguments. When the session resumed, the bench finally declared it would not interfere with the Bombay High Court's decision, though it added a caveat – prompted by Solicitor General Tushar Mehta – that the bail order should not influence the trial. The lawyers, smiling widely, were the first to come over to congratulate me. It was unbelievable that I could be free soon.

Now came the challenge of securing the court order in time for my release the next day. Rashmi persuaded the lawyers to expedite the formalities. It was a Friday, the week's last working day. A delay would mean waiting until Monday to get the order, with my release being pushed to Tuesday. My lawyers and Rashmi literally ran around the corridors of the Mumbai court to complete the formalities towards securing the order. The court was kind enough to issue the order, which now needed to reach the jail in time so as to ensure my release the next day.

While returning from the court we always had great fun, singing and eating the special food our friends arranged for us over the hour or so of travel it entailed. At times the guards threw tantrums about the food, but most times we had it unhindered. The entertainment master was usually Surendra, who had an inexhaustible store of songs and scripts. There was a battery of poets and singers among the group – Sudhir, Sagar and Ramesh, with occasional contributions by Gautam, Rona and others. There was an edge of positivity to this revelry that evening with my bail – the first one on merit granted in our case; the previous two had been by 'default' and 'medical'.

As we returned to the jail, word of my bail had already spread among the staff and our friends. The jailers supervising the prisoners' *zadati* congratulated me, though this did not exempt me from the routine strip search. Even the babas at the booth seemed more casual, their officers adopting a friendlier tone. Inside, fellow prisoners congratulated me warmly. Once in my cell, I began packing my belongings. My notebooks, containing the drafts of four books – a letter to Babasaheb, over a hundred-odd notes that I wrote inspired by my stay there, part of which are consumed in this book; a book on nationalism, and another on the making of the constitution – were already packed. It didn't take long to stuff my three bags and boxes containing the items sent from outside. I stacked everything neatly against the wall and retired for the night.

I found myself reflecting on the past thirty-one months – the longest stretch I had ever spent in one place since my college days. For most of my life I had constantly been on the move, whether on work, conferences, for social causes or personal reasons. Over the past two decades I had averaged three to four foreign trips annually, travelling for office work and to attend academic conferences across the globe. Many of these destinations were fascinating places I had hoped to revisit after retirement with my family, as those official trips rarely left me with time to explore the places or enjoy them fully.

In my hectic life, I had never paused to plan for retirement or even settle in a permanent home. For over five decades I had led a nomadic life, moving between company accommodations or institutional quarters, constantly travelling to address meetings, deliver lectures, lead struggles and support victims of human rights violations – often more actively than a professional politician. Incarceration had abruptly brought all of this to a standstill.

While in Goa, we had thought about buying a house to spend the rest of our lives in. A beautiful two-storeyed bungalow, owned by a Britisher planning to return to his homeland, was offered to me at a substantial discount as the seller came to learn about my activism. It was an idyllic spot, perfect for the slower pace of life I had envisioned for myself. Goa seemed ideal for the future, with its tranquillity and a network of friends nearby. I had decided to rekindle my passion for painting, which had been dormant for over four decades, and dedicate my remaining years to writing on issues I had always cared about.

There were also plans of long stays abroad, this time with the freedom to immerse myself in the experience – perhaps even through teaching assignments at universities. I wanted to see and experience as much of the world as I could while time allowed it.

But all these dreams came crashing down. Just as I was finalising the purchase of the house in Goa, the Bhima-Koregaon case engulfed me, and everything was derailed.

Even my last professional project – development of a full-fledged centre at GIM for Big Data and research into emerging areas like Internet of Things (IoT) and artificial intelligence, natural language processing, etc. – was stalled indefinitely. What was meant to be a serene and creative chapter of my life gave way to uncertainty and upheaval, leaving all those plans in ruins. Even my commitment to my students would be jeopardised. My job at GIM constituted the least cost among all these.

A whirlwind of memories from my prior days often haunted my mind while I was in prison. They rushed in and out as I lay in my bed, jostling with the thoughts that came later to mind. Chief among them were reflections on my family's journey – from struggling through abject poverty to building a foundation that allowed future generations to chart their own paths.

I often thought back to Rajur, a place that was neither fully a village nor quite a town. It was a strange blend of tradition and the stirrings of modern life. The place itself was neither black nor white – half the settlement was cloaked in the black dust of coal mines, while the other half was covered in a thick layer of lime. Growing up there instilled in me an appreciation for the 'greys' of life – a reminder that the world is rarely as simple as it seems.

Rajur, otherwise an unremarkable place, had given me this valuable perspective. We owned nothing but a mud house at the very edge of the Dalit *basti*, barely large enough to shelter the ten of us, and with plenty of rats and serpents that occasionally showed up. Yet that humble home was where our resilience was forged. The labour of my father, mother and all of us shaped us, making it easy for us to appreciate Marx's labour theory of value and his call to change the world. And the fiery Ambedkar, who had been a beacon of inspiration since childhood.

Most of my siblings eventually settled not far from Rajur, except for one sister who made her life in Bhopal. They knew the extended family – my uncles, aunts, their children – whom I, despite being the eldest, barely got to know. Life's circumstances often kept me away from Rajur, but the memories of those early years remain vivid, shaping who I am today.

The next morning began like any other, though anxiety gnawed at me. I dreaded the possibility of yet another delay. What if the order didn't reach the jail in time? The thought of spending two more nights in jail felt unbearable.

Arnab Goswami's brief stint in Taloja jail had sent shock waves through the corridors of power, prompting the constitution of a special bench on a Saturday to hear his bail plea and secure his immediate release. Unlike his case, mine barely raised an eyebrow. The Supreme Court's famous remark in Goswami's case – 'Deprivation of liberty even for a single day is one day too many' – rang hollow when juxtaposed against our prolonged detentions.

As legal scholar Gautam Bhatia aptly observed, this lofty rhetoric on liberty seemed hypocritical when weighed against the years of incarceration endured by us, the Bhima-Koregaon accused, without trial or bail. My release, delayed by even two days, would not make the news or stir the public conscience.

Around mid-morning, as I was getting a shave during the weekly barber rounds, the jailer arrived with a guard, instructing me to report to the office immediately. Once the orders were issued, implementation was swift. The kamwalla rushed in to pack my remaining things and carried the bags away. I hurriedly bid goodbye to the inmates who had helped me survive prison life. At the gate, the babas meticulously inventoried my belongings before escorting me upstairs for the paperwork. The superintendent had especially summoned me to his office – a rare gesture. I expected a touch of humanity, now that I was no longer his prisoner, but his demeanour remained cold and unsmiling. He informed me that a crowd awaited me outside and, upon my request, expedited the formalities, which still took more than an hour.

Finally, I stepped out. Walking through the gate felt surreal, as though I were escaping a hellhole, emerging alive from the jaws of death. A chilling thought crossed my mind: had I not survived the COVID-19 outbreak in 2020, it might have been my corpse leaving the jail instead.

Outside the red gate, my bags were already placed. I waved to friends, among them Kapil Patil, a noted social worker and long-time member of the Legislative Council of Maharashtra and one who had accompanied me and seen me off at the NIA office on 14 April 2020 – the day of my surrender and arrest; his younger brother, Yeshu Patil, the editor of *Shabd*, a progressive Marathi monthly, and owner of the publication house of the same name. My wife, daughter and others were waiting nearby with vehicles. Someone had already collected my bags at the gate and loaded them into vehicles. I was driven to the visitors' booth, where a larger crowd of friends and media awaited. To the journalists, I expressed gratitude for their presence but refrained from speaking much. When asked how I felt, I replied, 'Happy to be out, but angry about wasting my precious thirty-one months in the fakest case.' It was widely carried by newspapers and news portals. I met most of my friends who had turned up there to affectionately welcome my liberty, and proceeded out.

On the way home, Rama learned a media contingent was waiting at Rajgruha. To avoid them, we made a detour to visit our lawyer friend Mihir Desai. By the time we returned, it was past 3 p.m. and the reporters had dispersed. Rama had already prepared the house for our stay, having vacated our residence on the GIM campus and moved our belongings to a small flat I had bought in Mumbai during my IIT days. I realised that one of my bags, the contents of which I didn't recall, had been lost in the melee.

From the next day, friends from across the country and abroad began visiting. Our new home – a modest two-unit set-up in Rajgruha extension, meant to be a student hostel – was ideal for its proximity to the police station and court but too small for hosting many visitors at once. Somehow we managed, scheduling visits and reciprocating everyone's affection over the first two months.

Returning to Goa was no longer an option. I requested GIM to settle my dues, as the thought of teaching management students under the shadow of terror charges felt unbearable. This time everything was different. My former students had known me, trusted me and shared a deep camaraderie with me. But now the campus no longer felt familiar. All the faculty I had personally recruited and forged into a spirited team to realise my vision had resigned after my entanglement in this case. Adding to the pain, one of my closest colleagues and a pillar of support, Professor Hemant Kumar Padhiari, had passed away during my incarceration. His absence would haunt me if I ever returned to that campus.

The thought of walking through those once-familiar corridors now filled me with dread. The place, now strange and unfamiliar, would likely be rife with suspicious glances and whispered judgements. I couldn't bring myself to face the poisoned perceptions that would inevitably follow me there.

In the end, I resolved not to take up another job but to focus on completing my books and to wait for the political climate to improve for activism.

Since 2018, when my name first surfaced in the Bhima-Koregaon case, life took on a different tone, even though we tried to carry on as normally as possible. But with my arrest in April 2020, our world was turned upside down.

Coming out of jail, however, was a relief. The immediate priority was to arrange surety for my bail – a process that seemed simple but turned into a bureaucratic nightmare. Surprisingly, a ration card – a document meant for accessing subsidised food – was required to prove solvency. The irony was not lost on us: Why would a person relying on subsidised food grains be considered financially solvent? Nonetheless, the authorities insisted on it. It was a daunting task to find someone with a valid ration card in Mumbai willing to stand surety for us.

Even after securing the required documents – ration card, bank statements, immovable property records, Aadhaar card and PAN card – a complication arose. The person standing surety for me had a note on his ration card indicating he had stood surety for someone else over twenty years ago. Although that person had been acquitted, the remark still remained. It required additional proof of the acquittal, and it took weeks of running around to get the remark cancelled. My wife and I spent anxious days at court until the issue was resolved.

The process of recovering the ₹1 lakh deposit my daughter Rashmi had paid for my release was equally absurd. The court demanded a long list of documents, including the original receipt, bank passbook, Aadhaar card, PAN card and proof of address. It was baffling that the court – after holding me in custody for thirty-one months – needed such extensive documentation to verify my identity. All that should have been required was my bank account details for the refund. But in the labyrinth of bureaucracy, nothing is ever straightforward. Needless to say, each of these absurdities entailed the greasing of hands.

After gathering the necessary documents, a mismatch in the spelling of my name across them caused more trouble, requiring yet another affidavit to resolve. Oddly enough, the receipt for the deposit – arguably the most crucial document – could also be substituted with an affidavit. Eventually, the registrar approved the refund, and I was pleasantly surprised when the money was credited to my account sooner than expected.

With the bail matters finally settled, I turned my attention to the financial chaos that had piled up during my imprisonment. Reward points on credit cards and airline loyalty programmes worth lakhs of rupees had expired. My Google account, which held crucial financial information, and my half-finished writings and researches, remained inaccessible because I no longer had the password to them. Even though the charge sheet in my case had been filed, there was no valid rational reason for withholding the Google password. Yet, given my experiences, pursuing the matter in court seemed futile.

I underwent a full medical check-up, which had not been done in over three years. Many health issues had worsened during my time in jail. Despite the doctors' prescriptions, routine tests like PSA for my prostate were ignored. An MRI scan for suspected cervical and lumbar damage – recommended before my arrest by JJ Hospital – was persistently declined and was finally arranged in 2022, only after a court order. Now out of jail, I could finally prioritise my health.

Gradually, I adjusted to life outside. I resumed my editing of the biography of Babasaheb Ambedkar, which had been paused during my incarceration. My contract to do a textbook on management of Big Data projects, which could be the first one of its kind, with a reputed international publisher had to be terminated because of the case. I began keying in my books handwritten in the jail and also started work on a book on the state of human rights during BJP rule, which was conceived in jail.

Amid this, came a pleasant surprise: the Karnataka government announced that I had been selected for the Basava Rashtriya Puraskar for 2022, their highest honour. The selection committee, composed entirely of intellectuals and social workers, reached out through activist friends for my consent. Years ago I had declined to accept a nomination from the Maharashtra government to some committee and had declared that I would never accept any government nomination or award, believing it conflicted with my moral right to critique the state on behalf of the people. I had reiterated this resolve publicly, and no government had approached me since.

This time, however, friends urged me to reconsider my decision. They pointed out that the award was a recognition of the struggles of countless activists against the right-wing BJP regime. They likened it to my earlier acceptance of an honorary doctorate from the Karnataka State Open University, where there was no government involvement in the decision. After much deliberation, and in light of the political shifts in the country, I decided to accept the award.

With the court's permission, I travelled to Bengaluru to receive the honour in person. Shortly after, I was invited to a Constitution Day conference organised by the Karnataka government, which too I attended with the court's approval. The court was kind enough to grant me permissions twice to travel to Chennai, once for the release of a book on Babasaheb Ambedkar produced by the publishing house Anand Vikatan, and also for the release of my book *Iconoclast: A Reflective Biography of Dr Babasaheb Ambedkar*, recently published by Penguin. The second time it was to attend a symposium on the Constitution on Republic Day in 2024, where I had been invited to be the chief guest.

Life after incarceration was not the same, but I had begun piecing it back together – one step at a time.

As we unpacked the parcels sent from Goa, I was pleasantly surprised to find yet another honour – the Dr APJ Abdul Kalam Lifetime Achievement National Award (2020) – conferred on me. While in jail, we had also learned about the Shakti Bhatt Human Rights Award (2020) being jointly awarded to me and my co-accused Gautam Navlakha. These acknowledgements carried deep symbolic meaning. Despite the government's accusations against us and our ordeal of being implicated in the Bhima-Koregaon case, these awards – like many others conferred post-Bhima-Koregaon – were a reminder that civil society did not share the state's verdict. In fact, they continued to recognise and honour us as human rights defenders.

Life had adjusted to the new realities. For the first time I found myself without a salaried job, yet paradoxically busier than ever. There was a mountain of reading I wanted to complete and countless writings waiting to be finished.

Still, I often find myself reflecting on the surreal nature of these years – marked by endless encounters with police, lawyers, courts and judges. There was a constant, pervasive sense of helplessness as I witnessed the inversion of truth and meaning.

They say we now live in a post-truth world, where truth no longer exists but is manufactured. The term gained global prominence during Trump's 2016 campaign, but in India this post-truth phenomenon had already taken root two years earlier.

Here, the electoral majority seems conditioned to accept a grotesque reality, where lies parade as truth, communalism wears the mask of secularism, bigotry is promoted as tolerance, autocracy is sold as democracy and the very destroyers of the nation are hailed as *deshbhakt*s. Unlike anywhere else, this world has been constructed with a deadly mix of religion, caste and patriotism – a toxic combination so potent it feels almost insurmountable.

When my thoughts begin to spiral into this dark abyss, I draw strength from a powerful image: the monstrous structure of the Anda barrack loomed like a relic of tyranny, its bulk swallowed by the darkness of nightfall. Here and there, slivers of light escaped through the narrow cell openings – brief, broken beams that tore through the black like cries through silence. They caught the glint of layered steel: bars, grills, gates – each one a cold incision into our freedom. Yet even in this cavern of captivity, the air pulsed with resistance. Voices rose – raw, resolute – breaking through walls, shattering the hush with defiant echoes. Faiz's words surged through the gloom like a promise. Not merely remembered, but lived… *'Hum Dekhenge'*.[1]

Appendix 1

ORDERS OF VIOLENCE

9-10 April, 2018

Keynote Speaker Etienne Balibar

The American University of Paris
6, rue du Colonel Combes 75007 Paris

THE AMERICAN UNIVERSITY of PARIS 55 YEARS

GEORGE AND IRINA SCHAEFFER CENTER FOR THE STUDY OF GENOCIDE, HUMAN RIGHTS AND CONFLICT PREVENTION

For more information contact Lissa Lincoln llincoln@aup.edu

Orders of Violence Program

Monday April 9

Session I
1:30–5:30
1:30–1:40   Welcome and Opening Remarks (Lissa Lincoln)
1:40–2:30   Anand Teltumbde 'The Political Economy of Caste'
2:30–2:50   Discussion
2:50–3:40   Nicolas Jaoul 'The Dalit Panther's Response to Caste Violence in Uttar Pradesh'
3:40–4:00   Discussion
4:00–4:20   *pause café*

Session II
4:20–5:00   Round Table Discussion: 'The Politics of Representation: Filming Violence' Romain Huet, Nicolas Jaoul, Chowra Makaremi, (Lissa Lincoln, chair)
5:00–5:30   Discussion
5:30–6:30   Break
6:30   Keynote Address: Etienne Balibar 'From Violence as Anti-politics to Politics as Anti-Violence' (respondent: Anupama Rao)

Tuesday April 10

Session I
9:30–10:00	Coffee
10:00–10:50	Shailaja Paik 'Double Discrimination: Dalit Women in India'
10:50–11:10	Discussion
11:10–12:00	Vanessa Watts 'Claiming Place Through Death: Indigenous Lives and the Intensification of Canadian Frontiers'
12:00–12:20	Discussion
12:20–2:00	Lunch
2:00–2:50	Chowra Makaremi 'Red Lines: An Archeology of Violence in Iran'
2:50–3:10	Discussion
3:10–4:00	Ziad Majed 'Class, Gender and Social Representation in the Syrian Conflict'
4:00–4:20	Discussion
4:20–4:40	*pause café*
5:00–5:50	Closing address: Anupama Rao 'Existence and Insurgence: Reflections on Damaged Life'
5:50–6:15	Discussion
6:15	*Remerciements* and Closing Remarks

Appendix 2

Some Salient Draconian Laws

- The Maintenance of Internal Security Act, 1971 (MISA)
- The Terrorism and Disruptive Activities (Prevention) Act, 1987
- The Prevention of Terrorism Act, 2001 (POTA)
- National Security Act (1980, amended 1984 and 1987) (NSA)
- The Unlawful Activities (Prevention) Act, 1967 (UAPA)
- The Unlawful Activities (Prevention) Amendment Act, 2004 (as amended)
- The Essential Services Maintenance Act, (1981) (ESMA)
- The Maharashtra Control of Organised Crime Act, 1999 (MCOCA)
- DELHI – Maharashtra Control of Organised Crime Act, 1999 is applicable to Delhi
- The Karnataka Control of Organised Crime Act, 2000 (KCOCA)
- The Andhra Pradesh Control of Organised Crime Act, 2001 (APCOCA)
- The Uttar Pradesh Gangsters and Anti-Social Activities (Prevention) Act, 1986
- The Uttar Pradesh Control of Goondas Act, 1970 & Uttar Pradesh Control of Goondas Rules, 1970
- The Nagaland Security Regulation Act, 1962
- The Assam Maintenance of Public Order (Autonomous District) Act, 1952
- The Assam Preventive Detention Act, 1980
- The Assam Disturbed Areas Act, 1955
- The Armed Forces (Assam and Manipur) Special Powers Act, 1958
- The Punjab Disturbed Areas Act, 1983
- The Armed Forces (Punjab and Chandigarh) Special Powers Act, 1983
- The Bihar Maintenance of Public Order Act, 1947
- The Bihar Control of Crimes Act, 1981
- The Bombay Public Safety Act, 1947
- The Madras Suppression of Disturbances Act (1948)

Appendix 2

- The Jammu and Kashmir Public Safety Act, 1978
- The Jammu and Kashmir Disturbed Areas Act, 1990
- The Armed Forces (Jammu & Kashmir) Special Powers Act, 1990
- The Madhya Pradesh Rajya Suraksha Adhiniyam, 1990
- The Chhattisgarh Special Public Security Act, 2005
- The Anti-Hijacking Act, 1982
- The Chandigarh Disturbed Areas Act, 1983
- The Gujarat Prevention of Anti-Social Activities Act, 1985
- The Andhra Pradesh Prevention of Dangerous Activities of Bootleggers, Dacoits, Drug Offenders, Goondas, Immoral Traffic Offenders and Land Grabbers Act, 1986
- The Suppression of Unlawful Acts Against Safety of Civil Aviation Act, 1982
- The Terrorist Affected Areas (Special Courts) Act, 1984
- The National Security (Second Amendment) Ordinance, 1984
- The National Security Guard Act, 1986
- The Criminal Courts and Security Guard Courts Rules, 1987
- The Jammu and Kashmir Prevention of Illicit Traffic in Narcotic Drugs and Psychotropic Substances Act, 1988
- The Karnataka Prevention of Dangerous Activities of Bootleggers, Drug Offenders, Gamblers, Goondas, Immoral Traffic Offenders and Slum-Grabbers Act, 1985
- The Maharashtra Prevention of Communal, Anti-Social and Other Dangerous Activities Act, 1980
- The Maharashtra Prevention of Dangerous Activities of Slum Lords, Bootleggers and Drug Offenders Act, 1981
- Tamil Nadu Prevention of Dangerous Activities of Bootleggers, Drug Offenders (Forest Offenders), Goondas, Immoral Traffic Offenders and Slum-Grabbers Act, 1982
- The Chhattisgarh Special Public Security Act, 2005
- The Madhya Pradesh Special Public Security Act, 1999

Acknowledgements

The legal teams that defended me from the time of the first raid on my house through various courts to my release on bail:
- Kapil Sibal, Aparna Bhat, Mihir Desai in the Supreme Court
- Mihir Desai, Devyani Kulkarni in the Bombay High Court, Saranga in Goa
- Sudeep Pasbola, R. Satyanarayan, Arif Siddiqui, Susan Abraham, Neeraj Yadav, Larsen Furtado in the NIA Court Mumbai
- Maharukh Adenwala and Nilesh Ukey in NIA custody
- Pradeep Mandian, Anand – during the ACP interrogation in Pune
- Rohan Nahar and Parth Shah in the Pune Sessions Court

Civil society activists and organisations that stood in solidarity with me and campaigned for my release:
- Martin Macwan and his team of Navasarjan
- Subhasini Ali, Sitaram Yechuri, Dr Ashok Dhawale and all leaders and cadres of the CPM
- Dr Thol Thirumavalavan, Dr Ravi Kumar, leaders and cadres of the Viduthalai Chiruthaigal Katchi, Tamil Nadu

My alma maters and the academic institutes I worked for, which stood in solidarity with me and campaigned for my release:
- Faculty and students of the Goa Institute of Management for standing with me during my incrimination in the case
- Faculty, students, staff and alumni of all IIMs and IITs, particularly my alma maters IIM Ahmedabad and IIT Kharagpur having taken a lead to campaign for my release
- Alumni, students and faculty of Visvesvaraya National Institute of Technology, Nagpur, my alma mater
- Faculty and students of many universities in the US, UK, Spain, France, Canada and elsewhere who protested my arrest and campaigned for my release

Journalists who spoke out for me:
Nidhi Razdan, Sreenivasan Jain, Ravish Kumar, Nikhil Wagle, and many others in vernacular press and channels across India.

Organisations I was associated with: All India Forum for Right to Education (AIFRTE).

Acknowledgements

Academicians and organisations in Canada who actively campaigned for my release:

Chinmoy Bannerjee, Harindra Mohil of Hari Sharma Foundation, Canada; Jai Birdi, Chetana Association of Canada; Samir Gandesha, Simon Fraser University; Sara Schneiderman, Ajay Bharadwaj, Jessica Main and others, University of British Columbia; Raja Swamy, India Civil Watch (ICW), Canada; South Asian Network for Secularism and Democracy (Sansad), CERAS, Montreal; Democracy, Equality and Secularism in South Asia Winnipeg (DESSA); Punjabi Literary and Cultural Association, Winnipeg University, Canada; Dr Ambedkar Memorial Lecture Committee, Canada; Gurpreet Singh, *Radical Desi*, Canada.

Academicians and organisations in the United States who actively campaigned for my release:

Partha Chatterjee and Akeel Bilgrami of Columbia University; Thomas Bloom-Hansen of Stanford University; Rajeshwari Sundar Rajan and David Ludden of New York University; Barbara Harriss-White and Karin Kapadia of Oxford University; Sangeeta Kamat of the University of Massachusetts at Amherst; Elizabeth Woods of Yale University; Cornel West and Doris Sommer of Harvard University; Robin Kelley and Eric Sheppard of UCLA, Mriganka Sur of MIT, and Cindi Katz of the City University of New York and many others.

Prominent individuals, scholars, intellectuals who protested my arrest and demanded my release:

Noam Chomsky, Gayatri Spivak, Sukhadeo Thorat, Cornel West, Angela Davis, Rajmohan Gandhi, Arundhati Roy, T.M. Krishna, Kshama Sawant, Ramachandra Guha, Prakash Ambedkar, Anand Patwardhan, Robin D.G. Kelley, Justice Kolse-Patil, Partha Chatterjee, Arjun Appadurai, Akeel Bilgrami, Jean Dreze, Rajeshwari Sunder Rajan, Justice P.B. Sawant, Chandra Talpade Mohanty, Surinder Jodhka, V. Geetha, Manoranjan Mohanty, Dileep Menon, Aparna Sen, Zoya Hasan, Shabnam Hashmi, Sudipta Kaviraj, Ania Loomba, Suvir Kaul, Bruce Robbins, Nandini Sundar, Narendra Subramanian, Susie Tharu, John Dayal, Ram Puniyani, S. Anandhi, Alf Gunvald Nilsen, Shamshul Islam, Subir Sinha, Geeta Kapur, Priyamvada Gopal, Aakash Rathore, Ritty Lukose, Christophe Jaffrelot, Pratap Bhanu Mehta, Aijaz Ahmad, David Mosse, Barbara Harriss-White, Sushruth Jadhav, Prabhat Patnaik, Utsa Patnaik, Neera Chandoke, Karin Kapadia, S.V. Rajadurai, Sankalp Meshram, Jairus Banaji,

Swapan Chakravorty, Uma Chakravarti, Anand Chakravarti, Anil Sadgopal, Amit Bhaduri, Vinay Lal, Amit Chaudhury, Achin Vanaik, Jan Myrdal, Nandita Haksar, Niraja Jayal, Anjali Arondekar, Shailaja Paik, Meena Dhanda, Sudesh Ghoderao, Lawrence Simon, Gary Tartakov, Bill Fletcher, Joseph Tharamangalam, Christopher Queen, Sujata Patel, Nancy Holmstrom, Dilip Simeon, M.A. Baby, Roger Jeffrey, Kumkum Roy, Pritam Singh, G.N. Devy, Feroze Mithiborwala, Cedric Prakash, Sangayya Hiremath, K. Stalin, Cynthia Mckinney, John Harriss, Anil Sadgopal, Sudesh Ghoderao, Narendra Nayak, G. Haragopal, Jagmohan Singh, Madhu Prasad, Nandita Narain, Ganesh Devy, Chaman Lal, K. Chakradhar Rao, Manoranjan Mohanty, Meena Kandasamy, Alpa Shah, Teesta Setalwad, Rana Ayyub, Jignesh Mevani, Sagarika Ghosh, Kunal Kamra, Kapil Patil, Yogendra Yadav, Vijay Prashad, Sudhanva Deshpande, Kavita Krishnan, Kavita Shrivatsava, and many others.

Kapil Patil, Yeshu Patil, Prakash Ambedkar, Gurbir Singh, and friends who saw me off at NIA Mumbai and received me at the Taloja Central prison.

All activists' groups in India and abroad who stood in solidarity with me and my co-accused.

My family who stood, struggled and suffered along with me – Rama, my wife; Prachi and Rashmi, my daughters; Vinayak (son-in-law); my mother for her forbearance; and my brother Kishor and sister Vishakka for taking care of her.

My publisher Chirag Thakkar for believing in the book.

Notes

Prologue

1. Jacob Koshy, 'WHO Estimates 4.7 Million COVID-19-Linked Deaths in India', *The Hindu*, 6 May 2022, https://www.thehindu.com/sci-tech/health/who-estimates-47-million-covid-linked-deaths-in-india-10-times-official-count/article65385669.ece, accessed 23 March 2025.

Chapter 1 Portent of the Peril

1. Mridula Chari, Abhishek Dey and Shreya Roy Chowdhury, '13 Letters Leaked by Pune Police Show Why It's Hard to Believe Claims about a Maoist Conspiracy', Scroll.in, 9 September 2018, https://scroll.in/article/893686/13-letters-leaked-by-pune-police-show-why-it-s-hard-to-believe-claims-about-a-maoist-conspiracy, accessed 18 March 2025.
2. Ibid.
3. Ibid.
4. Ibid.
5. Scroll Staff, 'If the Accused Have Set Up an Anti-Fascist Front, They're, in Fact, Acting in Defence of Democracy', Scroll.in, 30 August 2018, https://scroll.in/article/892553/if-the-accused-have-set-up-an-anti-fascist-front-theyre-in-fact-acting-in-defence-of-democracy, accessed 23 March 2025.
6. *Romila Thapar vs Union of India*, 28 September 2018, https://indiankanoon.org/doc/52834611/?type=print, accessed 23 March 2025.

Chapter 2 Hope and Dejection

1. 'Bhima Koregaon Violence: "Why Did You Hold Press Conference when Matter Is Sub-Judice?", Bombay HC Lashes Out at Maharashtra Police', India Tv News, 3 September 2018, https://www.indiatvnews.com/news/india-bhima-koregaon-violence-why-did-you-hold-press-conference-when-matter-is-sub-judice-bombay-hc-lashes-out-at-maharashtra-police-461238, accessed 23 March 2025.
2. '"Must be More Responsible": Supreme Court Pulls up Pune Police over Press Meet on Arrests of Activists', News18, 6 September 2018, https://www.news18.com/news/india/must-be-more-responsible-supreme-court-pulls-up-pune-police-over-press-meet-on-arrests-of-activists-1869597.html, accessed 23 March 2025.
3. '"Police Should Be More Responsible": SC on Bhima Koregaon Case', The Quint, 6 September 2018, https://www.thequint.com/news/india/

supreme-court-on-maharashtra-police-bhima-koregaon#read-more, accessed 23 March 2025.
4. Ibid.
5. Chandan Haygunde and Sushant Kulkarni, 'Retired Supreme Court Justice Slams Pune Police for Turning Conversation into Chargesheet Statement', *Indian Express*, 7 December 2018, https://indianexpress.com/article/cities/pune/retired-supreme-court-justice-slams-pune-police-for-turning-conversation-into-chargesheet-statement-5482274/, accessed 23 March 2025.
6. Yogesh Joshi, 'ACP, Who Probed Elgar Parishad Case, Awarded by Union Home Ministry', *Hindustan Times*, 12 August 2020, https://www.hindustantimes.com/pune-news/acp-who-probed-elgar-parishad-case-awarded-by-union-home-ministry/story m4DQR3B6vI5wdoH0lKc1yJ.html, accessed 23 March 2025.
7. Srishti Deoras, 'AIM Data Science Education Ranking 2020: Top Full-Time PG Programmes In India', Analytics India Magazine, 5 November 2020, https://analyticsindiamag.com/ai-insights-analysis/aim-data-science-education-ranking-2020-top-full-time-pg-programmes-in-india/, accessed 23 March 2025.
8. Saurabh Vaktania, 'Non-bailable Warrant Issued against Former Mumbai Top Cop Param Bir Singh in Extortion Case', *India Today*, updated 28 October 2021, https://www.indiatoday.in/india/story/non-bailable-warrant-issued-against-former-mumbai-police-commissioner-param-bir-singh-in-extortion-case-1870705-2021-10-28, accessed 23 March 2025.
9. Priyanka Kakodkar, 'Maharashtra Govt Begins Process to Declare Param Bir Singh "Absconder"', *Times of India*, updated 26 October 2021, https://www.indiatoday.in/india/story/non-bailable-warrant-issued-against-former-mumbai-police-commissioner-param-bir-singh-in-extortion-case-1870705-2021-10-28, accessed 23 March 2025.
10. 'Mumbai Court Declares IPS Officer Param Bir Singh "Proclaimed Offender" in Extortion Case', *The Hindu*, updated 17 November 2021, https://www.thehindu.com/news/cities/mumbai/mumbai-court-declares-ips-officer-param-bir-singh-proclaimed-offender-in-extortion-case/article37541337.ece, accessed 23 March 2025.
11. Kamlesh Damodar Sutar, 'Param Bir Singh Faces Suspension for Violation of Service Rules, Action Likely in a Week: Sources', *India Today*, updated 26 November 2021, https://www.indiatoday.in/india/story/non-bailable-warrant-param-bir-singh-scrapped-sachin-vaze-extortion-1881174-2021-11-26, accessed 23 March 2025.
12. Yogesh Naik, 'Former Mumbai Top Cop Param Bir Singh Suspended', *Indian Express*, 3 December 2021, https://indianexpress.com/article/cities/mumbai/former-mumbai-top-cop-param-bir-singh-suspended-7652707/, accessed 5 December 2021.

13. Swati Deshpande, 'Param Bir Singh Has the Last Laugh, Maharashtra Revokes Ex-Top Cop's Suspension', *Times of India*, 13 May 2023, https://timesofindia.indiatimes.com/city/mumbai/state-drops-charges-revokes-suspension-of-ex-cp-param-bir/articleshow/100196267.cms, http://timesofindia.indiatimes.com/articleshow/100196267.cms?utm_source=contentofinterest&utm_medium=text&utm_campaign=cppst, accessed 23 March 2025.
14. Anandita Mishra and Tanmay Singh, 'Pegasus Investigation Report to Remain in Sealed Cover Despite Containing Evidence That 5 Phones Had Malware', Internet Freedom Foundation, 26 August 2022, https://internetfreedom.in/pegasus-investigation-report-to-remain-in-sealed-cover-even-though-it-contains-evidence-that-5-phones-had-malware/, accessed 23 March 2025.
15. Kanu Sarda, 'Explained: What Is Sealed Cover Method Used in Courts?', *India Today*, 2 June 2022, https://www.indiatoday.in/law/story/explained-sealed-cover-method-courts-malayalam-news-channel-media-one-supreme-court-1957628-2022-06-02, accessed 23 March 2025.
16. Anand Teltumbde, 'I Need Your Support at Sanhati', Sanhati, 17 January 2019.
17. Martin Niemöller: 'First They Came. . .', *Holocaust Encyclopedia*.

Chapter 3 Brush with Arrest

1. Purva Chitnis, 'Court Calls Arrest of Activist Accused in Koregaon Bhima Case "Illegal"', NDTV, https://www.ndtv.com/india-news/bhima-koregaon-police-arrest-activist-anand-teltumbde-from-mumbai-1987157, accessed 23 March 2025.

Chapter 4 Protests and Support

1. 'IITs and IIM Ahmedabad Fraternity Stand with "Role Model" Anand Teltumbde', *The Caravan*, 6 April 2020, https://caravanmagazine.in/noticeboard/iit-iim-fraternity-stand-with-anand-teltumbde, accessed 23 March 2025.
2. The Wire Staff, 'Faculty, Students at IIMs, IIT Condemn "False" Charges against Anand Teltumbde', The Wire, 29 January 2019, https://thewire.in/rights/faculty-students-and-iims-iit-condemn-false-charges-against-anandteltumbde, accessed 23 March 2025.
3. Ibid.
4. Nivedita Menon, 'Statement against Police Action on Professor Anand Teltumbde and Others– Students, Faculty and Alumni of IIT Kharagpur', Kafila, 2 September 2018, https://kafila.online/2018/09/02/statement-against-police-action-on-prof-anand-teltumbde-and-others-students-faculty-and-alumni-of-iit-kharagpur/, accessed 23 March 2025.

5 Gauri Malkarnekar, 'Goa Institute of Management Stands by Its Big Data Analytics Head', *Times of India*, 3 February 2019, https://timesofindia.indiatimes.com/city/mumbai/goa-institute-of-mgmt-stands-by-its-big-data-analytics-head/articleshow/67811077.cms, accessed 23 March 2025.

6 Gauri Malkarnekar, 'GIM Introduces Country's First Programme in Big Data Analytics', 29 May 2018, *Times of India*, https://timesofindia.indiatimes.com/city/goa/gims-introduces-countrys-first-programme-in-big-data-analytics/articleshow/64310930.cms, accessed 23 March 2025.

7 Srishti Deoras, 'Top 10 Full Time Data Science Courses in India – Ranking 2018', Analytics India Magazine, 15 November 2018, https://analyticsindiamag.com/ai-features/top-10-full-time-data-science-courses-in-india-ranking-2018/, accessed 23 March 2025.

8 Sunil Ramanand, *Cops in a Quagmire* (Pune: Vishwakarma Publications, 2020).

9 Anand Teltumbde, 'Cruel, Colonial and "High on Theatrics": Why India's Police Are the Way They Are', The Wire, 20 July 2024, https://thewire.in/books/india-police-quagmire-book-sunil-ramanand, accessed 23 March 2025.

10 Ramanand, *Cops in a Quagmire*, 274.

11 Spoorthidhama, https://spoorthidhama.com/ambedkar-habba/, accessed 23 March 2025.

Chapter 5 Theatre of the Absurd

1 'Dubious Decision: On NIA Takeover of Bhima Koregaon Case', *The Hindu*, updated 27 January 2022, https://www.thehindu.com/opinion/editorial/dubious-decision-the-hindu-editorial-on-nia-taking-over-bhima-koregaon-case-probe/article30659880.ece, accessed 23 March 2025.

2 'Activists' Arrest in Elgar Parishad Case Wrong, Form SIT to Probe Police Action: Sharad Pawar', *Economic Times*, updated 21 December 2019, https://economictimes.indiatimes.com/news/politics-and-nation/activists-arrest-in-elgar parishad-case-wrong-form-sit-to-probe-police-action-sharad pawar/articleshow/72914706.cms?from=mdr, accessed 23 March 2025.

3 'Bhima Koregaon Violence Was Pre-Planned, Says Maharashtra Minister Nawab Malik', *New Indian Express*, updated 24 February 2020, https://www.newindianexpress.com/nation/2020/Feb/24/bhima-koregaon-violence-was-pre-planned-says-maharashtra-minister-nawab-malik-2107767.html, accessed 23 March 2025.

4 'Will Ask Chief Minister to Form SIT to Investigate Bhima Koregaon Case Properly: NCP Chief Sharad Pawar', ANI, 21 December 2019, https://www.aninews.in/news/national/general-news/will-ask-chief-minister-to-form-sit-to-investigate-bhima-koregoan-case-

properly-ncp-chief-sharad-pawar20191221154036/, accessed 23 March 2025.
5. 'Sharad Pawar Seeks SIT Probe in Bhima Koregaon Cases, Writes to Uddhav', *Indian Express*, updated 24 January 2020, https://indianexpress.com/article/india/sharad-pawar-writes-to-uddhav-thackeray-seeks-sit-probe-in-bhima-koregaon-cases-6233248/, accessed 23 March 2025.
6. 'Central Agency NIA Takes Over Koregaon-Bhima Case, Maharashtra Furious', NDTV, 24 January 2020, https://www.ndtv.com/india-news/central-agency-nia-takes-over-koregaon-bhima-case-maharashtra-furious-2169359, accessed 23 March 2025.
7. Vijaita Singh, 'Bhima-Koregaon Case Transferred to NIA, Confirms Home Ministry', *The Hindu*, 25 January 2020, https://www.thehindu.com/news/national/bhima-koregaon-case-transferred-to-nia-confirms-home-ministry/article30651042.ece, accessed 23 March 2025.
8. 'Centre Transferred Bhima Koregaon Probe to NIA Without State Consent: Maha Home Minister', ThePrint, 25 January 2020, https://theprint.in/india/centre-transfers-bhima-koregaon-probe-to-nia-without-state-consent/354376/, accessed 23 March 2025.
9. '"Centre Fears . . .": Sharad Pawar on NIA Taking Koregaon-Bhima Case', NDTV, 25 January 2020, https://www.ndtv.com/india-news/bhima-koregaon-case-taken-over-by-nia-centre-fears-exposure-says-sharad-pawar-rahul-gandhi-criticise-2169654, accessed 23 March 2025.
10. Shiv Sena's ambivalence was reflected in its support of the initial arrests as a threat to national security but later raising doubts about the police's justification for the arrests. See 'Shiv Sena Questions Arrests of Five Activists', *National Herald*, 3 September 2018, https://www.nationalheraldindia.com/india/shiv-sena-questions-arrests-of-five-activists, accessed 23 March 2025.
11. Shubhangi Khapre and Sadaf Modak, 'Sharad Pawar Ping Pong and Politics of Bhima Koregaon Violence Probe', *Indian Express*, 7 May 2022, https://indianexpress.com/article/cities/mumbai/sharad-pawar-ping-pong-and-politics-of-bhima-koregaon-violence-probe-7904960/, accessed 23 March 2025.
12. Radhika Ramaswamy, 'Maharashtra Govt Opposes Transfer of Elgar Parishad Case to NIA Court, Says Pune Police Has Ample Proof', News18, updated 7 February 2020, https://www.news18.com/news/india/maharashtra-govt-opposes-transfer-of-elgar-parishad-case-to-nia-court-says-pune-police-has-ample-proof-2491503.html, accessed 23 March 2025.
13. Ibid.

CHAPTER 6 SURRENDER DURING THE PANDEMIC

1. Towards the end of the year 2019, a new type of coronavirus called Severe Acute Respiratory Syndrome Coronavirus 2 (SARS-CoV-2) was

identified as causing COVID-19. By March 2020, the WHO declared this COVID-19 outbreak as a pandemic. 'Naming the coronavirus disease (COVID-19) and the virus that causes it', World Health Organisation, https://www.who.int/emergencies/diseases/novel-coronavirus-2019/technical-guidance/naming-the-coronavirus-disease-(covid-2019)-and-the-virus-that-causes-it, accessed 23 March 2025.
2. Nidhi Jacob, 'Data Proves Uttarakhand Top Cops Wrong, Kumbh Was a "Super Spreader"', FactChecker, 4 June 2021, https://www.factchecker.in/fact-check/data-proves-uttarakhand-top-cops-wrong-kumbh-mela-was-a-super-spreadercovid-19-753292, accessed 23 March 2025.
3. Ibid.
4. 'Over 5,000 Test Covid19 Positive at Kumbh Mela', Northeast Now, 17 April 2021, https://nenow.in/top-news/over-5000-test-covid19-positive-at-kumbh-pm-modi-appeals-to-keep-kumbh-mela-symbolic.html, accessed 23 March 2025.
5. 'Ahead of His Arrest, Activist Anand Teltumbde Writes an Open Letter', *Mumbai Mirror*, updated 13 April 2020, https://mumbaimirror.indiatimes.com/mumbai/other/ahead-of-his-arrest-activist-anand-teltumbdes-Writes-an-Open-Letter-to-the-People-of-india/articleshow/75121830.cms; 'Elgar Parishad Case: Anand Teltumbde Writes an Open Letter to People of India before NIA Arrest; Notable Parts You Don't Want to Miss', *New Indian Express*, 15 April 2020, https://www.newindianexpress.com/galleries/nation/2020/Apr/15/elgar-parishad-case-anand-teltumbde-writes-an-open-letter-to-people-of-india-before-nia-arrest-not-102833.html, accessed 23 March 2025.

Chapter 8 Black Flag over Rajgruha

1. 'Maharashtra: VBA Chief Calls Teltumbde Arrest Shocking, Hoists Black Flag at Rajgruha', *Indian Express*, updated 15 April 2020, https://indianexpress.com/article/cities/mumbai/maharashtra-vba-chief-calls-teltumbde-arrest-shocking-hoists-black-flag-at-rajgruha-6363029/, accessed 23 March 2025.
2. As per the National Crime Research Bureau's *Crime in India 2022* report, there have been a total of 954 murders and 4,241 rapes of Dalit (SC) women, which works out to 2.61 murders and 11.61 rapes per day. See Table 7A.2: https://www.ncrb.gov.in/uploads/nationalcrimerecordsbureau/custom/1702027966TABLE7A2.pdf, accessed 23 March 2025.
3. 'Maharashtra: Dalit Anger Leaves 4 Dead, 60 Injured', Rediff.com, 30 November 2006.
4. Bhimrao Ramji Ambedkar, 'Ranade, Gandhi, and Jinnah', https://franpritchett.com/00ambedkar/txt_ambedkar_ranade.html.
5. 'Maharashtra: VBA Chief Calls Teltumbde Arrest Shocking, Hoists Black Flag at Rajgruha', *Indian Express*, accessed 23 March 2025.

6. 'Prakash Ambedkar, Family Express Concern over Pune Police Hounding Anand Teltumbde', The Wire, 1 March 2020, https://thewire.in/politics/prakash-ambedkar-anand-teltumbe, accessed 23 March 2025.

CHAPTER 10 AND I SURVIVED COVID-19

1. Vijay Kumar Yadav, 'Varavara Rao Released from Hospital after Covid Treatment; Back in Jail', *Hindustan Times*, 28 August 2022, https://www.hindustantimes.com/india-news/varavara-rao-released-from-hospital-after-covid-treatment-back-in-jail/story-OpdlkcToUZ45sOcHRDmbQI.html, accessed 23 March 2025.
2. 'Elgaar Parishad case: Varavara Rao Discharged from Hospital, Sent Back to Taloja Jail in Navi Mumbai', *Indian Express*, 28 August 2022, https://indianexpress.com/article/india/elgaar-parishad-case-varavara-rao-discharged-from-hospital-sent-back-to-jail-6572761/, accessed 23 March 2025.
3. Ibid.
4. Vijay Kumar Yadav, 'Varavara Rao Released from Hospital after Covid Treatment; Back in Jail', *Hindustan Times*, 28 August 2022.
5. 'Give Report on Varavara Rao's Health in 2 Weeks', *Hindustan Times*, 18 July 2020, https://www.hindustantimes.com/mumbai-news/give-report-on-varavara-rao-s-health-in-2-weeks/story-g4VYZk88ZklJNZ497abDPP.html, accessed 23 March 2025.
6. Ibid.
7. 'Varavara Rao Shifted to Nanavati Hospital post NHRC Notice to Government', *Indian Express*, 20 July 2020, https://indianexpress.com/article/india/varavara-rao-shifted-to-nanavati-hospital-post-nhrc-notice-to-government-6513974/, accessed 23 March 2025.
8. 'Maharashtra Govt Agrees to Shift Jailed Poet Varavara Rao to Nanavati Hospital', BW Legal World, 19 November 2020, https://bwlegalworld.com/article/maharashtra-govt-agrees-to-shift-jailed-poet-varavara-rao-to-nanavati-hospital-344171, accessed 23 March 2025.
9. Sharmeen Hakim, 'Bombay High Court Grants Varavara Rao Bail for 6 Months on Medical Grounds in Bhima-Koregaon Case', Live Law, 22 February 2021, https://www.livelaw.in/top-stories/bombay-high-court-grants-varavara-rao-bail-for-6-months-on-medical-grounds-in-bhima-koregaon-case-170205, accessed 23 March 2025.

CHAPTER 11 WE LOST STAN

1. Swati Deshpande, 'Elgar Case: Bombay HC Extends Stan Swamy's Hospitalization at Holy Family in Bandra', *Times of India*, 17 June 2021, https://timesofindia.indiatimes.com/city/mumbai/

elgar-case-hc-extends-activist-stan-swamys-stay-at-private-hospital-till-july-5/articleshow/83605441.cms, accessed 23 March 2025.

2. 'Father Stan Swamy's Death Highlights the Inhumanity of India's Justice System', *The Caravan*, 6 July 2021; PTI, 'Parkinson Patient Stan Swamy's Wait for Straw, Sipper Gets Longer as NIA Denies Confiscating Them', *Indian Express*, 26 November 2020, https://indianexpress.com/article/cities/mumbai/stan-swamys-wait-for-straw-and-sipper-gets-longer-also-seeks-bail-7069538/, accessed 23 March 2025.

3. Sadaf Modak, 'Stan Swamy, 83, Waits as the Buck Is Passed on His Sipper and Straw', *Indian Express*, 28 November 2020, https://indianexpress.com/article/india/stan-swamy-sipper-and-straw-nia-uapa-elgar-parishad-7071253/, accessed 23 March 2025.

4. 'Stan Swamy Finally Given Straw, Sipper by Jail Authorities', *Telegraph*, 4 December 2020, https://www.telegraphindia.com/india/stan-swamy-finally-given-straw-sipper-by-jail-authorities/cid/1799515, accessed 23 March 2025.

5. Alok Pandey, '"Government Should Apologise": Doctor Jailed over UP Child Deaths Cleared', NDTV, 28 September 2019, https://www.ndtv.com/india-news/gorakhpur-child-deaths-dr-kafeel-khan-jailed-for-63-child-deaths-in-hospital-cleared-of-charges-2108033, accessed 23 March 2025.

6. 'WHO Says Millions of Covid Deaths Went Unreported in India; Centre Questions Methodology', *Times of India*, 5 May 2022, https://timesofindia.indiatimes.com/india/who-says-millions-of-covid-deaths-went-unreported-in-india-centre-strongly-objects-methodology-key-points/articleshow/91349479.cms, accessed 23 March 2025; 'The Modi Government's Authoritarian Response to the Pandemic', *The Caravan*, 1 June 2022.

7. Sharmeen Hakim, '"Victimized for Demanding Their Rights as Prisoners": Kin of Bhima-Koregaon Move Bombay High Court against Prison Transfer Orders', Live Law, 3 August 2021, https://www.livelaw.in/top-stories/bombay-high-court-kin-of-bhima-koregaon-elgar-parishad-accused-challenge-prison-transfer-orders-citing-victimization-178766, accessed 23 March 2025.

8. 'How Stan Swamy Exposed India's UAPA Problem', Scroll.in, 7 July 2021.

9. 'Stan Takes a Stand', Indian Cultural Forum, 25 May 2021, https://indianculturalforum.in/2021/05/25/stan-takes-a-stand/, accessed 23 March 2025.

10. 'Father Stan Swamy, Arrested in Bhima Koregaon Case, Dies at 84', The Wire, 5 July 2021.

11. 'Mumbai: 84-Year-Old Fr Stan Swamy Tests Positive for Covid, in ICU', *Times of India*, 31 May 2021, https://timesofindia.indiatimes.com/city/mumbai/

mumbai-84-year-old-fr-stan-tests-positive-for-covid-in-icu/articleshow/83098636.cms, accessed 23 March 2025.
12. 'Stan Swamy: India Outrage over Death of Jailed Activist', BBC News, 7 July 2021, https://www.bbc.com/news/world-asia-india-57718361, accessed 23 March 2025.
13. Stan Swamy, United States Commission on International Religious Freedom, https://www.uscirf.gov/religious-prisoners-conscience/forb-victims-database/stan-swamy, accessed 23 March 2025.
14. 'Fr. Swamy's Death Will "Remain a Stain" on India's Human Rights Record: U.N. Expert Mary Lawlor', *The Hindu*, 9 July 2021; 'UN Expert: Stan Swamy Jail Death a "Stain" on India's Rights Record', Al Jazeera, 8 July 2021.
15. Gokul Rajendran, 'Native Village Viragalur Mourns Fr Stan Swamy', *Times of India* 6 July 2021, http://timesofindia.indiatimes.com/articleshow/84155460.cms?utm_source=contentofinterest&utm_medium=text&utm_campaign=cppst, accessed 23 March 2025.

Chapter 12 The Killing of My Brother

1. D. Roy, 'The Women Who Killed a Rapist in an Indian Courtroom', *Guardian*, 25 November 2017, https://www.theguardian.com/world/2017/nov/25/the-women-who-killed-a-rapist-in-an-indian-courtroom, accessed 23 March 2025.
2. S. Biswas, 'How Indian Women Took Revenge on Rapist', BBC News, 11 August 2004, http://news.bbc.co.uk/2/hi/south_asia/3559160.stm, accessed 23 March 2025.
3. A. Choudhary, 'All Accused in 2004 Rape Revenge Case Acquitted', *Times of India*, 6 January 2016, https://timesofindia.indiatimes.com, accessed 23 March 2025.
4. 'Indian Women Take Revenge on Rapist', BBC News, 10 August 2004, http://news.bbc.co.uk/2/hi/south_asia/3558872.stm, accessed 23 March 2025.
5. D. Roy, 'The Women Who Killed a Rapist in an Indian Courtroom', *Guardian*, 25 November 2017, accessed 23 March 2025.
6. VICE, (2017). *Death of a Rapist* (Documentary). Available at: https://video.vice.com/en_us/video/death-of-a-rapist/58efeb6741f7e27d73b1df85, accessed 23 March 2025.

Chapter 14 A Broken System

1. *Madukar Bhagwan Jambhale vs State of Maharashtra* (1987, Mh. L. J.), para 11.
2. Ibid., para 13.
3. Ibid., para 17A.
4. AIR 1966 SC 424.

5. *Devangana Kalita vs Delhi Police*, WP (Crl) 898/2020 decided on 27.07.2020, para 25.
6. Confidential letters no. 91-A/2021 dated 30.06.2021, no. 113/2021 dated 28.07.2021 and no. 111/2021 dated 27.07.2021.
7. Sonam Saigal, '10 Elgaar Parishad Accused Allege "Political Censorship" by Jail Authorities', *The Hindu*, 22 November 2021, https://www.thehindu.com/news/national/10-elghar-parishad-accused-allege-taloja-superintendent-scans-and-saves-their-letters/article61425141.ece, accessed 23 March 2025.
8. Kay Dodhiya, 'Dr Anand Teltumbde Writing Suspicious Content in Letters: NIA Affidavit in HC', *Hindustan Times*, 22 October 2021, https://www.hindustantimes.com/cities/mumbai-news/dr-anand-teltumbde-writing-suspicious-content-in-letters-nia-affidavit-in-hc-101634916102045.html, accessed 23 March 2025.
9. Anand Teltumbde, 'Economic Goals Cannot Disavow Constitutional Vision: Anand Teltumbde Writes from Prison', *The Caravan*, 10 March 2021, https://caravanmagazine.in/economy/anand-teltumbde-writes-from-prison-economy-cannot-divorce-constitution, accessed 23 March 2025.
10. Hamza Lakdawala, 'Bhima Koregaon: Bombay HC Issues Notice on Petition by Rama Anand Teltumbde, Susan Abraham Gonsalves against Jail Authorities Withholding Letters to and from Their Jailed Husbands', The Leaflet, 3 July 2021, https://theleaflet.in/bhima-koregaon-bombay-hc-issues-notice-on-petition-by-rama-anand-teltumbde-susan-abraham-gonsalves-against-jail-authorities-withholding-letters-to-and-from-their-jailed-husbands/, accessed 23 March 2025.

Chapter 15 And Bhola Hanged Himself

1. Stewart Gordon, *The Marathas 1600–1818* (Cambridge University Press, 2007), 15–16.
2. Abdul Wahid Shaikh, *Begunah Qaidi: Aatankwaad Ke Jhootey Muqaddmon Mein Phasaaye Gaye Muslim Nau Jawanon Ki Daastaan*. It details how after this shocking terror attack, the police rounded up Muslim youth, tortured them to get them to sign confession statements in police custody and put them in jails. Wahid is the only one out of the thirteen arrested who got acquitted by a special court in 2015 after spending a decade in prison. The book sheds light on the flaws in the Indian criminal justice system, particularly concerning wrongful arrests, media trials and the struggles of Muslims falsely implicated in terrorism cases.

Chapter 16 The Proximity of Captivity

1. Howard Zinn, *You Can't Be Neutral on a Moving Train: A Personal History of Our Times* (Beacon Press, 1994), 173.

2. Bureau of Police Research and Development, *Model Prison Manual* (Ministry of Home Affairs, Government of India), 2.14.2, https://www.mha.gov.in/sites/default/files/2022-12/ModelPrisonMan2003_14112022%5B1%5D.pdf, accessed 23 March 2025.
3. 'Air Hostesses Used to Visit Subrata Roy in Jail, I Informed Kejriwal: Former Tihar Official's Explosive Claim', *Times of India*, 25 February 2025, https://timesofindia.indiatimes.com/india/air-hostesses-used-to-visit-subrata-roy-in-jail-i-informed-kejriwal-former-tihar-officials-explosive-claim/articleshow/118562050.cms, accessed 23 March 2025.
4. Rutuja Gaidhani, 'Yes Bank Loan Case: Court Asks St George's Hospital to Decide Whether Avinash Bhosale Needs Further Hospitalisation', *Hindustan Times*, 5 May 2024, https://www.hindustantimes.com/cities/mumbai-news/yes-bank-loan-case-court-asks-st-george-s-hospital-to-decide-whether-avinash-bhosale-needs-further-hospitalisation-101714850212599.html, accessed 23 March 2025.
5. Ibid.
6. Ibid.
7. Ibid.

Chapter 17 Jai Bhim Syndrome

1. Constituent Assembly Debates, Vol. 11, Constitution of India, https://www.constitutionofindia.net/constituent-assembly-debate/volume-11/, accessed 23 March 2025.

Chapter 18 Thou Shalt Not Speak

1. Urvi Mahajani, 'Can't Allow Phone Call Access to Jailed Activist Navalakha as He Faces Terrorism Charges: Maharashtra Govt Tells HC', Free Press Journal, 20 July 2022, https://www.freepressjournal.in/legal/cant-allow-phone-call-access-to-jailed-activist-navlakha-as-he-faces-terrorism-charges-maharashtra-govt-tells-hc, accessed 25 June 2025.
2. Sonam Saigal, 'Bhima Koregaon Accused Calls off Hunger Strike', *The Hindu*, updated 28 May 2022, https://www.thehindu.com/news/cities/mumbai/bhima-koregaon-accused-calls-off-hunger-strike/article65467729.ece, accessed 23 March 2025.

Chapter 19 POCSO's Dalit Victims

1. 'The Decision on LGBTQ+ in India', Legal Service India, https://www.legalserviceindia.com/legal/article-15537-the-decision-on-lgbtq-in-india.html, accessed 25 June 2025.

Chapter 20 Abolish Prisons?

1. This study examined juvenile offenders in Michigan and found that longer incarceration periods did not reduce recidivism and, in some cases, led to worse outcomes. T.A. Loughran et al., 'Estimating a Dose-Response Relationship Between Length of Stay and Future Recidivism in Serious Juvenile Offenders', *Criminology* 47, no. 3 (2009): 699–740.
2. A meta-analysis concluding that incarceration generally has a null or criminogenic effect (increases reoffending) compared to community-based sanctions. Daniel S. Nagin et al., 'Imprisonment and Reoffending', *Crime and Justice* 38, no. 1(2009): 15–200.
3. The study found that prison sentences had no significant deterrent effect and sometimes increased recidivism compared to probation. William D. Bales and Alex R. Piquero, 'Assessing the Impact of Imprisonment on Recidivism', *Journal of Experimental Criminology* 8, no. 1 (2011): 71–101.
4. A systematic review showing that incarceration does not reduce recidivism and may worsen it for low-risk offenders. Patrice Villettaz et al., 'The Effects of Custodial vs. Non-Custodial Sentences on Re-offending: A Systematic Review', *Campbell Systematic Reviews* 11, no. 1 (2015).
5. The study found that longer prison sentences in Italy did not reduce recidivism and even increased it for some offenders. Francesco Drago, 'The Deterrent Effects of Prison: Evidence from a Natural Experiment', *Journal of Political Economy* 117, no. 2 (2009): 257–280.
6. It concluded that increasing incarceration length does not deter crime and may increase recidivism. 'Five Things About Deterrence', *National Institute of Justice*, 5 June 2016, https://nij.ojp.gov/topics/articles/five-things-about-deterrence.
7. 'More Imprisonment Does Not Reduce State Drug Problems', *PEW*, 8 March 2018, https://www.pewtrusts.org/en/research-and-analysis/reports/2018/03/more-imprisonment-does-not-reduce-state-drug-problems.
8. B. Johnsen & P. K. Granheim, 'Prison Size and Recidivism Rates: The Role of Prison Climate', *Prison Journal* 92, no. 1 (2012): 27–46.
   Norway is known for its progressive, humane prison system that emphasises rehabilitation over punishment, often incorporating nature and outdoor activities.
9. S. Klein, 'The Menendez Brothers' Prison Garden: Can Horticulture Reform Inmates?' *Los Angeles Magazine*, 2018.
   Lyle and Erik Menendez, incarcerated at Mule Creek State Prison, initiated a garden and beautification project that improved inmate morale and reduced disciplinary issues.

10   India's prisons house over 554,000 inmates (5.54 lakh) across 1,401 facilities, with 77.1 per cent being undertrial prisoners (awaiting trial). Many face prolonged detention due to case backlogs. National Crime Records Bureau (NCRB), Prison Statistics India (Ministry of Home Affairs, Government of India, 2022), https://www.ncrb.gov.in/en/prison-statistics-india, accessed 23 March 2025.
11   'What Is Prison Abolition?', Critical Resistance (n.d.), https://criticalresistance.org, accessed 23 March 2025.
12   Natalie Moore, 'Finland's Open Prisons', Pulitzer Centre, https://pulitzercenter.org/projects/finlands-open-prisons, accessed 23 March 2025.
13   Astrid Prange de Oliveira, 'The Story Behind the Netherlands' Empty Prisons', DW, 20 October 2024, https://www.dw.com/en/the-story-behind-the-netherlands-empty-prisons/a-70544397, accessed 23 March 2025.
14   David Downes, 'Visions of Penal Control in the Netherlands', *Crime and Justice in Historical Perspective* 36 (2007): 93.
15   Ibid.
16   Meagan Denny, 'Norway's Prison System: Investigating Recidivism and Reintegration,' *Bridges: A Journal of Student Research* 10, no. 10 (2016), https://digitalcommons.coastal.edu/bridges/vol10/iss10/2, accessed 23 March 2025.
17   'What We Can Learn from Norway's Prison System: Rehabilitation & Recidivism', First Step Alliance, 1 May 2024, https://www.firststepalliance.org/post/norway-prison-system-lessons, accessed 23 March 2025.
18   Ibid.
19   M. Killias et al., 'Electronic Monitoring and Recidivism: A Meta-Analysis', *Crime & Delinquency* 56, no. 1 (2010): 123–146.
20   I. Wennerberg, *The Development and Use of Electronic Monitoring in Sweden in Electronically Monitored Punishment: International and Critical Perspectives*, eds M. Nellis et al. (Routledge, 2012), 75–92.
21   Ibid.
22   P. Smith and T. Ugelvik, *Prisons and Penal Policy in Scandinavia: The Exceptionalism Debate* (Oxford University Press, 2017).
23   Ibid.
24   'Prison and Penal Reform: The Need for Change', United Nations Office on Drugs and Crime, https://www.unodc.org/unodc/en/justice-and-prison-reform/prison-reform-and-alternatives-to-imprisonment.html, accessed 23 March 2025.
25   Helmut Kury, 'Rehabilitation in Prison German Experiences and What Can Be Done Better', *Romanian Journal of Sociological Studies*, no. 1 (2018): 19–36, https://journalofsociology.ro/wp-content/uploads/2018/09/04-Helmut.pdf, accessed 23 March 2025.

26. F. Dünkel et al., 'Resocialisation and Rehabilitation: European Approaches' in *Crime Policy in Europe: Good Practices and Promising Examples* (Routledge, 2010).
27. C.E. Hughes and A. Stevens, 'What Can We Learn from the Portuguese Decriminalization of Illicit Drugs?', *British Journal of Criminology* 50, no. 6 (2010): 999–1022.
28. Ibid.
29. M.F. Aebi and N. Delgrande, *Council of Europe Annual Penal Statistics: SPACE I – Prison Populations Survey 2014* (Strasbourg: Council of Europe, 2015).
30. Ibid.
31. 'Māori Pathways: A New Approach to Reducing Reoffending by Māori', New Zealand Department of Corrections, 2017. Retrieved from New Zealand Department of Corrections website.
32. Ibid.

Chapter 21 A Nation of Anti-Nationals

1. Jeffrey Gettleman et al., '"If We Kill You, Nothing Will Happen": How Delhi's Police Turned against Muslims', *New York Times*, 12 March 2020.
2. Nupur Thapiyal, '"Sorry State of Affairs, Lackadaisical": 10 Times When Courts Slammed Delhi Police over Riots Probe in 2021', Live Law, 31 December 2021, https://www.livelaw.in/top-stories/10-times-when-courts-slammed-police-over-delhi-riots-probe-2021-188556, accessed 23 March 2025.
3. 'Kapil Mishra Warns Cops: Clear Road in 3 Days . . . After That We Won't Listen to You', *Hindustan Times*, 24 February 2020; 'Two Complaints Filed against BJP Leader Kapil Mishra for Inciting Violence in North-East Delhi', DNA India, 25 February 2020.
4. 'Delhi Riots: Why Failure to Mention Evidence on Role Played by "Hindu" Nationalists?', Counterview, 19 August 2020, https://www.counterview.in/2020/08/delhi-riots-why-failure-to-mention.html, accessed 23 March 2025.
5. 'Delhi High Court Judge Justice Muralidhar's Transfer Triggers War of Words', *The Hindu*, updated 28 February 2020, https://www.thehindu.com/news/national/justice-murlidhar-transferred-to-punjab-and-haryana-high-court/article30928647.ece, accessed 23 March 2025.
6. Krishna Thevar, 'Bhima Koregaon Violence: Criminal Case Filed against Jignesh Mevani, Umar Khalid', *Economic Times*, 5 January 2018, https://economictimes.indiatimes.com/news/politics-and-nation/bhima-koregaon-violence-fir-against-jignesh-mevani-umar-khalid/articleshow/62364835.cms?from=mdr, accessed 23 March 2025.

7. 'JNU Sedition Case: Kanhaiya Kumar, Umar Khalid and 8 Others to Be Charged Today', *India Today*, 14 January 2019, https://www.indiatoday.in/india/story/jnu-sedition-case-chargesheet-kanhaiya-kumar-umar-khalid-1430284-2019-01-14, accessed 23 March 2025.
8. Manoj Mitta, 'Afzal Guru's Secret Hanging a Human Rights Violation: Prosecutor', *Times of India*, 13 February 2013, https://timesofindia.indiatimes.com/india/afzal-gurus-secret-hanging-a-human-rights-violation-prosecutor/articleshow/18474808.cms, accessed 23 March 2025.
9. Sandeep Bhushan, 'How Television Media Uncritically Reproduced the Sangh's Narrative of "Nationalist" Versus "Anti-Nationalist"', *The Caravan*, 28 February 2016, https://caravanmagazine.in/vantage/media-uncritically-reproduced-nationalist, accessed 23 March 2025.
10. Scroll staff, '"My Conscience Has Started to Revolt": A Zee News Producer Quits over Channel's Handling of JNU Row', Scroll.in, 21 February 2016, https://scroll.in/article/803943/my-conscience-has-started-to-revolt-a-zee-news-producer-quits-over-channels-handling-of-jnu-row, accessed 23 March 2025.
11. 'Afzal Guru Row: JNU Panel Finds 21 Students Guilty, Fine Reduced for Few', *Economic Times*, updated 23 August 2016, https://economictimes.indiatimes.com/news/politics-and-nation/afzal-guru-row-jnu-panel-finds-21-students-guilty-fine-reduced-for-few/articleshow/53831664.cms?from=mdr, accessed 23 March 2025.
12. 'Two of Seven JNU Videos Manipulated, Finds Forensic Probe', *The Hindu*, 26 November 2021, https://www.thehindu.com/news/cities/Delhi/JNU-row-Two-of-seven-videos-manipulated-says-forensic-probe-report/article60515298.ece, accessed 23 March 2025.
13. Kingshuk Chatterjee, 'Finding the Malaise That Ails JNU', *New Indian Express*, 1 May 2022, https://www.newindianexpress.com/lifestyle/books/2022/Apr/30/finding-the-malaise-thatails-jnu-2447605.html, accessed 23 March 2025.
14. Anand Teltumbde, 'Rohith Vemula's Death: A Noose around the BJP's Neck', Countercurrents, 8 February 2016, https://www.countercurrents.org/teltumbde080216.htm.
15. Amritha Mohan, 'Justice for Rohith Vemula: Students, Faculty Burn Roopanwal Commission Report', Newslaundry, 25 August 2017, https://www.newslaundry.com/2017/08/25/roopanwal-rohith-vemula-hyderabad-university, accessed 23 March 2025.
16. 'India Today Sting Impact: Attacker Lawyer Yashpal Singh Arrested', *India Today*, 23 February 2016, https://www.indiatoday.in/india/story/india-today-sting-impact-attacker-lawyer-yashpal-singh-arrested-310191-2016-02-23, accessed 23 March 2025.
17. Shubhomoy Sikdar, 'JNU Event Footage Authentic, Says Report', *The Hindu*, 18 October 2016, https://www.thehindu.com/news/cities/

Delhi/JNU-event-footage-authentic-says report/article14414770.ece, accessed 23 March 2025.

18 Leela Jacinto, 'How Indian Authorities "Weaponised" a *New York Times* Report to Target the Press', France 24, 6 October 2023, https://www.france24.com/en/asia-pacific/20231006-how-the-indian-state-weaponised-a-new-york-times-report-to-target-the-press, accessed 23 March 2025.

19 Smita Narula, 'Confronting State Violence: Lessons from India's Farmer Protests', *Columbia Human Rights Law Review* 54, no. 1 (2022), https://hrlr.law.columbia.edu/files/2022/12/Narula_Finalized-12.08.22.pdf, accessed 23 March 2025.

20 Rishab Gaur and Ryan Thomas, 'Campus Insecurity', *The Caravan*, 23 February 2025, https://caravanmagazine.in/crime/jamia-students-detention-delhi-police-anti-caa-dissent-suspension, accessed 23 March 2025.

21 Nilanjana Bhowmick, '"Women Don't Give Up." Why Female Protesters Are at the Forefront of India's Resistance Movement', *TIME*, 15 January 2020, https://time.com/5765702/india-protests-women/, accessed 23 March 2025.

22 Kavitha Iyer, 'Delhi Riots: How BJP Leaders Created a Powderkeg That Led to 2020 Hindu-Muslim Violence', Article 14, 11 October 2022, https://article-14.com/post/delhi-riots-how-bjp-leaders-created-a-powderkeg-that-led-to-2020-hindu-muslim-violence – 6344d8d280625.

23 'BJP MP Parvesh Verma in Hate Row as Pitch Turns Communal', *Hindustan Times*, 29 January 2020, https://www.hindustantimes.com/india-news/bjp-mp-in-hate-row-as-pitch-turns-communal/story-EFllHZQcaw9IXibYxRMibP.html, accessed 25 June 2025.

24 Archis Chowdhury, 'Fact Check: Did Union Minister Anurag Thakur Raise Goli Maro Slogan?', Boom Fact Check, 2 March 2020, https://www.boomlive.in/fake-news/fact-check-did-union-minister-anurag-thakur-raise-goli-maro-slogan-7087, accessed 25 June 2025.

25 Aman Sharma, 'We Can't Leave Delhi in Anarchy: Modi', *Economic Times*, updated 4 February 2020, https://economictimes.indiatimes.com/news/elections/assembly-elections/delhi/we-cant-leave-delhi-in-anarchy-modi/articleshow/73921498.cms?from=mdr; '2020 Delhi Pogrom: Citizens' Chargesheet against Hate-Mongering', Maktoob Media, 26 February 2023, https://maktoobmedia.com/india/2020-delhi-pogrom-citizens-chargesheet-against-hate-mongering/, accessed 23 March 2025.

26 Sagar Kulkarni, 'Delhi Polls: PM Modi Sees Design in Shaheen Bagh Protest, Asks Delhi to Vote Out Anarchy', *Deccan Herald*, 3 February 2020, https://www.deccanherald.com/india/delhi-polls-pm-modi-sees-design-in-shaheen-bagh-protest-asks-delhi-to-vote-out-anarchy-801252.html, accessed 23 March 2025.

Chapter 22 Of Labels and Labelling

1. Karl Marx and Friedrich Engels, *Collected Works*, Vol. 46, Letters, 1880–1883 (London: Lawrence & Wishart, 1982), 356.
2. Dr Ambedkar's significant struggle for abolishing the oppressive Khoti system – a kind of zamindari system, prevalent in the Konkan region of Maharashtra – was joined by the communist leaders. It culminated in a march of 25,000 peasants, both the Dalits and non-Dalits, to the Bombay Council Hall on 12 January 1938. See Anand Teltumbde, *Iconoclast: A Reflective Biography of Dr Babasaheb Ambedkar* (Gurugram: Penguin, 2024), 243–244.
3. A massive protest of the workers called by Ambedkar's Independent Labour Party was joined by the communists on 4 January 1938 against the Industrial Dispute Bill that was condemned by him as 'Workers' Civil Liberties Suspension Act'. See Teltumbde, *Iconoclast*, 246–247.
4. The first post-Ambedkar land struggle took place from 26 July 1959 under the leadership of Dadasaheb Gaikwad which was massively supported by the communists. See Teltumbde, *Iconoclast*, 521–522.

Epilogue

1. The nazm was composed as a medium of protest against Zia Ul Haq's oppressive regime by Faiz Ahmad Faiz, included in his seventh poetry book, *Mere Dil Mere Musafir*. It gained a rapid cult following as a leftist song of resistance and defiance after a public rendition by Iqbal Bano at Alhamra Arts Council on 13 February 1986 that ignored the ban on Faiz's poetry. See Kaveree Bamzai, 'Modi's India Unhappy with Protesters Singing Faiz's Hum Dekhenge. Zia's Pakistan Was too', ThePrint, 2 January 2020, https://theprint.in/opinion/modi-india-unhappy-with-faizs-hum-dekhenge-zias-pakistan-was-too/343560/, accessed 23 March 2025.

   The translation of the nazm in English is as follows:

   We Shall See
   We shall see
   It is certain, that we too shall see –
   That day which has been promised to us,
   Which is written on the tablet of eternity.
   When these towering mountains of tyranny and oppression
   Will be blown away like cotton in the wind.
   When beneath the feet of the subjugated,
   The earth will tremble and throb with defiance.
   And over the heads of the rulers and masters,
   Lightning will crackle and thunder.
   When from the sacred land of God's Kaaba,

Every idol will be lifted and cast away –
Then we, the pure-hearted, the banished of the sanctum,
Shall be seated upon thrones of dignity.
All crowns will be tossed in the air,
All thrones will be toppled to the ground.
Only the name will remain – of God,
Who is both present and unseen –
Who is both the witness and the vision.
And a cry shall rise: Ana al-Haqq! (I am the Truth)
Which means: I too am God – and so are you.
And the people of God shall rule –
Those who are I, and you, and all of us.

About the Author

Anand Teltumbde is a prominent Indian scholar, writer and social activist. In 2018, he was implicated in the Elgar Parishad–Bhima-Koregaon case and spent thirty-one months in prison before being released on bail in November 2022.

A prolific author and public intellectual, he has written over thirty books, many of which have been translated into several Indian languages. He is also a regular contributor to *Economic and Political Weekly, Outlook, Frontline, The Caravan*, The Wire and Scroll, as well as national dailies including *Indian Express, The Hindu* and *Times of India*.